SUPERMAN BATMAN

SAGA OF THE

SUPER SONS

BATMAN created by **BOB KANE** with **BILL FINGER**

SUPERMAN created by **JERRY SIEGEL** and **JOE SHUSTER**
By special arrangement with the Jerry Siegel family

AQUAMAN created by **PAUL NORRIS**

SUPERMAN/BATMAN: SAGA OF THE SUPER SONS

Published by DC Comics. Compilation and all new material Copyright © 2017 DC Comics. All Rights Reserved.

Originally published in single magazine form in WORLD'S FINEST COMICS 215, 216, 221, 222, 224, 228, 230, 231, 233, 238, 242, 263, ELSEWORLDS 80-PAGE GIANT 1. Copyright © 1972, 1973, 1974, 1975, 1976, 1980, 1999 DC Comics. All Rights Reserved. All characters, their distinctive likenesses and related elements featured in this publication are trademarks of DC Comics. The stories, characters and incidents featured in this publication are entirely fictional. DC Comics does not read or accept unsolicited submissions of ideas, stories or artwork.

DC Comics, 2900 West Alameda Ave., Burbank, CA 91505
Printed by LSC Communications, Owensville, MO, USA. 1/6/17. First Printing.
ISBN: 978-1-4012-6968-5

Library of Congress Cataloging-in-Publication Data is available.

"One generation passeth away, and another generation cometh; but the earth abideth forever..."
— Ecclesiastes

SUPERMAN AND BATMAN

TWO FAMED, FAMILIAR FIGURES SIDE BY SIDE IN MAHOGANY COFFINS!? CAN IT BE? IT *MUST* BE! DEATH, THE PALE HORSEMAN HAS CLAIMED...

YES, ONE GENERATION PASSETH AWAY--BUT WHO ARE THOSE TWO STALWART FORMS, STIFLING MANLY TEARS? *SUPERMAN* AND *BATMAN?* SURELY, THEY DO NOT MOURN THEMSELVES! AND THOSE TWO VEILED, GRIEF-STRICKEN WOMEN, WHO ARE THEY? AND WHO IS THE TALL, STERN MAN WHO VOWS VENGEANCE?

CLARK... MY SON!

BRUCE, MY SON!

OH, CLARK... MY DARLING!

BRUCE... MY BABY...

I SHALL AVENGE YOUR DEATHS, YOUNG CUBS!

A MILLION REGRETS, BOYS! Rocco

DID YOU EVER WONDER IF ONE DAY *SUPERMAN* AND *BATMAN* HAD SONS...WHAT THEY WOULD BE LIKE?? HEROIC CHIPS OFF THE OLD BLOCKS--OR SUPER DUDS? WONDER NO MORE, FAITHFUL ONES! IMAGINATION? PUT-ON? *NO!* FOR NOW, HERE, REVEALED IN ALL ITS SHOCK AND HUMAN ANGUISH, THE SENSATIONAL TOP-SECRET *WORLD'S FINEST* STORY THAT CRIED OUT TO BE TOLD...

"SAGA OF THE SUPER SONS!"

ART BY: DICK DILLIN AND HENRY SCARPELLI   STORY BY: BOB HANEY

A FEW WEEKS BEFORE, A CALM, SUNNY MORNING IN A MODEST MIDDLE-CLASS HOME IN METROPOLIS, U.S.A....

HERE, SPEAK TO YOUR SON! ASK HIM WHY HE HASN'T BEEN HOME TO SEE US FOR DAYS!

HMMM-- ALL RIGHT, DEAR!

NOT MANY BLOCKS AWAY, A STOREFRONT COMMUNITY CENTER-- WHERE GOOD INTENTIONS AND YOUNG IDEALS STRUGGLE AGAINST THAT OCTOPUS OF DESPAIR... THE GHETTO!

JOB TRAINING HERE TODAY

PEOPLE ARE OUR BAG!

CLARK? DAD! WHY HAVEN'T WE SEEN YOU LATELY?

...ARE A BAD TRIP!

UHH, SORRY, DAD-- BUT I'VE BEEN BUSY!

I'VE DONE SOME DO-GOODING IN MY LIFE, TOO! BUT AT YOUR AGE I HAD A JOB... I KNEW WHO I WAS AND WHERE I WAS GOING...!

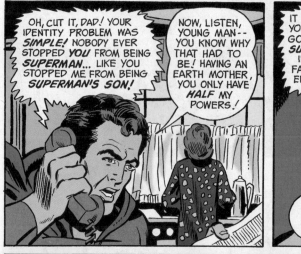

OH, CUT IT, DAD! YOUR IDENTITY PROBLEM WAS SIMPLE! NOBODY EVER STOPPED YOU FROM BEING SUPERMAN... LIKE YOU STOPPED ME FROM BEING SUPERMAN'S SON!

NOW, LISTEN, YOUNG MAN-- YOU KNOW WHY THAT HAD TO BE! HAVING AN EARTH MOTHER, YOU ONLY HAVE HALF MY POWERS!

IT WAS FOR YOUR OWN GOOD! ONE SUPERMAN IN THE FAMILY'S ENOUGH!

SURE, SO I HAVE TO BE THE OFFSHOOT OF AN IDENTITY YOU MADE UP... A SOFTIE NAMED CLARK KENT!

THAT'S THE FATHER IMAGE I HAVE TO COPY!

DON'T PUT THE PHONE DOWN-- I'M TALKING TO YOU! WHAT WAS THAT?

KERRRASSSSSSSSSSH

BABY, HAVE FEAR-- SATAN'S SOCKERS ARE HERE! AND WE'RE GONNA REALLY SOCK IT TO YA!

2

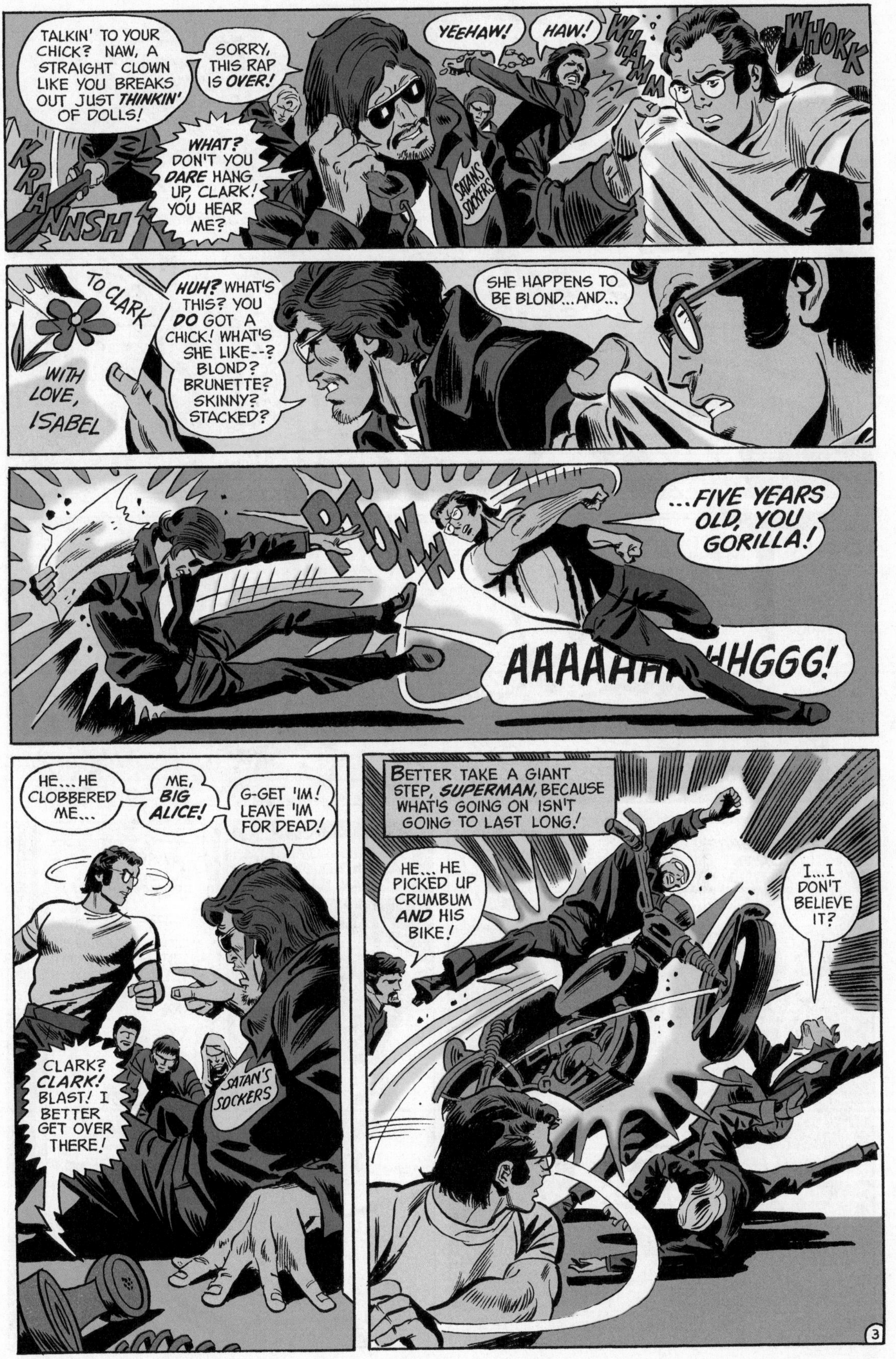
TALKIN' TO YOUR CHICK? NAW, A STRAIGHT CLOWN LIKE YOU BREAKS OUT JUST THINKIN' OF DOLLS!
SORRY, THIS RAP IS OVER!
WHAT? DON'T YOU DARE HANG UP, CLARK! YOU HEAR ME?
KRANNSH
SATAN'S SOCKERS
YEEHAW!
HAW!
WHAMM
WHOKK
TO CLARK
WITH LOVE, ISABEL
HUH? WHAT'S THIS? YOU DO GOT A CHICK! WHAT'S SHE LIKE--? BLOND? BRUNETTE? SKINNY? STACKED?
SHE HAPPENS TO BE BLOND...AND...
PTOWWH
...FIVE YEARS OLD, YOU GORILLA!
AAAAAHHHHGGG!
HE...HE CLOBBERED ME...
ME, BIG ALICE!
G-GET 'IM! LEAVE 'IM FOR DEAD!
CLARK? CLARK! BLAST! I BETTER GET OVER THERE!
SATAN'S SOCKERS
BETTER TAKE A GIANT STEP, SUPERMAN, BECAUSE WHAT'S GOING ON ISN'T GOING TO LAST LONG!
HE... HE PICKED UP CRUMBUM AND HIS BIKE!
I...I DON'T BELIEVE IT?
3

UNNNNHH!

WHAAAAM

EEEYYUUUH!

SPLIT! THAT GUY'S A SUPERMAN!

SUDDEN QUIET, THEN A DEEP VOICE, A TITANIC TORSO FILLING THE DOORWAY...

PRETTY, CLARK! VERY PRETTY! YOU HEARD THEM -- NOW THEY SUSPECT YOU REALLY ARE A SUPERMAN!

HALF--- REMEMBER, DAD?

SORRY, I JUST LOST MY HEAD! CLARK KENT, JR. KIND OF WENT UP IN ANGRY SMOKE AND SOMEBODY ELSE TOOK HIS PLACE!

I KNOW, SUPERMAN, JR.! WELL, FORGET IT! YOUR LIFE'S GOING TO BE DIFFERENT! I PROMISED YOUR MOTHER THAT--

I WON'T LISTEN TO YOU ANYMORE!

COME BACK!

AT THIS MOMENT, A PENTHOUSE IN GOTHAM CITY, U.S.A....

ALFRED! DOUSE THAT FREAKY LIGHT!

SORRY, MASTER BRUCE --BUT YOUR PARENTS WOULD LIKE YOU TO JOIN THEM ON THE TERRACE...FOR LUNCH!

4

SHORTLY...

WELL, WELL, AT LAST! WHERE WERE YOU ALL NIGHT, BRUCE?

SWINGING, DAD! BEFORE I KNEW IT, ROSY-FINGERED DAWN WAS GILDING GOTHAM'S SKYLINE!

YOU'RE WASTING YOUR YEAR OFF FROM COLLEGE! WHEN I WAS YOUR AGE--

I KNOW YOU WERE LIVING LIKE A MONK AND TRAINING LIKE A DEMON TO BATTLE THE UNDERWORLD ON WHICH YOU'D SWORN REVENGE!

IN SHORT, AN OBSESSED, NO-FUN FREAK!

BRUCE! YOU SPEAK THIS WAY TO YOUR FATHER?

SORRY, MOTHER-- UNTIL TWO YEARS AGO, THE ONLY FATHER IMAGE I HAD WAS BRUCE WAYNE, PLAYBOY! DON'T BLAME ME FOR ACTING LIKE ONE NOW!

THAT WAS TO HIDE MY BATMAN IDENTITY-- AND YOU WERE TOO YOUNG TO BE TOLD EARLIER!

BUT NOT TOO YOUNG TO BE HURT BY NOT KNOWING I WAS BATMAN'S SON!

SHARPER THAN A SERPENT'S TOOTH, A CHILD'S JUDGMENT OF HIS PARENT!

THE NOON NEWS... I BELIEVE IS ON NOW!

KLIK

LAST NIGHT, BATMAN "DROPPED IN" ON AUGIE BECK, AS THE LONGSHOREMAN LEADER ADDRESSED HIS FOLLOWERS!

5

AFTER CLOBBERING BECK AND DELIVERING HIM TO THE JAILHOUSE, BATMAN VANISHED!

HIS ATTORNEY HAD HIM RELEASED FOR LACK OF EVIDENCE, AND BECK VOWS TO SUE BATMAN AND GOTHAM CITY FOR FALSE ARREST AND ASSAULT!

WHAT? I...I DID NO SUCH CRAZY THING LAST NIGHT!

PERHAPS YOU DIDN'T, SIR...

...BUT SOMEONE WEARING YOUR EXTRA COSTUME DID! I FOUND IT IN MASTER BRUCE'S ROOM!

ALFRED, YOU TRAITOR!

NO TRAITOR, YOUNG SIR... BUT ONE WHO LOVES AND SERVES ALL WITH THE WAYNE NAME!

YOU YOUNG FOOL! PLAYING BATMAN!! I WARNED YOU NEVER TO TRY THAT! NOW LOOK WHAT'S HAPPENED!

BUT EVERYONE KNOWS BECK'S THE WATER-FRONT'S RACKET KING... A KILLER--!

BUT YOU MUST HAVE EVIDENCE! YOU CAN'T PLAY VIGILANTE! YOU'VE PUT ME IN A BAD SPOT--YOU GO BACK TO COLLEGE...TONIGHT!

I'M FED UP! GOODBYE!

MY GOD-- HE'S JUMPING--!!

THE NEXT MOMENT...

A ROPE TO THE NEXT BUILDING! THE YOUNG TRICKSTER!

HE MUST WANT TO PLAY BATMAN PRETTY BADLY!

YES, MR. WAYNE, JUST LIKE ANOTHER YOUNG MAN DID YEARS AGO... REMEMBER?

6

LATER, THE JET ROUTES BETWEEN *METROPOLIS* AND *GOTHAM CITY*...

ONE HUNDRED MILE LEAPS ARE MY LIMIT-- BUT THIS WILL GET ME TO GOTHAM!

HWEST ORIENT

STEWARDESS! NO MORE COCKTAILS FOR ME--I JUST SAW A GUY GO PAST MY WINDOW!!

AND THAT EVENING...

BRUCE, LOVER-- WHY SO DOWN? COME DANCE WITH DEBBIE!

NO CHANCE, DOLL-- I'M WAITING FOR SOMEONE-- SOMEONE I NEED LIKE BAD!

HEY, I THOUGHT I WAS YOUR CHICK THIS WEEK!

CLARK KIDDO! AM I EVER GLAD TO SEE *YOU*, SPIRITUAL BROTHER!

HI, BRUCE! I CAME AS SOON AS I COULD! GUESS WE BOTH HAD THE SAME NEED!

LET'S HIT THE COBBLES--AND RAP!

BUDDY, WE'VE GOT A HEAVY PROBLEM! WE'RE THE SONS OF THE WORLD'S TWO GREATEST HEROES...

BUT IF WE TRY TO LIVE UP TO OUR FATHERS, WE GET CLOBBERED BY THE *GENERATION GAP!*

YEAH, I CAN'T BELIEVE THEY'RE OUR FATHERS-- THEY'RE BOTH SO YOUNG AND RIGHT ON--!

PLUS I'M NOT SURE I COULD LIVE UP TO MY DAD--HE'S JUST AS TOUGH AND FAST AS EVER!

CHECK! I'LL NEVER BE MORE THAN *HALF* THE MAN *MY* DAD IS!

IF ONLY THEY'D UNDERSTAND WE DON'T WANT TO *REPLACE* THEM-- WE JUST NEED TO GET OUT FROM UNDER THEIR SHADOWS!

MAN, TALK ABOUT YOUR IDENTITY CRISIS--AND COMMUNICA- TIONS GAP-- WE'VE GOT *SUPER* ONES!

7

Not too far away, a special room in a certain penthouse...

BUT WE CAN'T JUST WALLOW IN NEUROTIC SELF-PITY, CLARK! SOMETHING'S *GOT* TO GIVE!

YES, BRUCE-- BUT IT WON'T BE OUR FATHERS! I LOVE *SUPERMAN*... BUT SOMETIMES I ALMOST HATE CLARK KENT, SR.!

HEARD ENOUGH FROM THAT ELECTRONIC BUG ALFRED HID IN MY SON'S CLOTHES?

CLICK

WE'VE GOT TO DO *SOMETHING* ABOUT THE BOYS! MY WIFE MADE ME PROMISE THAT!

BRUCE'S MOTHER TWISTED *MY* ARM, TOO! IT'S AN OLD STORY-- THE YOUNGER GENERATION'S ITCHING TO PROVE ITSELF!

YES, BUT *ANOTHER SUPERMAN*... *ANOTHER BATMAN*... ALSO OPERATING NOW? AND HOW DO WE KNOW WHAT THEY *CAN* DO? YOU CAN'T RUN A TEST ABOUT REAL LIFE!

CRIME FILE

MAYBE WE *CAN!* MY CRIME FILES SHOW THAT ROCCO KRUGGE, HEAD OF THE RACKETS IN SPARTA CITY, IS GETTING OLD... LOSING HIS GRIP!

WHAT IF WE SEND THE BOYS OUT THERE TO TOPPLE HIS ORGANIZATION... AS A NICE, *EASY* TEST?

HMMM, YES-- BUT I DON'T LIKE USING A WHOLE CITY AS TEST TUBE FOR HOT-HEADED, INEXPERIENCED--

WAIT A MINUTE! MAYBE I'VE GOT AN *IMPROVEMENT* ON YOUR IDEA!

I'LL CREATE A *DUPLICATE* SPARTA CITY-- EXACTLY LIKE THE *REAL* ONE-- EXCEPT THAT WHEN THE EXPERIMENT'S OVER, IT'LL *VANISH* AND NO ONE-- EXCEPT *US*-- WILL BE THE WISER!

8

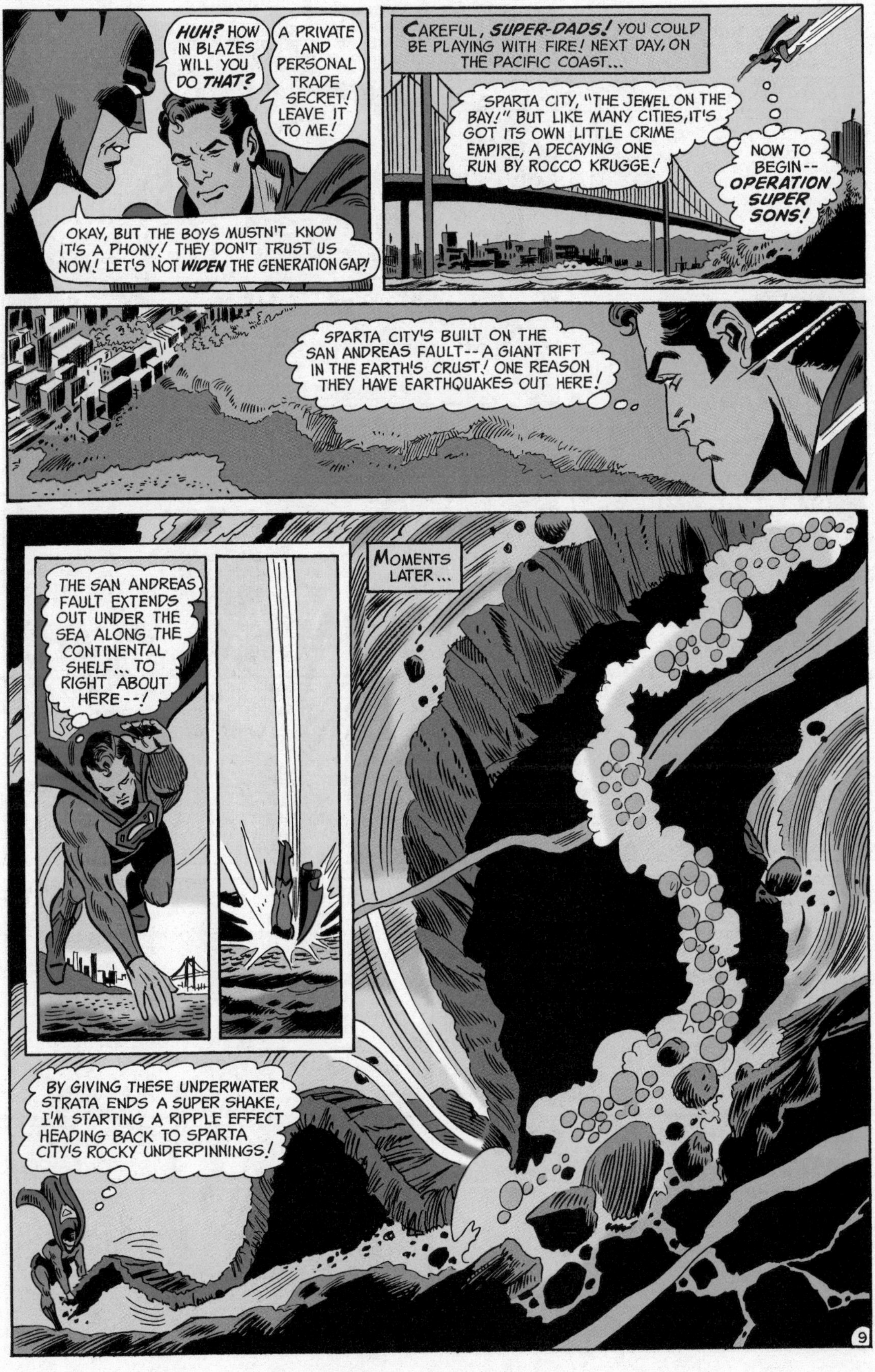
HUH? HOW IN BLAZES WILL YOU DO THAT?
A PRIVATE AND PERSONAL TRADE SECRET! LEAVE IT TO ME!
OKAY, BUT THE BOYS MUSTN'T KNOW IT'S A PHONY! THEY DON'T TRUST US NOW! LET'S NOT WIDEN THE GENERATION GAP!
CAREFUL, SUPER-DADS! YOU COULD BE PLAYING WITH FIRE! NEXT DAY, ON THE PACIFIC COAST...
SPARTA CITY, "THE JEWEL ON THE BAY!" BUT LIKE MANY CITIES, IT'S GOT ITS OWN LITTLE CRIME EMPIRE, A DECAYING ONE RUN BY ROCCO KRUGGE!
NOW TO BEGIN-- OPERATION SUPER SONS!
SPARTA CITY'S BUILT ON THE SAN ANDREAS FAULT-- A GIANT RIFT IN THE EARTH'S CRUST! ONE REASON THEY HAVE EARTHQUAKES OUT HERE!
THE SAN ANDREAS FAULT EXTENDS OUT UNDER THE SEA ALONG THE CONTINENTAL SHELF... TO RIGHT ABOUT HERE--!
MOMENTS LATER...
BY GIVING THESE UNDERWATER STRATA ENDS A SUPER SHAKE, I'M STARTING A RIPPLE EFFECT HEADING BACK TO SPARTA CITY'S ROCKY UNDERPINNINGS!
9

TIME AND *SPACE* ARE BASED ON THE SPEED OF *LIGHT!* AS YOU APPROACH THAT SPEED, TIME SLOWS DOWN AND SPACE IS ALTERED!

WHEN THE RIPPLE HITS SPARTA CITY, BECAUSE OF THE SAN ANDREAS FAULT...

...THE CITY'S ROTATIONAL AND ORBITAL SPEEDS WILL BE SLIGHTLY ACCELERATED AT A SPECIFIC RATE!

THUS WILL BE CREATED A *TEMPORARY DUPLICATE CITY*, SLOWED IN TIME AND SPACE TO ONE DAY IN THE *PAST!*

WHEW! SOME *SUPER-SKULL*, THAT *SUPERMAN!* BUT AS HE WORKS HIS SCIENTIFIC WIZARDRY, LET'S LOOK IN ON THE BARONIAL HOME OF ROCCO KRUGGE, CRIME BOSS OF SPARTA CITY...

MAREK, MY FATHER *CAN'T* BE DISTURBED--HE'S OLD AND SICK! BESIDES, THAT MEDICAL QUACK, DOCTOR GAVILAN, IS TREATING HIM NOW!

HE'LL *HAVE* TO BE DISTURBED-- AFTERWARDS! THE ORGANIZATION'S BREAKING UP! LOTS OF PUNKS ARE HOLDING OUT, NOT TAKING ORDERS!

LET IT BREAK UP! THEN MAYBE THE KRUGGE FAMILY CAN LIVE NORMAL LIVES!

IF YOU WEREN'T SO SOFT, *YOU'D* TAKE CHARGE YOUR-SELF! IF SOMEONE DOESN'T START MAKING THE RIGHT DECISIONS, WE'RE FINISHED!

THE HOUSE... *SHAKING--?!*

JUST ANOTHER EARTH-QUAKE TREMOR! THAT DOESN'T SCARE A TOUGH OLD HOOD LIKE *YOU*, MAREK!

10

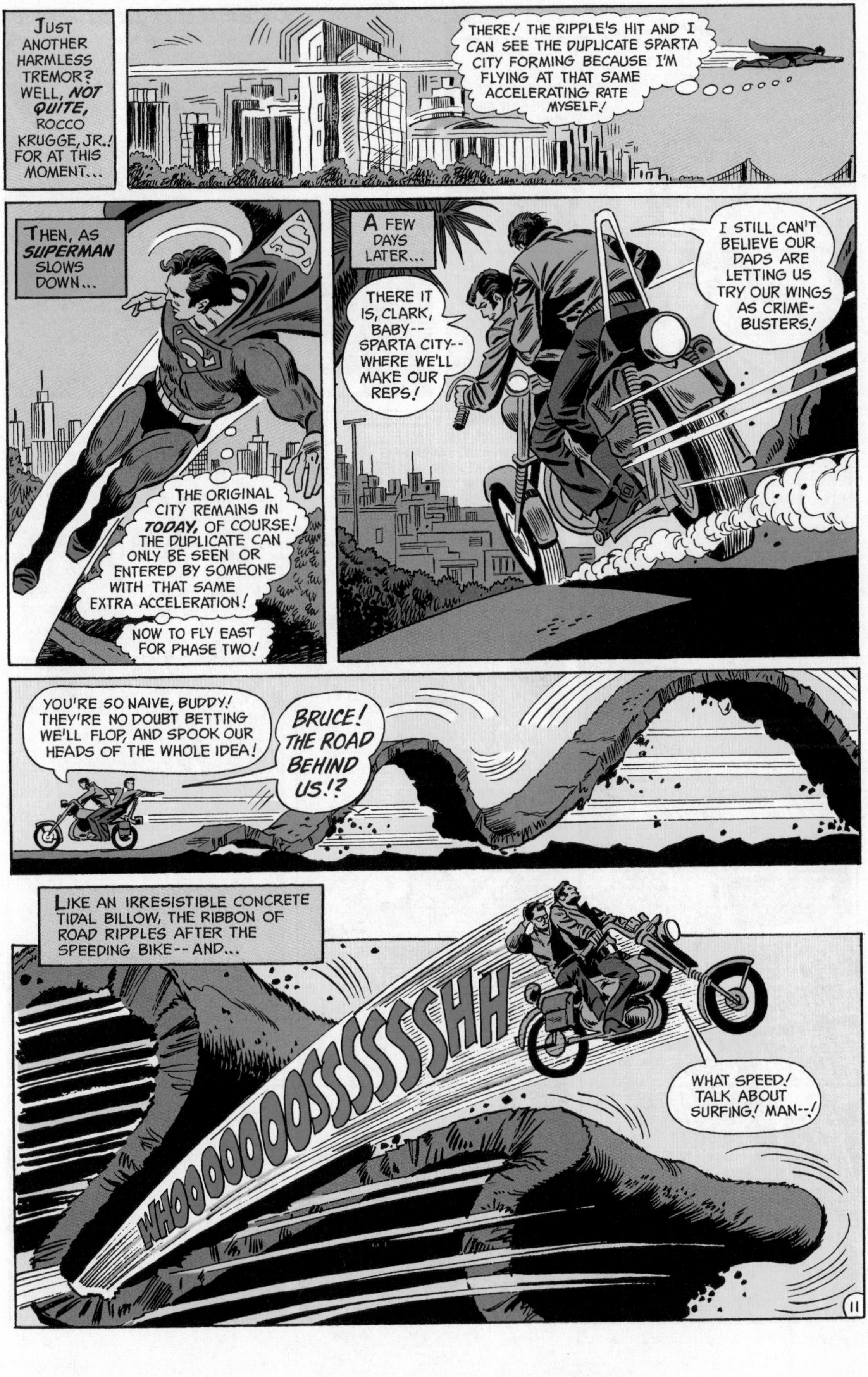
JUST ANOTHER HARMLESS TREMOR? WELL, *NOT QUITE,* ROCCO KRUGGE, JR.! FOR AT THIS MOMENT...
THERE! THE RIPPLE'S HIT AND I CAN SEE THE DUPLICATE SPARTA CITY FORMING BECAUSE I'M FLYING AT THAT SAME ACCELERATING RATE MYSELF!
THEN, AS *SUPERMAN* SLOWS DOWN...
THE ORIGINAL CITY REMAINS IN *TODAY,* OF COURSE! THE DUPLICATE CAN ONLY BE SEEN OR ENTERED BY SOMEONE WITH THAT SAME EXTRA ACCELERATION!
NOW TO FLY EAST FOR PHASE TWO!
A FEW DAYS LATER...
THERE IT IS, CLARK, BABY-- SPARTA CITY-- WHERE WE'LL MAKE OUR REPS!
I STILL CAN'T BELIEVE OUR DADS ARE LETTING US TRY OUR WINGS AS CRIME-BUSTERS!
YOU'RE SO NAIVE, BUDDY! THEY'RE NO DOUBT BETTING WE'LL FLOP, AND SPOOK OUR HEADS OF THE WHOLE IDEA!
BRUCE! THE ROAD BEHIND US!?
LIKE AN IRRESISTIBLE CONCRETE TIDAL BILLOW, THE RIBBON OF ROAD RIPPLES AFTER THE SPEEDING BIKE-- AND...
WHOOOOOOOSSSSSSSHH
WHAT SPEED! TALK ABOUT SURFING! MAN--!
11

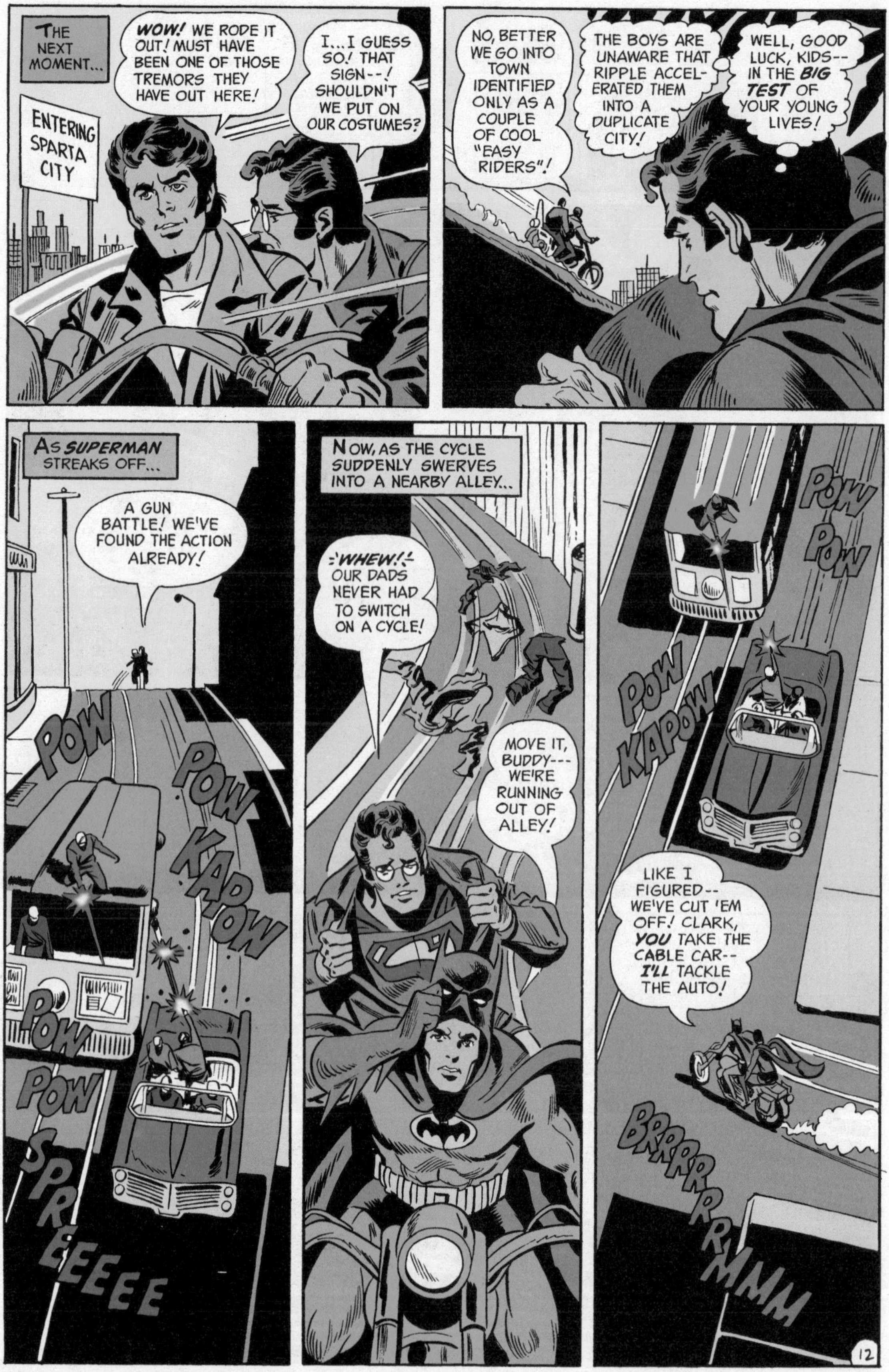
THE NEXT MOMENT...
WOW! WE RODE IT OUT! MUST HAVE BEEN ONE OF THOSE TREMORS THEY HAVE OUT HERE!
ENTERING SPARTA CITY
I...I GUESS SO! THAT SIGN--! SHOULDN'T WE PUT ON OUR COSTUMES?
NO, BETTER WE GO INTO TOWN IDENTIFIED ONLY AS A COUPLE OF COOL "EASY RIDERS"!
THE BOYS ARE UNAWARE THAT RIPPLE ACCELERATED THEM INTO A DUPLICATE CITY!
WELL, GOOD LUCK, KIDS-- IN THE BIG TEST OF YOUR YOUNG LIVES!
AS SUPERMAN STREAKS OFF...
A GUN BATTLE! WE'VE FOUND THE ACTION ALREADY!
POW
POW KAPOW
POW POW SPREEEEEE
NOW, AS THE CYCLE SUDDENLY SWERVES INTO A NEARBY ALLEY...
WHEW! OUR DADS NEVER HAD TO SWITCH ON A CYCLE!
MOVE IT, BUDDY--- WE'RE RUNNING OUT OF ALLEY!
POW POW
POW KAPOW
LIKE I FIGURED-- WE'VE CUT 'EM OFF! CLARK, YOU TAKE THE CABLE CAR-- I'LL TACKLE THE AUTO!
BRRRRRRMMM
12

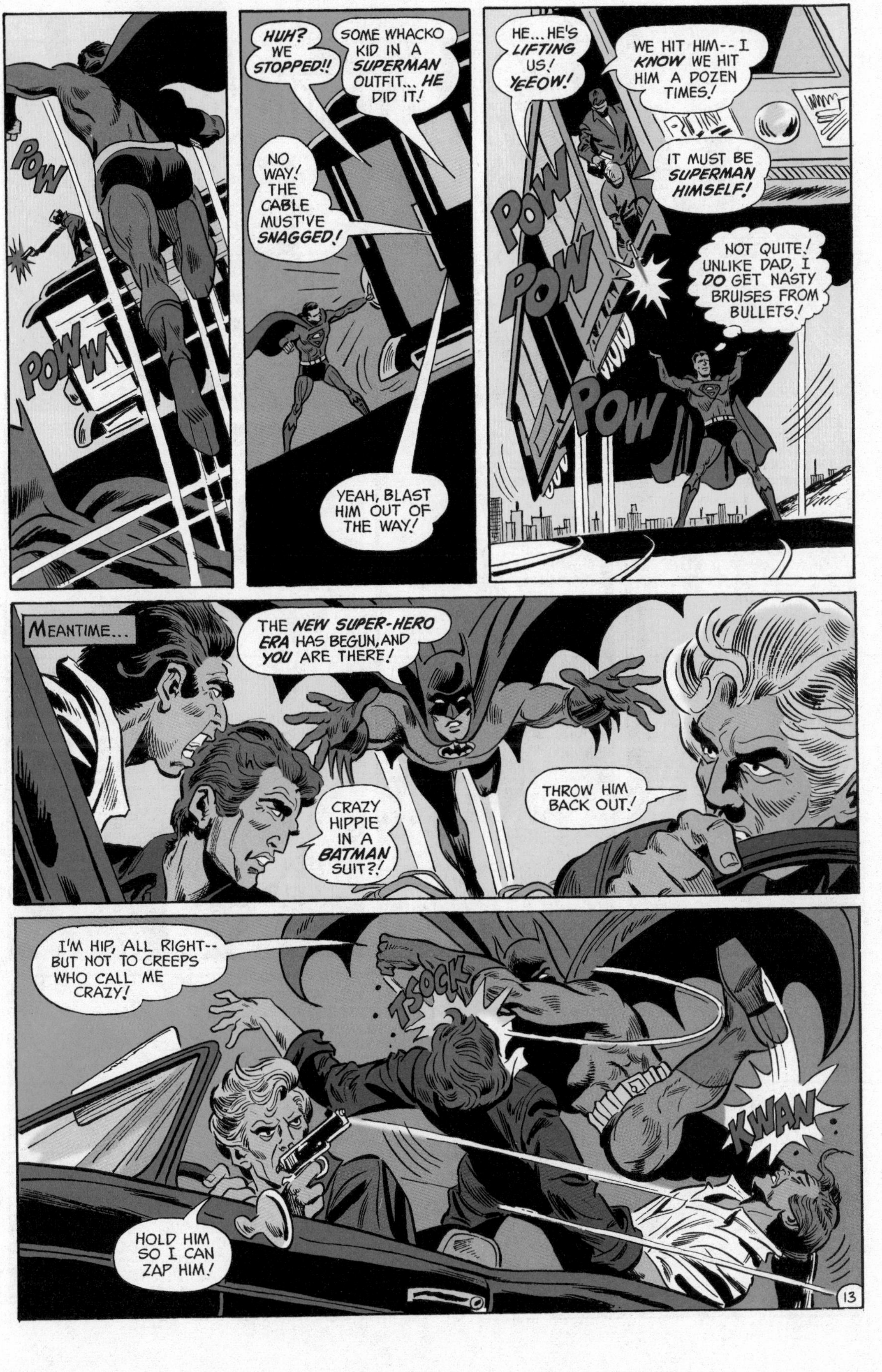
POW
POWW
HUH? WE STOPPED!!
SOME WHACKO KID IN A SUPERMAN OUTFIT... HE DID IT!
NO WAY! THE CABLE MUST'VE SNAGGED!
YEAH, BLAST HIM OUT OF THE WAY!
HE... HE'S LIFTING US! YEEOW!
WE HIT HIM-- I KNOW WE HIT HIM A DOZEN TIMES!
IT MUST BE SUPERMAN HIMSELF!
POW
POW
POW
NOT QUITE! UNLIKE DAD, I DO GET NASTY BRUISES FROM BULLETS!
MEANTIME...
THE NEW SUPER-HERO ERA HAS BEGUN, AND YOU ARE THERE!
CRAZY HIPPIE IN A BATMAN SUIT?!
THROW HIM BACK OUT!
I'M HIP, ALL RIGHT-- BUT NOT TO CREEPS WHO CALL ME CRAZY!
TSOCK
KWAN
HOLD HIM SO I CAN ZAP HIM!
13

DON'T TRY TO TURN AROUND TO SHOOT SOMEONE BEHIND WHEN YOU DRIVE BECAUSE--

KHRAAAA-A-WHAAAMMM

A FEW MOMENTS LATER, AS POLICE SIRENS SHRILL...

WHOOOOEEEEEEE

COURTESY OF BATMAN, JR. & SUPERMAN, JR.

LATER, IN THE BARONIAL HOME OF ROCCO KRUGGE...

WHAT?! I SEND A HIT SQUAD AFTER THOSE PUNKS HOLDING OUT ON THE ORGANIZATION, AND TWO KIDS, SAYING THEY'RE THE SONS OF SUPERMAN AND BATMAN, NAIL THEM?

KWAM

WHAT? IS THIS THE SAME MAN WE SAW SICK, OLD AND DYING...?

BOSS--THEY MUST BE THE REAL ONES! DIDN'T THEY HANDLE TOP GUNS LIKE THEY WERE PUSHOVERS?

I DON'T CARE! I WANT THOSE COSTUMED CREEPS HIT! I WILL SMASH ANYONE WHO DEFIES MY POWER ...LIKE SO!

KRCHUNCH

NOW GET OUT-- I MUST MAKE DECISIONS!

YOUR FATHER'S RECOVERY'S A MIRACLE, ROCCO. HE'S LIKE HE WAS YEARS AGO--TOUGH, SMART, RUTHLESS!

IT MUST BE A MIRACLE! VERY STRANGE...

THE FOLLOWING DAY...

DIG THAT, CLARK! WE'RE FAMOUS ALREADY! SET FOR MORE?

YES, IF IT'S AS EASY AS YESTERDAY-- THEN IT'S GOODBYE TO CLARK KENT, JUNIOR SQUARE-- AND HELLO TO SUPERMAN II!

SPARTA CITY TRIBUNE
SUPER-SONS OPEN CRIME WAR!

BUT I THOUGHT HEROES LIVED BETTER THAN IN THIS DINGY RENTED ROOM, RICH PLAYBOY-FRIEND!

HA! HA! SORRY, BUDDY-- BUT IF I'M GOING TO CHANGE MY IMAGE WITH DAD, IT'S CHEAPSVILLE FOR US!

14

SHORTLY, AS THE TWO COMRADES RIDE AWAY FROM THE RUN-DOWN NEIGHBORHOOD...

ROCCO KRUGGE IS SUPPOSED TO BE LOSING HIS GRIP! LET'S LOOSEN IT A BIT MORE BY CHECKING OUT HIS GAMBLING SET-UP!

HMMM, THE CYCLE'S ACTING FUNNY! IT HAD A ROUGH DAY YESTERDAY!

CHUFF-CHUFF-CHUGG

BRUCE...GET OFF! GET OFF!!

WH--??!

THE NEXT MOMENT...

WHRRAAAAAMM

OH, MY GOD--

CLARK!... CLARK, YOU OKAY?

SURE--YOU KNOW BOMBS CAN'T KILL ME-- JUST STUN ME! LUCKY I SAW IT STUCK TO THE EXHAUST AND TOSSED YOU CLEAR!

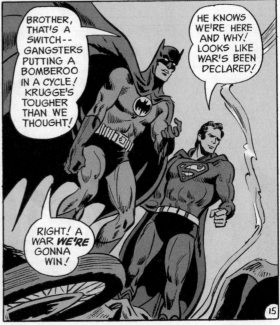

BROTHER, THAT'S A SWITCH-- GANGSTERS PUTTING A BOMBEROO IN A CYCLE! KRUGGE'S TOUGHER THAN WE THOUGHT!

HE KNOWS WE'RE HERE AND WHY! LOOKS LIKE WAR'S BEEN DECLARED!

RIGHT! A WAR WE'RE GONNA WIN!

15

IN THE NEXT FEW DAYS, THE YOUNGSTERS WADE INTO BATTLE...

AND SOON...

POLICE PR____

CHALK UP ANOTHER ARREST! BUT ALL WE'RE DOING IS NETTING *LITTLE FISH!* WE'RE NO NEARER TO THE OLD SHARK HIMSELF--*ROCCO KRUGGE!*

THAT TAKES EVIDENCE THAT'LL STAND UP IN COURT!

YOU SOUND LIKE DAD--BUT YOU'RE *RIGHT!* BUT IT TAKES EXPERIENCE TO GET THAT!

16

HOW TRUE! AND ONLY THE OLD HAVE EXPERIENCE! LIKE ROCCO KRUGGE, SR., FOR INSTANCE...

THIS *SUPERMAN, JR.*... HE *IS* LIMITED IN POWERS! WE SAW THAT WHEN THE BOMB ONLY STUNNED HIM! THOUGH THE STRONGER, PERHAPS *HE* IS THE KEY TO MY PLAN TO DESTROY THEM BOTH!

AND *YOU*, ROCCO, MY OWN SON, WILL MAKE IT WORK!

I...I FATHER--?

THE NEXT NIGHT...

WHAT FANTASTIC LUCK! KRUGGE'S SON CALLS AND SAYS TO MEET HIM HERE AND HE'LL GIVE US EVIDENCE TO CONVICT HIS OLD MAN!

HIS *OWN* FATHER!? I'M SUSPICIOUS! IT COULD BE A *TRAP!*

HE SAYS HE'S FED UP--WANTS HIS GENERATION TO LIVE STRAIGHT! I'LL SMELL A TRAP FASTER THAN *YOU*--BUT YOU HIDE NEARBY AND COVER ME, CHUM!

ALL I GET IS FLATTERY! BUT BE *CAREFUL*, GENIUS--I'M FOND OF YOUR VULNERABLE HIDE!

MINUTES PASS-- AND THEN A LONE ARRIVAL...

THIS IS DYNAMITE! IT COULD PUT YOUR OLD MAN AWAY FOR GOOD!

YES, IT'S GENUINE, ALL RIGHT... BECAUSE I KNEW PHONY EVIDENCE...

...WOULDN'T KEEP YOU OFF-GUARD LONG ENOUGH FOR ME TO PRODUCE-- *THIS!*

HUH? SO THIS *IS* A TRAP!

WASTE OF TIME, ROCCO! MY *SUPER*-CHUM'S NEARBY --HE'LL MAKE TIN SPAGHETTI OF THAT PISTOL!

17

THE NEXT INSTANT...AN EXPLOSION NEARBY...

BAAAAAARAAAMMM

YOU... YOU LOUSY CRUMB!

DON'T TRY ANYTHING! HE'S **NOT** DEAD--BUT THAT BOMB WAS BIG ENOUGH TO KNOCK HIM OUT!

NOW, COME! MY FATHER IS WAITING--!

SHORTLY...

KRUGGE, YOUR TRICK WON'T WORK! WHEN MY BUDDY WAKES, HE'LL CLOBBER YOU!

A HOLLOW BOAST, SINCE HE THEN WILL BE INSIDE A CONCRETE TOMB...ONE HUNDRED FEET THICK!

SOON, THE SITE OF A HUGE, HALF-COMPLETED DAM IN THE CANYONS BEYOND SPARTA CITY...

NO! HOW-- HOW CAN YOU DO THIS?

TO RETAIN POWER, ONE MUST BE **RUTHLESS!**

GET RID OF HIM!

MY PAL! WE'VE **FAILED**... FAILED OUR FATHERS AND OURSELVES!

I LIKE YOUR TENDER FEELINGS FOR YOUR COMRADE, BUT IT IS A HARSH WORLD, YOUNG CUB!...

...NOW TONS OF WET CONCRETE SEAL HIM IN THE DAM FOREVER... FOR EVEN HIS LIMITED SUPER-STRENGTH CANNOT CRACK FREE WHEN HE AWAKES!

KRUGGE CONTR

SPOOOOOOSH

18

HOW LONG CAN EVEN *HE* LAST WITHOUT AIR? A FEW DAYS! NOW IT IS *YOUR* TURN TO DIE! BUT THE DEATH OF YOUNG MEN SADDENS ME!

ROCCO, YOU HAVE PLEASED ME TO-NIGHT! NOW PLEASE ME MORE AND GET RID OF THIS ENEMY OF OUR FAMILY!

AS YOU WISH, FATHER!

A FEW MOMENTS LATER...

POW

IT IS DONE! MY SUDDEN RETURN TO HEALTH--THE DEFEAT OF THESE YOUNG ENEMIES-- SURELY A NEW DAY HAS DAWNED FOR THE KRUGGES!

MEANWHILE, BACK IN METROPOLIS...

CLARK, I'M WORRIED ABOUT JUNIOR! WE HAVEN'T HEARD A *WORD!*

UH... BELIEVE ME, DEAR--HE'S IN *LITTLE* DANGER! OLD KRUGGE'S A PUSHOVER FOR HIM AND YOUNG BRUCE!

AND IN GOTHAM CITY...

I'M UPSET ABOUT OUR SON! I HAVE A FEELING SOMETHING'S GONE WRONG!

NONSENSE, DARLING! *SUPERMAN* AND I SET UP AN EASY, FOOLPROOF TEST!

BUT WORRIED MOTHERS HAVE A WAY OF GET-TING THEIR WAY-- AND SHORTLY...

I'M SURE THE BOYS ARE OKAY--BUT TO KEEP *BATMAN* AND ME FROM BEING NAGGED, I'LL CHECK UP ON THEM!

DUPLICATE SPARTA CITY AHEAD--!

KRUGGE-- SURROUNDED BY NEWSMEN? AND HE LOOKS SO HEALTHY?

THOSE YOUNG MEN WERE *HEROES!* THEY DIED FIGHTING THE CRIMINAL ELEMENTS STRANGLING OUR FAIR CITY!

CITY HALL

19

AS A CONCERNED AND GRIEVING CITIZEN, I'M GIVING THEM THE FINEST FUNERAL MONEY CAN BUY! AND I SWEAR TO HELP FIND THEIR VICIOUS KILLERS!

WHAT'S HAPPENED HERE?

AT SUPER-SPEED, THE *MAN OF METROPOLIS* INVESTIGATES--AND SOON...

CLARK AND BRUCE ARE *DEAD*--AND IT'S ALL *MY* FAULT!

I'VE JUST BEEN TO THE *REAL* SPARTA CITY! THE ROCCO KRUGGE THERE IS OLD AND WEAK...

...BUT IN THE DUPLICATE CITY, HE'S *STRONG* AND *RUTHLESS!* WHEN I GAVE THE CITY THAT EXTRA SPACE SPIN, KRUGGE WAS BEING TREATED BY SOME DOCTOR'S WEIRDO MACHINE!

SOMEHOW THE TREMOR CAUSED A SHORT-CIRCUIT!

...AND BY AN IRONIC FLUKE MADE THE *DUPLICATE* KRUGGE INTO A FEARSOME FOE WHO DESTROYED OUR SONS!

NOW FOR THE HARDEST THING I'VE DONE-- BREAKING THE TERRIBLE NEWS TO THEIR MOTHERS AND *BATMAN!*

AND SO, IT HAS COME TO PASS, THAT THE SAD WORLD IS TURNED UPSIDE-DOWN, AND ONE GENERATION PASSETH AWAY--WHILE THE WRONG GENERATION MOURNS...

SO LONG, BOYS!

THAT HYPOCRITICAL SWINE! WE *KNOW* HE'S THEIR KILLER! *LET ME AT HIM!*

NO, OLD FRIEND! WOULD YOU DISHONOR OUR SONS' MEMORIES BY ILLEGAL REVENGE? HOW CAN WE PROVE IT? BLAME FATE...BLAME *ME*--!

20

IT *IS* YOUR FAULT! MY BRUCE...BURIED HERE IN THIS DUPLICATE DEATH TRAP!

SUPERMAN-- I...I *NEVER* WANT TO SEE YOU AGAIN!

BATMAN!

AND WHEN FRIENDS FALL OUT AND TRAGEDY SEEMS TRIUMPHANT...

I *LOVE* BIG FUNERALS! NOBODY CAN SAY ROCCO KRUGGE DIDN'T DO RIGHT BY THOSE BOYS!

THE EVIDENCE WE USED TO TRAP THEM-- IT COULD BE DANGEROUS! WHERE IS IT?

WHERE *NO ONE* WILL FIND IT UNTIL ETERNITY! HA-HA-HA!

THAT NIGHT...

UHNNN?... *YOU TWO?!* N-NO!

AND SHORTLY, A FRIGHTENED, NERVOUS MAN DRIVES ALONE TO...

...THE CEMETERY! I MUST MAKE SURE!

THEIR GRAVES *OPEN*...THE BODIES *GONE!*

AIEEEEEEE!

WE'RE *NOT* GHOSTS, KRUGGE! *WE'RE ALIVE!*

BUT I SAW YOU BOTH DEAD... *BURIED!?*

SUSPENDED ANIMATION-- EASY ENOUGH FOR ME WITH MY POWERS!

AND NOT TOO TOUGH FOR ME, USING A SPECIAL DRUG EVEN A *JUNIOR BATMAN* CARRIES!

21

BUT *YOU* WERE FOUND SUFFOCATED IN THE DAM-- WHEN A ROUTINE STRUCTURAL TEST DETECTED SOMETHING FOREIGN IN THE CONCRETE!

I SAW IT IN THE NEWSPAPERS--!

"THE STORY WAS SLIGHTLY ALTERED TO FOOL YOU, KRUGGE! I WAS CHIPPED FREE *BEFORE* THE TWO DAYS I CAN LIVE WITHOUT AIR WERE UP!"

CHECK! BECAUSE *I* TOLD THE DAM ENGINEERS HE WAS THERE!

BUT *YOU* WERE ALREADY DEAD... SLAIN BY MY OWN SON!?

NO, FATHER, I ONLY *PRETENDED* TO SHOOT HIM!

ROCCO! YOU BETRAYED ME!

NO, *YOU* BETRAYED THE WHOLE FAMILY BY MAKING CRIME OUR WAY OF LIFE!

AND WHEN YOU MADE *ME* TRAP THESE TWO, I FELT SHAME AND GUILT!

I ENVIED THEM THEIR COURAGE AND FRIENDSHIP! I WANTED TO CHANGE MY OWN LIFE-- SO I HELPED THEM!

BY FAKING DEATH, THEY WERE SAFE FROM YOUR KILLERS -- WHILE WE WAITED FOR YOU TO MAKE A MISTAKE!

BUT I MADE NO MISTAKES! AND NO JURY WOULD HONOR A SON'S TESTIMONY AGAINST HIS OWN FATHER!

WE DON'T NEED ROCCO, JR'S TESTIMONY, KRUGGE! *HERE'S* THE EVIDENCE YOU USED TO TRAP US! MY *X-RAY VISION* DETECTED WHERE YOU HID IT AS I LAY "DEAD!"

SKASSSSH

22

CLEVER IDEA--BUT YOUR SENTIMENTAL, OLD-STYLE GANGSTER MANIA ABOUT FUNERALS *BACKFIRED* ON YOU!

YOU WILL *NEVER* TAKE ME TO JUSTICE! THIS OLD LION RUNS TO FIGHT ANOTHER DAY!

DON'T LET HIM GET AWAY!

BUT THE NEXT MOMENT...

KPOW

A SHOT!!

HE... HE'S *DEAD!* TRIPPED OVER THAT TOMBSTONE AND HIS GUN WENT OFF!

ROCCO! THE STONE...?

MY MOTHER ALWAYS WANTED MY FATHER TO CHANGE HIS LIFE OF CRIME! NOW, AT LAST, THEY ARE *BOTH* AT PEACE!

MARIE KRUGGE 1910-1969

SOME TIME LATER, A UNIQUE REUNION...

VERY CLEVER THE WAY YOU TWO TURNED THE TABLES ON KRUGGE!

YOU ARE LEAVING SPARTA CITY COME AGAIN!

WE'RE *PROUD* OF YOU, AND YOUR MOTHERS ARE *OVERJOYED!*

GREAT! BUT THE GENERATION GAP'S *STILL* THERE! YOU WEREN'T STRAIGHT WITH US--YOU SET UP A PHONY TEST OF OUR AMBITIONS!

AND WHAT DID WE ACCOMPLISH? THE *REAL* ROCCO KRUGGE'S *STILL* CRIME KING OF THE REAL SPARTA CITY!

23

GUILTY AS CHARGED! BUT LOOK AT IT THIS WAY--SINCE THAT DUPLICATE KRUGGE WAS *TOUGHER* THAN THE ORIGINAL, THE TEST WAS TOUGHER, TOO!
IT MADE YOU *REALLY* PROVE YOURSELVES!
THE REAL ROCCO KRUGGE *IS* DEAD! THIS PAPER SAYS HE DIED OF A HEART ATTACK WHEN, AGAINST DOCTOR'S ORDERS, HE VISITED HIS WIFE'S GRAVE!
IRONIC, EH?
CRIME CHIEFTAN
GUESS THINGS TURNED OUT OKAY, AFTER ALL!
BUT YOU TWO CAN HAVE YOUR HERO BAG BACK FOR NOW! IT'S TOO GRIM! WE'RE OFF TO FIND SOME LAUGHS! SEE YA, *SUPER-DADS!*
24
The END

SUPERMAN and BATMAN

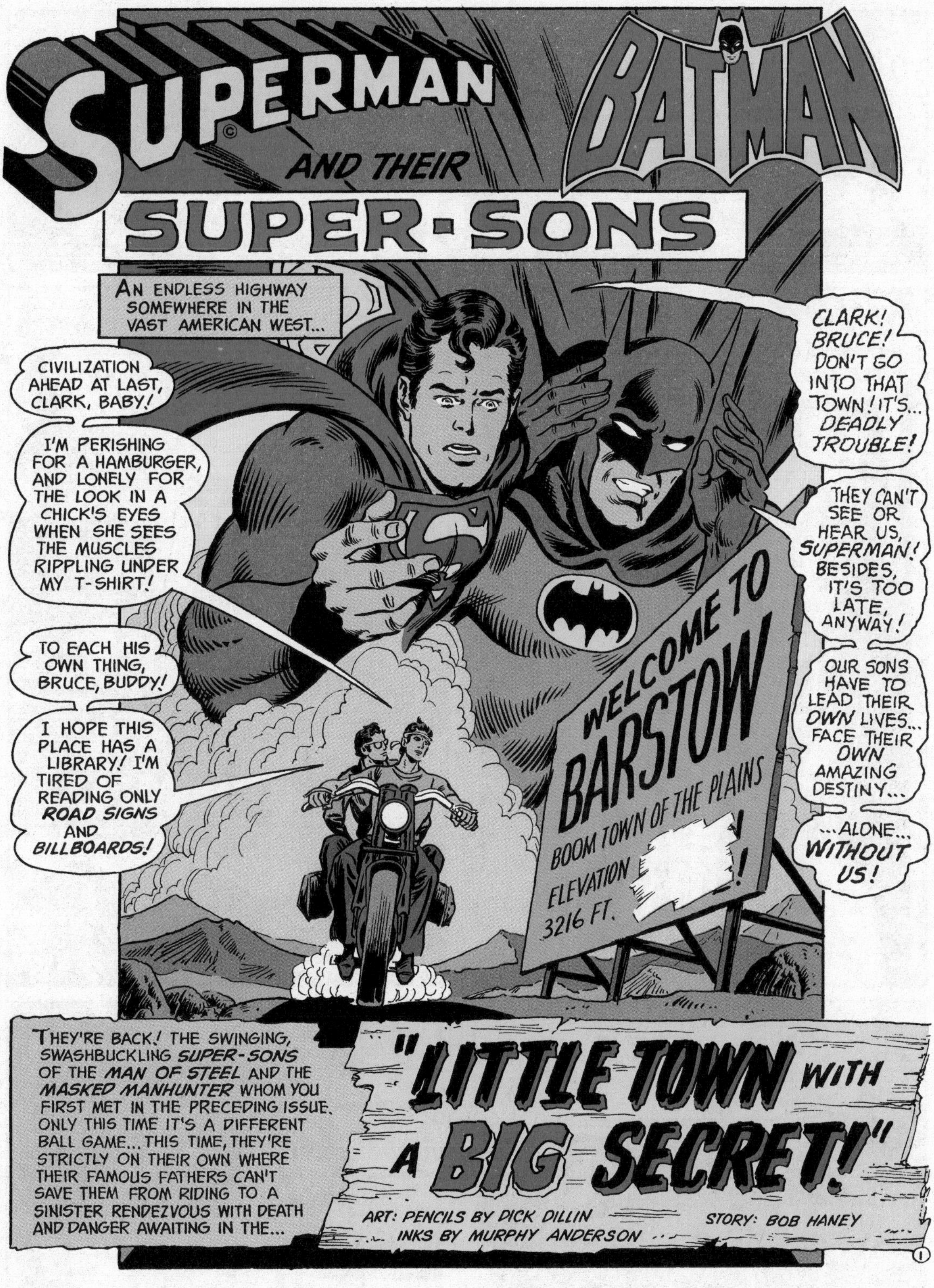
SUPERMAN
BATMAN
AND THEIR
SUPER-SONS
AN ENDLESS HIGHWAY SOMEWHERE IN THE VAST AMERICAN WEST...
CIVILIZATION AHEAD AT LAST, CLARK, BABY!
I'M PERISHING FOR A HAMBURGER, AND LONELY FOR THE LOOK IN A CHICK'S EYES WHEN SHE SEES THE MUSCLES RIPPLING UNDER MY T-SHIRT!
TO EACH HIS OWN THING, BRUCE, BUDDY!
I HOPE THIS PLACE HAS A LIBRARY! I'M TIRED OF READING ONLY ROAD SIGNS AND BILLBOARDS!
CLARK! BRUCE! DON'T GO INTO THAT TOWN! IT'S... DEADLY TROUBLE!
THEY CAN'T SEE OR HEAR US, SUPERMAN! BESIDES, IT'S TOO LATE, ANYWAY!
OUR SONS HAVE TO LEAD THEIR OWN LIVES... FACE THEIR OWN AMAZING DESTINY...
...ALONE... WITHOUT US!
WELCOME TO BARSTOW
BOOM TOWN OF THE PLAINS
ELEVATION 3216 FT.
THEY'RE BACK! THE SWINGING, SWASHBUCKLING SUPER-SONS OF THE MAN OF STEEL AND THE MASKED MANHUNTER WHOM YOU FIRST MET IN THE PRECEDING ISSUE. ONLY THIS TIME IT'S A DIFFERENT BALL GAME... THIS TIME, THEY'RE STRICTLY ON THEIR OWN WHERE THEIR FAMOUS FATHERS CAN'T SAVE THEM FROM RIDING TO A SINISTER RENDEZVOUS WITH DEATH AND DANGER AWAITING IN THE...
"LITTLE TOWN WITH A BIG SECRET!"
ART: PENCILS BY DICK DILLIN
INKS BY MURPHY ANDERSON
STORY: BOB HANEY
1

O'RYAN WAS HERE!

SPEAKING OF BILL-BOARDS...THAT ONE HAS SOME GRAFFITI PAINTED OVER... MY X-RAY VISION REVEALS IT TO BE... "O'RYAN WAS HERE!"

WHAT EVER HAPPENED TO KILROY?

FORGET IT, AND DIG THE WAY THAT TRUCK'S WEAVING ALL OVER!

MILK

YEEEOW! HE'S HOGGING US OFF THE ROAD!

SKREEEEEECH

BRRRRMMMM

HE WANTS THAT LANE-- OKAY, WE'LL TAKE THIS ONE!

WILD! HE'S SWUNG BACK!?

HEY, YOU CLOWN... GET OVER!!

HUH? NOBODY'S AT THE WHEEL--?!

BRUCE-- MY X-RAY SHOWS THE DRIVER'S ASLEEP!

I'VE GOT TO TAKE OVER! I'M BAILING OUT--

NOW!

I CAN'T HOLD HER!

MILK

KHAAA-

WHUMMMPP

THE NEXT MOMENT...

MILK

HAVE TO RISK TURNING THIS TANKER INTO A *SUPER MILK SHAKE*-- BUT HERE GOES!

MILK

HE BETTER HAVE A RELIEF DRIVER OR A LOT OF LUCK NEXT TRIP!

WHA--? MUSTA DOZED OFF! BUT THE OLD HANDS NEVER SLEEP! THEY KEPT ME HIGH-BALLING RIGHT DOWN THE OLD WHITE LINE!

AND AS THE TRUCK ROLLS AHEAD INTO BARSTOW...

CHITTER-CHEEE CHEEE

HA-HA! THAT PRAIRIE DOG'S GOT TO BE A "*HE*"-- BECAUSE HE CERTAINLY ISN'T ADMIRING YOUR RIPPLING MUSCLES, BRUCE! --HA-HA!

LAUGH, CLOWN, LAUGH!

WHILE *YOU* WERE PLAYING HERO, I WAS SAVING THE CYCLE FROM THE JUNK PILE!

LOOK, I'M SORRY IF I WAS BORN WITH SUPER STRENGTH! IT'S A BIG RESPONSIBILITY... AND IT DOESN'T GIVE ME TOTAL HAPPINESS!

3

OH, CUT THAT SHY-ADOLESCENT-WITH-A-HEAVY-PROBLEM ACT, BUDDY! I'M *SICK* OF IT!

YEAH? WELL, I'M SICK OF YOUR BIG HIPSTER ACT, TOO!

ONCE A PLAYBOY... ALWAYS A SPOILED PAIN, I SAY!

YOU WANT A SOCK IN THE NOSE?

YOU WANT A *SUPER* SOCK?

CLARK, BABY--WE MUST BE FLIPPIN'--YOU AND ME FIGHTING?! WE'VE BEEN ON THE ROAD TOO LONG!

IT'S MADE US BOTH UPTIGHT! WE NEED A CHANGE! LET'S HEAD INTO THIS TOWN--AND FIND IT!

SO CLARK KENT, JR. AND BRUCE WAYNE, JR. RIDE INTO BARSTOW AND THE ADVENTURE OF THEIR YOUNG LIVES!

HEY, THE PLACE IS FALLING APART!

AND YOU KNOW WHAT'S ODD? THERE ISN'T A *SINGLE PERSON* AROUND!

4

HI! MY NAME'S BOBBY!

WELL, AT LEAST THERE'S A *JUNIOR* CITIZEN!

HI, BOBBY...!

GET BACK IN HERE-- AND DON'T EVER TALK TO STRANGERS--

OR I'LL SEND YOU TO THE *ICE MAN!*

NO, MOMMY... NOT THAT! PLEASE...I'LL BE GOOD!

NOTICE HOW SCARED THAT KID WAS? I'VE HEARD OF PARENTS FRIGHTENING KIDS WITH ALL KINDS OF BOGEY MEN-- BUT NEVER AN... AN... *ICE MAN!?*

MAYBE BARSTOW'S GOT A PARTICU- LARLY NASTY GUY DELIVERING ICE!

NO WAY-- EVEN OUT HERE, THEY HAVE REFRIGERATORS, GENIUS!

LOOK, THERE'S THAT MILK TRUCK!

MILK

YESSIR, ED, I HAD A ROUGH TRIP... BUT I'M READY TO DELIVER THE MILK SO BARSTOW'S KIDS CAN GROW BIG AND STRONG, RIGHT?

CLARK, ARE YOU GETTING THE SAME VIBES I AM?

YES, BRUCE! THEY'RE BOTH HOSTILE TOWARD US... AND ARE TALKING LOUD SO WE'LL HEAR!

AND ALSO THAT DRIVER'S *LYING*-- THERE'S *NO* MILK IN THAT TRUCK!

5

IT'S FILLED WITH LIQUID, ALL RIGHT-- BUT AT HUNDREDS OF DEGREES *BELOW* ZERO!

WHEN I LIFTED THE TRUCK, THE METAL WAS SO COLD, IT WOULD'VE "BURNED" ORDINARY FLESH!

I DON'T GET IT! AT THAT TEMPERATURE, IT'D BE ONE BIG POPSICLE!

ONLY THING LIQUID AT THAT TEMPERATURE IS *GAS*... LIKE OXYGEN OR NITROGEN!

SO WHY THE PHONY MILK SIGN ON THAT RIG?

OH-OH-- HERE COMES "LAUGHING BOY!"

YOU BUYIN' SOMETHIN' OR JUST USING UP MY AIR?

WE'RE DOING A TEST ON TIRE AIR, MISTER... AND YOU'VE GOT THE BEST WE'VE COME ACROSS!

SAY, WHERE CAN WE GET A GOOD HAMBURGER?

WHAT? WELL, UH, ACROSS THE STREET! THEY'RE GOOD BECAUSE THEY'RE THE ONLY ONES IN TOWN!

YOU BOYS JUST PASSING THROUGH? COME ON IN! THE NAME'S SWEEPER WYATT-- I OWN THIS PLACE!

A FRIENDLY FACE AT LAST! WHAT'S WITH THIS TOWN, MR. WYATT? LOOKS LIKE A MOVIE SET *AFTER* THE CAMERAS STOPPED!

OH, BARSTOW'S A DYIN' TOWN! FIRST, THE MINES GAVE OUT... THEN WE HAD A MISSILE BASE... BUT THE GOVERNMENT CLOSED IT!

NOW THE OLD FOLKS DIE OFF, AND THE YOUNG ONES MOVE... AWAY!

YESSIR, BARSTOW'S FADIN' AWAY...

HI, BEAUTIFUL! I'M BRUCE, THE LOVER, AND THIS IS CLARK, THE READER! TWO BURGERS... *RARE!*

6

I'M LINDA, THE *COOKER*-- AND I PREFER READERS TO LOVERS!

OH-HO, SHE DIGS *YOU*, CLARK, BUT LOOKS LIKE WE'RE *BOTH* OUT OF LUCK!

SHE'S ALREADY GOT A GUY--CHECK THE PHOTO!

To LINDA, LOVE GAR O'RYAN

HE *WAS* MY BOYFRIEND... BUT HE'S ... HE'S *DEAD*!

DEAD? HEY, DOLL, DON'T CRY! I'M SORRY... I COULDN'T KNOW!

YOU UPSETTIN' THE GAL, BUSTER? I'M GONNA UPSET *YOU*!

WHA--??!

WE DON'T LIKE STRANGERS BUTTIN' IN-- UFFFFFFH!

WHAMMPF

THEN I'LL BUTT *OUT*--!

OH, THIS IS *TERRIBLE!* YOUR FRIEND WILL BE HURT! *HELP HIM!*

HE CAN TAKE CARE OF HIMSELF!

HMM, THAT PHOTO... REALLY INTERESTING! ESPECIALLY WITH *TELESCOPIC SCRUTINY!*

*B*RUCE, JR. FACING *BARSTOW* BULLIES-- AND CLARK, JR. STUDYING A SENTIMENTAL PHOTO! SEEMS A JUICY PLACE TO STOP *PART 1! PART 2* BUSTS WIDE OPEN ON THE NEXT PAGE !

7

PART TWO "THE PEOPLE WITHOUT SHADOWS"

YOU'LL GET A *KICK* OUT OF *THIS*, CHUM!

OW, THE THINGS I SAY UNDER PRESSURE!

WHOKK

GUESS THIS ONE NEVER TOOK A MAIL-ORDER JUDO COURSE -- OR HE'D NEVER HAVE *FALLEN* FOR *THIS*! OUCH! THAT HURTS EVEN *ME*!

KWAMM

⸓*WHEW!*⸓ THE THINGS THAT HAPPEN WHEN YOU ASK FOR A HAMBURGER IN THIS TOWN! THANKS FOR THE HELP, CLARK-BUDDY!

YOU'RE THE LOVER AND FIGHTER -- REMEMBER, BRUCE?

OH, IT'S ALL *MY* FAULT -- IF I HADN'T BROKEN DOWN....!

I KNOW THEY STARTED IT, YOUNG FELLA -- BUT MAYBE IT'S WISE IF YOU BOTH MOVE ON! DON'T MEAN TO BE UNFRIENDLY....!

WE GET THE VIBES, MR. WYATT! YOU'RE A RIGHT DUDE! SORRY IF WE CAUSED YOU ANY TROUBLE!

COME ON, CLARK!

BUT SOON A MILE OUT OF TOWN...

WE NEVER *DID* GET THOSE BURGERS ...SO IT'S BEANS AGAIN!

OUR COSTUMES?! I THOUGHT THIS WAS A VACATION FROM OUR SECRET IDENTITIES! WHAT GIVES?

SOMETHING VERY FUNNY GIVES BACK IN BARSTOW, BUDDY! A PHONY MILK TRUCK -- UPTIGHT PEOPLE IN A SEMI-GHOST TOWN -- KIDS BEING SCARED BY A FRIGID BOGEY MAN...

...IT *ALL* ADDS UP TO SOMETHING *WEIRD*!

8

AND LINDA'S BOY FRIEND'S NAME WAS O'RYAN, LIKE THE BILLBOARD'S PAINTED-OVER GRAFFITI! BUT EVEN WEIRDER... IN THE PHOTO LINDA HAD A SHADOW... *BUT HE DIDN'T!*

FAR OUT! OKAY, BARSTOW DIDN'T LIKE CLARK AND BRUCE-- LET'S SEE HOW THEY WELCOME *SUPERMAN, JUNIOR AND BATMAN, JUNIOR!*

SHORTLY, A FAMILIAR FIGURE FLIES OVER AN ARID LANDSCAPE...

THE PHONY MILK TRUCK TURNED OFF THE HIGHWAY... BUT THEN ITS TIRE TRACKS SUDDENLY STOP?!

MY *X-RAY* VISION REVEALS NOTHING UNDERGROUND... BUT THAT BIG RIG COULDN'T JUST *VANISH?!*

AND, BACK IN BARSTOW, IT IS *BATMAN'S* YOUNG HEIR WHO PROWLS...

DAD ALWAYS SAID A TOWN'S GRAVEYARD CAN TELL YOU LOTS ABOUT A PLACE AND ITS PEOPLE!

GUESS THIS IS BARSTOW'S BOOT HILL!

BUT AS THE *SON* OF THE *MAN OF STEEL* CIRCLES IN THE HOT SHIMMERING AIR...

HARD TO MAKE IT OUT-- BUT I'LL BET IT'S JUST WHAT I FEARED!... MUST WARN THE OTHERS--QUICKLY!

KELL
1850-1908

ERENEZ GORH

THESE THREE NAME-LESS TOMBSTONES ARE THE MOST RECENT-- BUT SWEEPER WYATT SAID BARSTOW'S OLD FOLKS WERE DYING OFF...

YET, NOBODY'S BEEN PLANTED HERE IN FOUR LONG YEARS! HMMMM?!

THEN AS DARKNESS CLOSES DOWN...

THE TOWN UNDERTAKER ...HE'S CLOSED UP AND GONE, TOO! THAT'S A REAL MIND-GRABBER!

MOMENTS LATER...

NOW LET'S SEE WHAT THE TOWN HALL RECORDS REVEAL ABOUT WEIRDSVILLE-ON-THE-PRAIRIE!

HMM, STRANGE KIND OF TOWN BUDGET ...AND WHAT'S THE GOLDEN TOMORROW FUND?

SUDDENLY...

A SEARCHLIGHT! SOMEBODY'S WISE I'M HERE!

GOT TO EXIT THIS WAY... OOUFF!

CRA SSH

STAGGERED BY THE SURPRISE BLOW, THE JUNIOR CAPED CRUSADER STILL MANAGES TO STAY ON HIS FEET, AND...

I HIT HIM-- BUT HE KEPT GOIN'!

WE'LL GET HIM, SHERIFF!

10

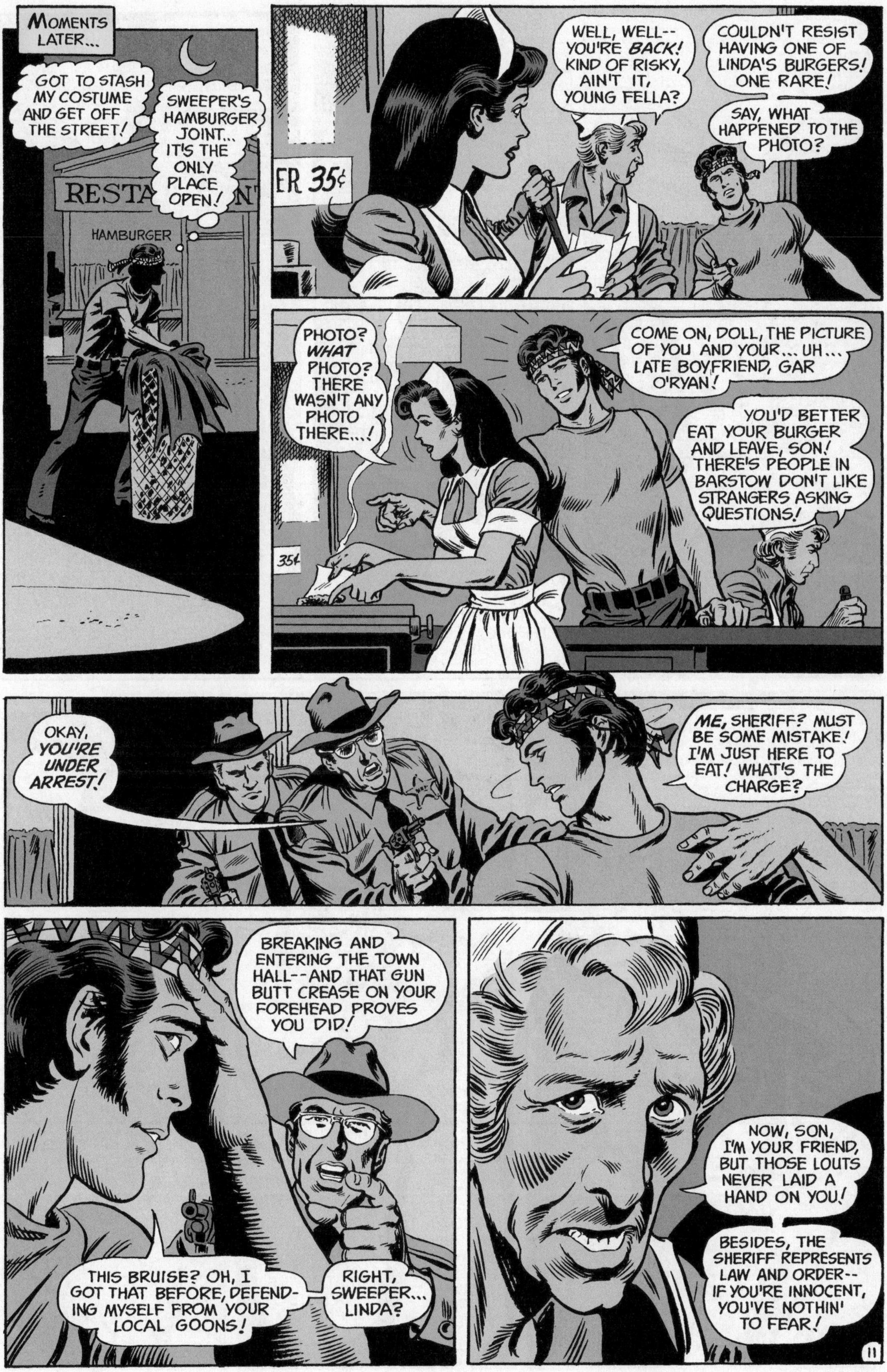
MOMENTS LATER...
GOT TO STASH MY COSTUME AND GET OFF THE STREET!
SWEEPER'S HAMBURGER JOINT... IT'S THE ONLY PLACE OPEN!
RESTA NT
HAMBURGER
ER 35¢
WELL, WELL-- YOU'RE BACK! KIND OF RISKY, AIN'T IT, YOUNG FELLA?
COULDN'T RESIST HAVING ONE OF LINDA'S BURGERS! ONE RARE!
SAY, WHAT HAPPENED TO THE PHOTO?
PHOTO? WHAT PHOTO? THERE WASN'T ANY PHOTO THERE...!
COME ON, DOLL, THE PICTURE OF YOU AND YOUR... UH... LATE BOYFRIEND, GAR O'RYAN!
YOU'D BETTER EAT YOUR BURGER AND LEAVE, SON! THERE'S PEOPLE IN BARSTOW DON'T LIKE STRANGERS ASKING QUESTIONS!
35¢
OKAY, YOU'RE UNDER ARREST!
ME, SHERIFF? MUST BE SOME MISTAKE! I'M JUST HERE TO EAT! WHAT'S THE CHARGE?
BREAKING AND ENTERING THE TOWN HALL--AND THAT GUN BUTT CREASE ON YOUR FOREHEAD PROVES YOU DID!
THIS BRUISE? OH, I GOT THAT BEFORE, DEFENDING MYSELF FROM YOUR LOCAL GOONS!
RIGHT, SWEEPER... LINDA?
NOW, SON, I'M YOUR FRIEND, BUT THOSE LOUTS NEVER LAID A HAND ON YOU!
BESIDES, THE SHERIFF REPRESENTS LAW AND ORDER-- IF YOU'RE INNOCENT, YOU'VE NOTHIN' TO FEAR!
11

LINDA... TELL THE SHERIFF HE'S GOT ME WRONG!

COME ON, BOY! YOU'RE COMING ALONG WITH US!

I COULD FIGHT MY WAY OUT--BUT THIS IS THE "LAW"! BETTER GO QUIETLY... AND SEE WHAT DEVELOPS! THAT'S WHAT DAD WOULD DO!

SOME TIME LATER...

YOU GOT A VISITOR, BOY!

CLARK! ABOUT TIME!

HI, BRUCIE! HOW'S THE LOVER? WHAT YOU WON'T GO THROUGH FOR A HAMBURGER!

THERE! NOW WE GOT BOTH YOU NOSEY TROUBLEMAKERS!

BUT YOU CAN'T HOLD HIM! YOU'VE NO RIGHT... NO CHARGES!

KALAAANNNG

I GOT ALL THE RIGHT AND CHARGES I NEED HERE--IN MY GUN!

YOU TWO ARE GOING TO BE SORRY YOU EVER CAME SNOOPIN' AROUND BARSTOW!

WOW! WE'RE IN LARGE TROUBLE, PAL! SOMETHING IS DEFINITELY WRONG IN THIS TOWN WHEN THE LAW'S PLAYING VIGILANTE!

CHECK! WHEN YOU DIDN'T SHOW UP AT OUR RENDEZVOUS, I FIGURED YOU WERE IN A JAM! NOW WE'D BETTER COMPARE WHAT WE'VE FOUND SO FAR...!

SHORTLY...

SO THE TRUCK VANISHED? JUST LIKE BARSTOW'S DISAPPEARING CITIZENS!

BUT HOW? AND WHY? I COULD BUST US OUT OF HERE...

12

NO WAY! THAT'D REVEAL YOUR SUPER IDENTITY... AND WHAT'S OUR NEXT MOVE, ANYWAY? ALL THESE CLUES COME TO A *DEAD END!*

RIGHT NOW, I WISH OUR DADS WERE HERE-- NOT *US!* I'D TRADE A LITTLE YOUTHFUL *ZING* FOR SOME OF THEIR *EXPERIENCE!*

CLARK! BRUCE!

LINDA?!

I...I'M SO SORRY THIS HAPPENED! I LIKE YOU BOTH-- AND WANT TO HELP, BUT I'M AFRAID!

EASY, DOLL! THE PICTURE-- WHY'D YOU *LIE* ABOUT IT?

I *HAD* TO! *THEY* MADE ME TAKE IT DOWN AND DESTROY IT-- JUST LIKE *GAR* WAS DESTROYED!

WHO ARE... *THEY?* WHAT DO YOU MEAN, LIKE *GAR* WAS DESTROYED?

SOMEONE'S COMING! I CAN'T STAY HERE!

RUNNING FOOTSTEPS, AND THEN...!

I GOT HER!

YOU'RE GOING TO SEE THE *ICE MAN,* NOW!

OH, PLEASE, NO... NO... NO!

THEY'VE GOT LINDA-- AND THE *ICE MAN'S* NO BOGEY JUST TO SCARE KIDS! WE'VE GOT TO BUST OUT!

WE'RE ALREADY ON OUR WAY!

THE SHERIFF'S GOT HER! IT'S *JUNIOR SUPER HERO* TIME AGAIN, TIGER!

FOLLOW THEM!

AS SOON AS I BEND THESE BACK...TO GIVE THEM SOMETHING TO WONDER ABOUT!

RESTAURA

13

IN A FEW MINUTES, A RED AND BLUE BLUR STREAKS ABOVE THE HIGHWAY OUT OF BARSTOW...

THEY'RE TURNING OFF ONTO THE SAME CROSS-COUNTRY ROUTE THE PHONY MILK TRUCK TOOK!

BUT AS *SUPERMAN, JR.* PLUMMETS DOWN THROUGH THE BILLOWING DUST PLUME CREATED BY THE SPEEDING AUTO...

GOT TO SNEEZE...

AAAAAAAACHAAAAAAAA-HAAAAWWW...

SOMERSAULTED BACKWARDS A HALF MILE BY THE FORCE OF HIS OWN SNEEZE, THE YOUTHFUL *SUPERMAN* STREAKS FORWARD AGAIN TO...

ALWAYS DID HAVE AN ALLERGIC REACTION TO DUST!

HUH? THE CAR VANISHED AT THE SAME SPOT AS THE TRUCK!

MY *X-RAY VISION* REVEALS NOTHING AGAIN...!

HOLD IT! I JUST REALIZED-- I'M NOT EVEN GETTING A NORMAL X-RAY VIEW OF UNDERGROUND STRATA!

SOMETHING'S BLOCKING THE X-RAYS... AND ONLY ONE THING CAN DO THAT-- *LEAD!*

THERE, I'VE THRUST MY FINGERS DOWN INTO THIS DUSTY HARDPACK,... TO A BIG METAL PANEL OR LID!

1A

THEN, WITH A POWERFUL TUG...

GREAT KRYPTON, AS DAD WOULD SAY -- AN UNDERGROUND MISSILE SILO! SWEEPER SAID THE GOVERNMENT CLOSED ONE DOWN AROUND HERE!

IT'S BIG ENOUGH TO SWALLOW THAT TRUCK, AND A DOZEN CARS!

THE DOORS MUST'VE BEEN COATED WITH LEAD TO SHIELD THE DELICATE MISSILE-AIMING EQUIP-MENT FROM ENEMY *ABM* RADIATION OR COSMIC RAYS!

BUT WHAT'S BARSTOW'S SHERIFF USING AN ABANDONED MISSILE SILO FOR... AND WHY THEY'D BRING LINDA HERE?

MAYBE THE ANSWER IS *THIS* WAY!

CONTROL CHAMBER

THIS IS *FANTASTIC!* BARSTOW'S MISSING CITIZENS... YOUNG AND OLD... ALL IN CRYOGENIC CAP-SULES... *FROZEN ALIVE!*

I'VE FOUND THE ANSWER TO PART OF THE MYSTERY!

THAT'S NOT *ALL* YOU'VE FOUND, CHIP-OFF-THE-OLD-SUPER-BLOCK!! TO WITNESS *SUPER, JR.'S* UPCOMING SUPER-TROUBLE, FLIP DIRECTLY TO *PART 3* -- BECAUSE THIS IS THE END OF *PART 2!* COLD TRUTH!

15

PART THREE CHILDREN OF THE UNIVERSE

GET INTO THE CAPSULE, GIRL! YOUR TIME HAS COME!

PLEASE, *NO!* I WASN'T TO GO FOR *WEEKS* YET! YOU'RE DOING THIS TO *PUNISH* ME!

LINDA! THEY'RE GOING TO *FREEZE* HER!

YOU WERE READY TO BETRAY US ALL TO THOSE TWO YOUNG STRANGERS!

IT WON'T HURT, GIRL! GET IT OVER WITH! IF YOU DON'T, WE'LL *FORCE* YOU, ANYWAY!

NO YOU WON'T!

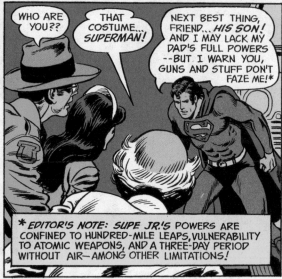

WHO ARE YOU??

THAT COSTUME... *SUPERMAN!*

NEXT BEST THING, FRIEND... *HIS SON!* AND I MAY LACK MY *DAD'S* FULL POWERS --BUT I WARN YOU, GUNS AND STUFF DON'T *FAZE* ME!*

*EDITOR'S NOTE: SUPE JR.'S POWERS ARE CONFINED TO HUNDRED-MILE LEAPS, VULNERABILITY TO ATOMIC WEAPONS, AND A THREE-DAY PERIOD WITHOUT AIR—AMONG OTHER LIMITATIONS!

NOW LET HER GO!

ALL WE'LL LET GO IS LIQUID NITROGEN RIGHT AT *YOU!*

SPOOOOSSHH

CAUGHT OFF-GUARD, THE INTENSELY COLD CRYOGENIC FLUID HITS LIKE A NUMBING SHOCKWAVE...

I-I'M STIFFENING UP! GOT TO GRAB THAT HOSE!

SPOOOSSHH

16

BUT WITHIN AN INSTANT HIS MOLECULES ARE SLOWED TO WHERE HIS STRENGTH IS REDUCED TO THAT OF AN *ORDINARY* MORTAL...

I'LL... CLOBBER... YOU... WHEN... I... CATCH... YOU...!

NO CHANCE!

SPOOOSSHH

AND IN ANOTHER TICK OF TIME...

YOU *DID* IT, *ICE MAN!* YOU STOPPED HIM *COLD!*

YOU... YOU *MONSTERS!*

IT WAS NECESSARY! THE *OUTSIDE* WORLD MUST NOT LEARN WHAT WE DO HERE!

NOW, IT'S *YOUR* TURN!

MEANTIME, ON A DESERTED ROAD JUST OUT OF TOWN...

A BURNT-OUT RUIN-- ALL THAT'S LEFT OF THE O'RYAN FAMILY HOME! I GOT ITS LOCATION FROM TOWN TAX RECORDS!

BUT *WHO WERE* THEY, REALLY?

EVIDENTLY THEY CAME TO BARSTOW SHORTLY BEFORE THEIR SON, GAR, DIED!

WHAT A BUBBLEBRAIN I'VE BEEN! THOSE THREE TOMBSTONES DIDN'T THROW SHADOWS, EITHER!

AND I THINK I KNOW *WHY* THE WHOLE O'RYAN FAMILY'S BURIED UNDER THEM!

BUT WHAT HAPPENED TO HIS *PARENTS*-- THE MOTHER AND FATHER OF THE KID WITHOUT A SHADOW?

AND NAMELESS GRAVES... AS IF THEIR DEATHS WERE SUSPICIOUS!

WHAT'S *THIS?* A FUNNY KIND OF COMPASS GIZMO? IT DOESN'T POINT NORTH... BUT *SOUTHWEST?*

17

As the son of the world's greatest detective follows another hunch...

I'VE FOLLOWED THIS GIZMO'S NEEDLE FOR MILES INTO THESE HILLS!

WHERE'S IT TAKING ME?

Soon, leaving his cycle, and moving ahead on foot...

A DEAD-END CANYON--

--AND HIDDEN IN IT... A SHIMMERING, SEAMLESS GIANT OBJECT!

Suddenly, a tumbling pebble shatters the stillness...

SWEEPER! SOMEHOW I FIGURED IT WAS YOU!

DON'T KNOW HOW YOU FOUND IT, FELLA-- BUT IT'LL DO YOU NO GOOD!

RAISE THOSE HANDS, IF YOU WANT TO KEEP ON LIVIN'!

THAT SPHERE'S OURS NOW... THE PEOPLE OF BARSTOW!

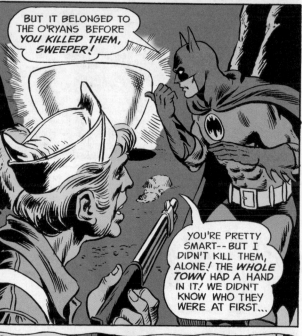

BUT IT BELONGED TO THE O'RYANS BEFORE YOU KILLED THEM, SWEEPER!

YOU'RE PRETTY SMART-- BUT I DIDN'T KILL THEM, ALONE! THE WHOLE TOWN HAD A HAND IN IT! WE DIDN'T KNOW WHO THEY WERE AT FIRST...

"SEEMED LIKE A NICE FAMILY MOVIN' IN FROM OUT OF STATE! THEN, ONE DAY, THEIR BOY, GAR, STARTED SHOWIN' OFF TO IMPRESS LINDA..."

GAR! YOU PASSED YOUR HAND RIGHT THROUGH THAT POST!

BECAUSE I'M NOT AN EARTHLING... I'M FROM SPACE... FROM THE CONSTELLATION ORION!

18

"LINDA GOT SCARED AND TOLD HER FOLKS. SOON, THE WHOLE TOWN WAS AROUSED..."

IT'S HORRIBLE-- *THEM* LIVING RIGHT AMONG US!

BUT THEY *LOOK* AND *ACT* LIKE US!

YEAH, THAT'S WHAT'S SO SCARY!

FUNNY HOW WE NEVER NOTICED THEY HAVE NO SHADOWS!

"BARSTOW HAD HAD A RUN OF BAD LUCK--THE MISSILE BASE CLOSIN'!.. FREAKISH WEATHER... PEOPLE DYIN' IN ACCIDENTS..."

IT'S *THEIR* FAULT! THEY'RE WORKING EVIL ON THE TOWN!

"I WAS IN THAT MAD CROWD AS WAS MOST OF BARSTOW! WHEN WE REACHED THE O'RYAN HOUSE, GAR'S FATHER FACED US..."

YES...IT'S *TRUE*--WE *ARE* FROM FAR SPACE! WE CAME HERE BY ACCIDENT WHEN OUR STAR-SHIP'S FUEL CORE MALFUNCTIONED!

THE SHIP IS NEAR HERE--*LOCKED*--AND WILL REPAIR ITSELF AUTOMATI-CALLY BY THE YEAR 1994!

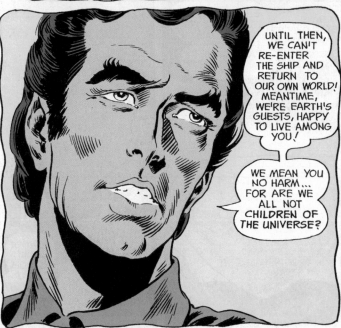

UNTIL THEN, WE CAN'T RE-ENTER THE SHIP AND RETURN TO OUR OWN WORLD! MEANTIME, WE'RE EARTH'S GUESTS, HAPPY TO LIVE AMONG YOU!

WE MEAN YOU NO HARM... FOR ARE WE ALL NOT CHILDREN OF THE UNIVERSE?

PLEASE, *PUT ASIDE* YOUR ANGER AND FEAR! AND WHEN THE SHIP RE-OPENS, WE'LL REWARD YOU ALL GREATLY! IT CONTAINS IMMENSE *RICHES*!

19

"GUESS HIS STRANGE TALK AND THE CROWD'S MOOD WAS LIKE GASOLINE AND MATCHES! SUDDENLY, THE O'RYAN HOUSE WAS ABLAZE..."

THEY'RE TRAPPED IN THERE!

SERVES 'EM RIGHT!

I CAN FILL IN THE REST! LATER, YOU ALL FELT GUILTY, AFRAID OF PUNISHMENT BY OUR LAW... OR PERHAPS FROM THE O'RYANS' WORLD!

SO *YOU,* SWEEPER, FIGURED A WAY TO EVADE JUSTICE AND YOUR OWN CONSCIENCES!

YOU BEGAN TO SLOWLY PHASE OUT THE WHOLE TOWN --USING MOST OF ITS BUDGET TO BUY CRYOGENIC EQUIPMENT TO PUT EVERY-ONE INTO DEEP FREEZE!

THAT WAS THE *GOLDEN TOMORROW FUND* I FOUND IN THE FILES!

YOU ALL *CONSPIRED* TO HIDE ANY CLUE TO THE O'RYANS' VERY EXISTENCE!

LIKE PAINTING OVER THE GRAFFITI GAR LEFT ON THE BILLBOARD...DESTROY-ING THAT PHOTO OF HIM AND LINDA....!

THEN, *YEARS FROM NOW,* WHEN YOU ALL THAWED OUT, YOUR COMMON CRIME WOULD BE ANCIENT HISTORY, AND YOU'D HAVE THE STAR-SHIP'S TREASURE!

YEAH, WE'D NEED THE TREASURE TO REBUILD! WE COULDN'T BRING BACK THE O'RYANS--

BUT WHY SHOULD WE ALL SUFFER FOR THE MIS-TAKES OF BARSTOW'S ONE BAD NIGHT?

BUT YOUR WAY IS *IMMORAL...CRAZY!* GIVE IT UP!

TOO LATE! I JUST DELIVERED THE LAST OF BARSTOW'S CITIZENS TO THE *ICE MAN!* IN 1994, THEY'LL THAW OUT INTO A BETTER WORLD!

YOU'RE GOIN' TO JOIN 'EM! MARCH!

20

NOT LONG AFTER...

YOU FROZE MY BUDDY... AND LINDA?

HAD TO! HIS STRENGTH COULD'VE WRECKED EVERYTHING!

FUNNY, TOO, BECAUSE WHEN I FIRST SPOTTED HIM FLYIN' AROUND, I MISTOOK HIM FOR AVENGERS FROM THE O'RYANS' PLANET!

THAT'S WHY WE SPEEDED UP THE PHASE-OUT... TILL NOW ONLY US THREE ARE LEFT, BESIDES YOU, FELLA!

AND YOU GOT TO BE FROZEN TO KEEP YOU QUIET!

NOW CLIMB INTO THAT CAPSULE AND SAY GOODBYE TO YOUR SUPER-BUDDY THERE UNTIL THE YEAR 1994!

AND MAYBE GOODBYE TO OUR PARENTS WHO MIGHT BE DEAD BY THEN! OUR FRIENDS WILL BE OLDER... OUR WORLD WILL BE DEAD, TOO!

IT CHILLS MY BLOOD JUST THINKING ABOUT IT!

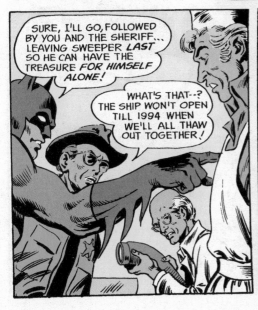

SURE, I'LL GO, FOLLOWED BY YOU AND THE SHERIFF... LEAVING SWEEPER LAST SO HE CAN HAVE THE TREASURE FOR HIMSELF ALONE!

WHAT'S THAT--? THE SHIP WON'T OPEN TILL 1994 WHEN WE'LL ALL THAW OUT TOGETHER!

WRONG, SHERIFF! IT'LL OPEN SOONER... MUCH SOONER-- AND SWEEPER KNOWS IT! MR. O'RYAN MISCALCULATED THE STRENGTH OF EARTH'S MAGNETIC FIELDS!

DON'T LISTEN TO HIM!

21

NO, LET'S HEAR HIM!

ANY OF YOU EVER BEEN NEAR THE SHIP?

WHY, NO--SWEEPER SAID ITS EXACT LOCATION SHOULD STAY WITH HIM ONLY... TO DECREASE CHANCES OF SOMEBODY BLABBING!

WELL, I'VE BEEN NEAR IT, AND MY WATCH HANDS ACCELERATED LIKE CRAZY... DAYS GOING BY IN MINUTES!

SWEEPER MUST HAVE NOTICED IT, TOO... THE SHIP'S ON DIFFERENT TIME DUE TO RESIDUAL MAGNETISM FROM ORION!

FREEZE HIM--OR I'LL SHOOT HIM!

I DO THE ONLY SHOOTING IN BARSTOW! TALK ON, SON!

BEFORE I FOUND THE SHIP, I CHECKED THE TOWN LIBRARY!

SWEEPER'S LIBRARY CARD SHOWED HE BORROWED A BOOK ON ASTROPHYSICS AND TIME-SPACE THEORY! I SAW THE BOOK, ITS UNDERLINED PASSAGES PROVE HE FIGURED OUT THE SHIP WILL OPEN... THIS YEAR... VERY SOON!

BARSTOW PUBLIC LIBRARY

___ SWEEP MUM

SPOOOOOOOSH

THAT'S REALLY WHY HE SPEEDED UP THE PHASE-OUT! HE NEVER INTENDED TO JOIN THE REST OF BARSTOW IN DEEP FREEZE...

BUT GRAB THE SHIP'S TREASURE AND TAKE OFF WITH IT!

I'LL QUIET YOU!

NO, YOU DON'T, SWEEPER!

22

WELL, I'LL BE--! SWEEPER WAS HOODWINKING US ALL!

BUT...BUT WHAT NOW? IF THE SHIP'S DUE TO OPEN, I CAN THAW OUT EVERYONE, AND BARSTOW COULD REBUILD ITSELF WITH THE TREASURE!

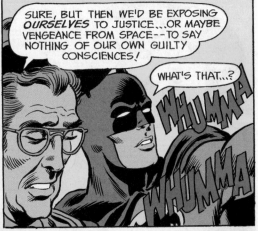

SURE, BUT THEN WE'D BE EXPOSING *OURSELVES* TO JUSTICE...OR MAYBE VENGEANCE FROM SPACE--TO SAY NOTHING OF OUR OWN GUILTY CONSCIENCES!

WHAT'S THAT...?

WHUMMA

WHUMMA

MOMENTS LATER, OUTSIDE...

THE O'RYANS' STAR-SHIP! JUST AS SWEEPER FIGURED, IT'S FIXED ITSELF...WAY AHEAD OF 1994!

WHUMMA WHUMMA

BUT THE TREASURE... THE RICHES WE ALL RANSOMED OUR FUTURES TO--?

LOOKS LIKE IT'S GOING BACK TO WHERE IT CAME FROM... THE FAR, FAR HOME OF THE O'RYAN FAMILY! IRONIC, EH?

SOME TIME LATER...

WELL, BARSTOW'S RETURNED TO LIFE...TO FACING THE CONSEQUENCES OF ITS ONE BAD NIGHT! THE GOVERNOR PARDONED THE TOWN FOR THE O'RYANS' DEATHS...

AND SWEEPER WYATT'S GONE...A DISCREDITED WANDERER!

23

IN RETURN FOR OUR GUARANTEE, BARSTOW WILL ALWAYS WELCOME ANY TRAVELER OR STRANGER WITH OPEN ARMS FOREVER MORE!

LIKE MR. O'RYAN SAID, WE'RE ALL EARTHLINGS AND ALIENS...CHILDREN OF THE UNIVERSE!

THAT MAKES ME SAD ABOUT THOSE TWO NICE STRANGERS WE PERSECUTED... BRUCE AND CLARK! AND HOW'D THEY ESCAPE FROM THE JAIL CELL?

MAYBE THEY WERE INSUBSTANTIAL SPACE BEINGS, TOO, LINDA!

ANYWAY, I'VE GOT A HUNCH YOU'LL BE SEEING THEM AGAIN ONE DAY!

24

SHORTLY...

SO LONG, CLARK AND BRUCE... FOR NOW! BUT YOU'LL BE BACK--AS WILL YOUR FAMOUS FATHERS, IN FAB FUTURE ISSUES OF *WORLD'S FINEST*! STAY WITH IT! NEVER *THE END*!

"CRY NOT FOR MY FORSAKEN SON!"

STORY: BOB HANEY

ART BY DICK DILLIN & MURPHY ANDERSON

TWO HOUSEHOLDS, SO *DIFFERENT* ON THE SURFACE, BUT YET SO UNIQUELY *ALIKE* WITH THEIR SPECIAL PROBLEM...

WHAT? YOU TWO HAVE SURE *REVERSED* YOURSELVES! BRUCE AND I ALREADY TRIED OUR SUPER-HERO WINGS AND WE DID OKAY!

WE CAN'T STOP *NOW!*

WHAT A SWITCH! CLARK AND I DID OUR THING TWICE AND SURVIVED-- WHAT'S DIFFERENT ABOUT *THIS* TIME?

ADULTS-- I'LL NEVER DIG THEIR HEADS!

I MUST ADMIT THE BOYS SURPRISED *BATMAN* AND ME BY "COMING BACK FROM THE DEAD" IN THEIR FIRST ADVENTURE TO WRECK A MAFIA GANG!

IT'S TRUE THE BOYS DID *SUPERMAN* AND ME PROUD BY SOLVING THE MYSTERY OF THAT PHONY WESTERN "GHOST TOWN" IN THEIR SECOND ADVENTURE!

BARSTOW HOTEL

BUT FATHERS, INWARDLY PROUD, ARE OFTEN *OTHER-WISE* ON THE OUTSIDE!

LISTEN HERE-- YOU MUST STOP NOW, BEFORE YOUR LUCK RUNS OUT! REMEMBER, YOUR POWERS AREN'T AS GREAT AS MINE!*

ALL THE *MORE* REASON I HAVE TO KEEP PROVING MYSELF!

*EDITOR'S NOTE: SUPES JR.'S POWERS ARE ROUGHLY HALF OF THOSE OF SUPES SR.-- BUT STILL DEVELOPING!

ONE MEMBER OF THE FAMILY RISKING HIS NECK'S ENOUGH-- AND YOUTHFUL SINEWS AND REFLEXES *AREN'T* ENOUGH! YOU NEED *EXPERIENCE!*

AND THE ONLY WAY TO GET THAT IS TO KEEP ON BEING *BATMAN JR.*

2

AND SONS, INWARDLY INSECURE, MUST BOLDLY CHALLENGE LIFE AND AUTHORITY ON THE OUTSIDE!

SORRY, FOLKS, MY DESTINY CALLS, CORNBALL AS THAT MAY SOUND!

HE'S BREAKING HIS MOTHER'S HEART!

SORRY, BUT I'M "TURNED ON" TO THE *BATMAN* BAG, AND YOU CAN'T TURN ME OFF!

HE'LL GIVE ME A BREAK-DOWN YET!

TWO UNIQUE YOUNG MEN WITH THE SAME PROBLEM--TWO LOVING FRIENDS WHO SOON MAKE A RENDEZVOUS IN GOTHAM CITY...

CLARK, BABY, WHAT TOOK YOU SO LONG?

HEAD WINDS EVERY MILE FROM *METROPOLIS*, BRUCE! BESIDES, I HAD A BIG HASSLE WITH MY PARENTS!

ME, TOO! MAN, I'M REALLY DRAGGED BEING *BATMAN'S* BOY SOMETIMES!

FORGIVE THE COMPARISON, BUDDY, BUT BEING *SUPERMAN'S* SCION IS EVEN *TOUGHER*! GUESS NO TWO GUYS EVER HAD *OUR* PROBLEMS!

FUZZ.... AFTER SOMEBODY! IT'S ACTION TIME, TIGER!

THE NEXT MOMENT, TWO LITHE FIGURES DROP FROM NOWHERE...

FAR ENOUGH!

3

COMMISSIONER GORDON! WHAT'S THE BEEF, SIR?

BATMAN JR. AND SUPERMAN JR.?! THIS PUNK JUST STOLE THAT CAR!

UP AGAINST THE WALL, BUSTER!

I JUST BORROWED IT....!

A LIKELY STORY!

BUT MOST LIKELY TRUE, SIR! CRIME STATISTICS PROVE MOST YOUNG CAR "THIEVES" RETURN THE VEHICLE SOON AFTER!

DANNY ORR, EH? EVER BEEN IN TROUBLE BEFORE?

NO WAY! I JUST BORROWED THE WHEELS TO GET AWAY FROM MY PROBLEMS!

HOW ABOUT RELEASING DANNY IN OUR CUSTODY? WE'LL VOUCH FOR HIM!

HMMM, YOU DID APPREHEND HIM-- AND I DO OWE YOUR DAD, THE BATMAN, A FEW FAVORS!

OKAY, DANNY, KEEP CLEAN FROM NOW ON!

THANKS, SIR! COME ON, DANNY, LET'S WALK AND RAP!

SHORTLY...

HEY, WE UNDERSTAND, FELLA-- WE GOT HANG-UPS, TOO! LIKE BEING THE SONS OF FAMOUS FATHERS!

YOU TWO CLOWNS MAKE ME SICK! YOU GOT PROBLEMS BECAUSE YOUR FATHERS ARE SO POWERFUL AND FAMOUS! HOW'D YOU LIKE A FATHER WHO'S A NOTHING... A NOBODY?!

COME ON, I'LL SHOW YOU MY OLD MAN!

4

SHORTLY, A FEW STREETS AWAY...

THAT'S *HIM*, JACK ORR, BOWING AND SCRAPING FOR TIPS! HE WEARS A UNIFORM, TOO-- BUT HE'S NO HERO!

A DOORMAN? WELL, IT'S *HONEST* WORK, DANNY!

THAT'S *ALL IT IS!* MY MOTHER'S DEAD AND WITH HIM WORKING LONG HOURS, I NEVER SAW MUCH OF HIM! BUT WHY SHOULD I CARE...

...THAT FAILURE'S *NOT* MY *REAL* FATHER! I JUST FOUND OUT TODAY I'M *ADOPTED!*

IT BLEW MY MIND... GUESS THAT'S WHY I "BORROWED" THAT CAR!

DANNY! WHERE ARE YOU GOING?

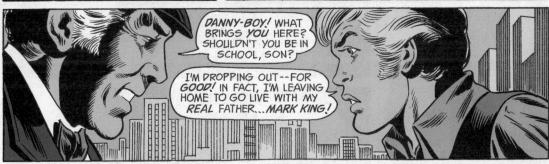

DANNY-BOY! WHAT BRINGS *YOU* HERE? SHOULDN'T YOU BE IN SCHOOL, SON?

I'M DROPPING OUT--FOR *GOOD!* IN FACT, I'M LEAVING HOME TO GO LIVE WITH MY *REAL* FATHER...*MARK KING!*

FOR A MOMENT, THE MIDDLE-AGED MAN STARES IN SHOCK...

SO YOU FOUND OUT SOMEHOW ...AT LAST! I...I'M SORRY, SON! I ALWAYS FEARED THIS DAY WOULD COME! I MEANT TO TELL YOU--

SURE, I'LL BET! HERE'S A TIP FOR PUTTING UP WITH ME ALL THESE YEARS!

SEE YOU AROUND, "*DAD*"!

WHAT A ROTTEN THING TO DO! I FEEL LIKE PADDLING HIS TAIL!

EASY, BUDDY! WE THOUGHT *WE* HAD PROBLEMS! DANNY'S ON A MUCH HEAVIER TRIP! HE NEEDS *HELP*-- NOT *HASSLES!*

I'LL SHADOW HIM WHILE YOU DO A LITTLE DETECTIVE WORK!

5

SOON, AT ONE OF GOTHAM'S NEWEST GLITTERING GLASS SKYSCRAPERS...

JUST TELL MR. KING HIS SON DANNY IS HERE!

KING BUILDING

DANNY! DANNY, MY OWN SON! THIS IS FANTASTIC!

OUT OF HERE, *ALL OF YOU!* I'VE GOT TO GET ACQUAINTED WITH MY BOY!

WHAT A SCENE-- *THIS* IS WHERE I BELONG! HE'S EVEN TALLER THAN I IMAGINED... AND WHEN HE TALKS... OTHER MEN *JUMP!*

DANNY, YOU REALLY GREW UP! HOW'D YOU FIND OUT ABOUT ME?

FROM AN OLD LETTER MY FOSTER-FATHER HAD HIDDEN AWAY! IT WAS SOME SHOCK!

I'LL BET! I *MEANT* TO LOOK YOU UP, KID... OFTEN... BUT I WAS SO BUSY BUILDING MY BUSINESS! AND I WASN'T SURE *YOU'D* WANT TO SEE ME...

I OFTEN WONDERED ABOUT THAT, BUT I'M WILLING TO FORGET THE PAST, DAD! IT'S *YOU* AND *YOUR* KIND OF LIFE I WANT AND NEED NOW!

YOU'RE A CHIP OFF THE OLD KING-BLOCK! ALL THESE YEARS APART DIDN'T MAKE YOU INTO A NO-WHERE-LOSER! YOU'RE A WINNER... JUST LIKE ME!

NOW, SON, WE'RE GOING TO MAKE UP FOR LOST TIME!

WELL, DANNY'S FOUND HIS *NEW* LIFE-- WONDER WHAT BRUCE'S FOUND OUT ABOUT HIS *OLD* ONE?

THAT WILL UNRAVEL IN *PART 2*--BECAUSE IT'S COMING RIGHT UP *NEXT!*

6

PART 2 — RENDEZVOUS ON MASSACRE ISLAND

IT IS A WHILE LATER, AND THE SONS OF THE WORLD'S GREATEST HEROES WATCH A TOUCHING SCENE...

THERE GOES DANNY, OFF WITH HIS NEW DAD! WHAT'D YOU FIND OUT, BRUCE?

JACK ORR AND MARK KING WERE FRIENDS AND PROSPECTING PARTNERS! THEY BOTH LOVED THE SAME GIRL, DANNY'S MOTHER!

"MARK KING WON OUT AND MARRIED HER...

SO LONG, DARLING! WE'LL BE BACK IN A FEW MONTHS AS MILLIONAIRES!

ANNE...YOU'RE MARK'S WIFE, BUT I'LL ALWAYS LOVE YOU!

SOUTHERN STAR

"DANNY'S MOTHER DIED IN CHILDBIRTH WHILE THE TWO MEN WERE STILL PROSPECTING IN CENTRAL AMERICA...

JACK, ANNE'S... DEAD! BUT IF I GO BACK NOW TO TAKE CARE OF THE KID--WE'LL LOSE OUR CHANCE TO MAKE A BIG EMERALD FIND!

YOU'RE THE MINERAL EXPERT, MARK...I CAN BE MORE EASILY SPARED! I'LL GO!

"BECAUSE HE HAD LOVED DANNY'S MOTHER SO MUCH, JACK ORR DID COME BACK TO TAKE CARE OF HIM...

ANNE KING RIP

"TIME WENT BY, AND JACK ORR RAISED YOUNG DANNY, AS MARK KING CONTINUED HIS FRANTIC SEARCH FOR RICHES, ALMOST COMPLETELY FORGETTING HIS SON..."

MARK KING MAKES HUGE EMERALD STRIKE

KING CLAIMED THE MINE FOR HIMSELF AND ORR WAS TOO PROUD TO ASK FOR A SHARE!

BESIDES, HE KNEW KING HAD BECOME CORRUPT! HE WANTED YOUNG DANNY BROUGHT UP STRAIGHT!

AND THAT'S THE "FAILURE FATHER" HE TRADED IN FOR THE BIG WHEEL! WOW!

7

IN THE DAYS THAT FOLLOW, DANNY ORR FINDS THE TASTE OF LIFE WITH HIS "NEW" OLD MAN VERY SWEET...

DAD, I'VE NEVER BEEN SO HAPPY... AND TO CELEBRATE OUR FINDING EACH OTHER I'M TAKING BACK MY *REAL* NAME--*KING!*

BEAUTIFUL! HERE'S TO THE GREATEST SON A GUY EVER HAD!

WORLD, I GIVE YOU... *DANNY KING!!*

SON, IT'S TIME YOU LEARNED ABOUT MY BUSINESS!

THE HEART OF IT IS THE EMERALD MINE IN CENTRAL AMERICA!

I'M SENDING *YOU* THERE AS MY PERSONAL REPRESENTATIVE!

TWO DAYS LATER, A SLEEK PRIVATE JET LANDS ON MATANZAS ISLAND, A JUNGLE-ENCARPETED CHUNK IN SHARK-INFESTED SEAS...

SEÑOR DANNY KING? I AM *BRAZOS*, THE MINE CHIEF! WELCOME!

KING ENTERPRISES

I'M HERE TO LEARN THE BUSINESS, BRAZOS! HOW ABOUT SHOWING ME THOSE BARRACKS FIRST?

KING MINES

8

NO, SEÑOR DANNY! YOU MUST *NEVER* GO THERE! THE MINERS LIVE IN THOSE BARRACKS! THEY ARE *THIEVES* AND *CUTTHROATS*, BUT THE ONLY WORKERS WE CAN FIND! YOU WOULD NOT BE SAFE AMONG THEM!

COME... YOU MUST REST!

MINING EQUIPMENT

LATER, AS NIGHT FALLS, IN A BIG STORAGE SHED...

DID WE HAVE TO COME THIS WAY? I COULD HAVE *FLOWN* US HERE *FIRST CLASS!*

SOME MINING EQUIPMENT--UNLESS THEY'RE DRILLING EMERALDS WITH *BULLETS* THESE DAYS!

DIG *THAT*, BUDDY! LOOKS LIKE A CONCENTRATION CAMP!

NO! NO!

I CAN'T TAKE NO MORE! LET ME OUT!

BUDDA

BUDDA

BUDDA

BLAZES, SUPES! THEY SHOT HIM DOWN...*IN COLD BLOOD!*

YEAH, MAYBE THAT'S WHY THEY CALL THIS *"MASSACRE ISLAND!"*

9

BRAZOS! I HEARD SHOOTING--

--THAT MINER...?

VERY REGRETTABLE, SEÑOR DANNY! WE HAD TO SHOOT HIM FOR STEALING SOME EMERALDS AND TRYING TO ESCAPE!

SEE? I FOUND THE STONES ON HIS BODY! HE WOULD CHEAT YOUR FATHER, HIS FAIR AND KIND EMPLOYER!

BRAZOS IS LYING! I SAW HIM WITH MY TELESCOPIC VISION PLANT THOSE EMERALDS ON THE BODY!

OKAY--TIME TO START EDUCATING DANNY TO THE REAL SCENE HERE!

SHORTLY, WHEN DANNY ENTERS HIS QUARTERS...

HUH? YOU TWO--!? YOU FOLLOWED ME ALL THE WAY HERE FROM GOTHAM CITY! BUT WHY...?

TO PROTECT YOU FROM YOURSELF AND OPEN YOUR EYES ABOUT THE REAL SET-UP DOWN HERE!

THAT MINER WASN'T A THIEF--BRAZOS HID THOSE EMERALDS ON HIM! HE JUST WANTED TO ESCAPE FROM THIS PLACE!

LOOK, THAT GUY'S DEATH BOTHERED ME, BUT I THINK YOU TWO BUSY-BODIES ARE LYING! THESE MINERS ARE ALL CRIMINALS!

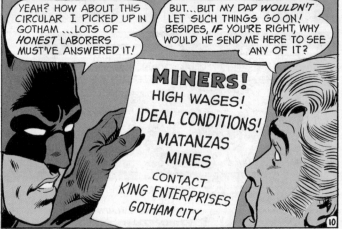

YEAH? HOW ABOUT THIS CIRCULAR I PICKED UP IN GOTHAM ...LOTS OF HONEST LABORERS MUST'VE ANSWERED IT!

BUT...BUT MY DAD WOULDN'T LET SUCH THINGS GO ON! BESIDES, IF YOU'RE RIGHT, WHY WOULD HE SEND ME HERE TO SEE ANY OF IT?

MINERS!
HIGH WAGES!
IDEAL CONDITIONS!
MATANZAS MINES
CONTACT
KING ENTERPRISES
GOTHAM CITY

10

BRAZOS MUST'VE HAD ORDERS TO GIVE YOU A PHONY GUIDED TOUR! WE DARE YOU TO GO ON A *REAL UN-OFFICIAL* INSPECTION!

OKAY, AND YOU'LL *BOTH* SEE YOU'RE WRONG!

MOMENTS LATER...

WE DON'T WANT TO ALARM THE GUARDS --GOING THROUGH THE WIRE IS OUT, *SUPES!*

SO WE'LL GO *UNDER* VIA A LITTLE SUPER-TUNNELING!

IN SECONDS...

AND SOON...

MADRE DE DIOS! SOMEONE TUNNELS THROUGH TO US?!

SEÑORES, YOU ARE TAKING A TERRIBLE CHANCE!

WE KNOW IT!

LOOK AROUND, DANNY! ARE THESE *IDEAL* CONDITIONS? ARE THESE MEN *THIEVES* AND *CUTTHROATS?*

YES, TAKE A *GOOD* LOOK, DANNY-BOY!

MY FOSTER-FATHER!? JACK ORR!?

A *GOOD* SHOCKING SPOT TO END *PART 2* -- BUT THE SHOCK WAVES ROLL ON IN *PART 3* -- ON THE *PAGE FOLLOWING.*

11

PART 3 JUST AN ORDINARY HERO

WHAT...WHAT ARE *YOU* DOING *HERE*?!

ONE OF THE GUYS HERE, AN OLD FRIEND, SMUGGLED A LETTER OUT TO ME, ASKING FOR HELP!

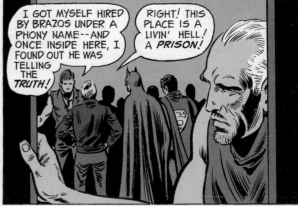

I GOT MYSELF HIRED BY BRAZOS UNDER A PHONY NAME--AND ONCE INSIDE HERE, I FOUND OUT HE WAS TELLING THE *TRUTH*!

RIGHT! THIS PLACE IS A LIVIN' HELL! A *PRISON*!

I ADMIT THINGS *LOOK* BAD--BUT MY DAD WILL PUT IT ALL RIGHT WHEN I GIVE HIM MY PERSONAL REPORT!

HATE TO PUT DOWN MY OLD PARTNER, BUT MARK KING *MUST* KNOW ABOUT ALL THIS...MAYBE HE EVEN *ORDERED* IT!

YOU CAN'T PROVE THAT! YOU HATE DAD BECAUSE MY MOTHER PREFERRED HIM AND HE BECAME A *SUCCESS*!

DANNY, I REALLY AM GOING TO PADDLE YOUR TAIL FOR TALKING THAT WAY!

HOLD IT! GUARDS COMING... A WHOLE ARMY OF THEM!

THEY'RE HEADING RIGHT FOR *THIS* BARRACKS!

HOW'D THEY KNOW?

BRAZOS HAS STOOL PIGEONS PLANTED *EVERYWHERE*!

12

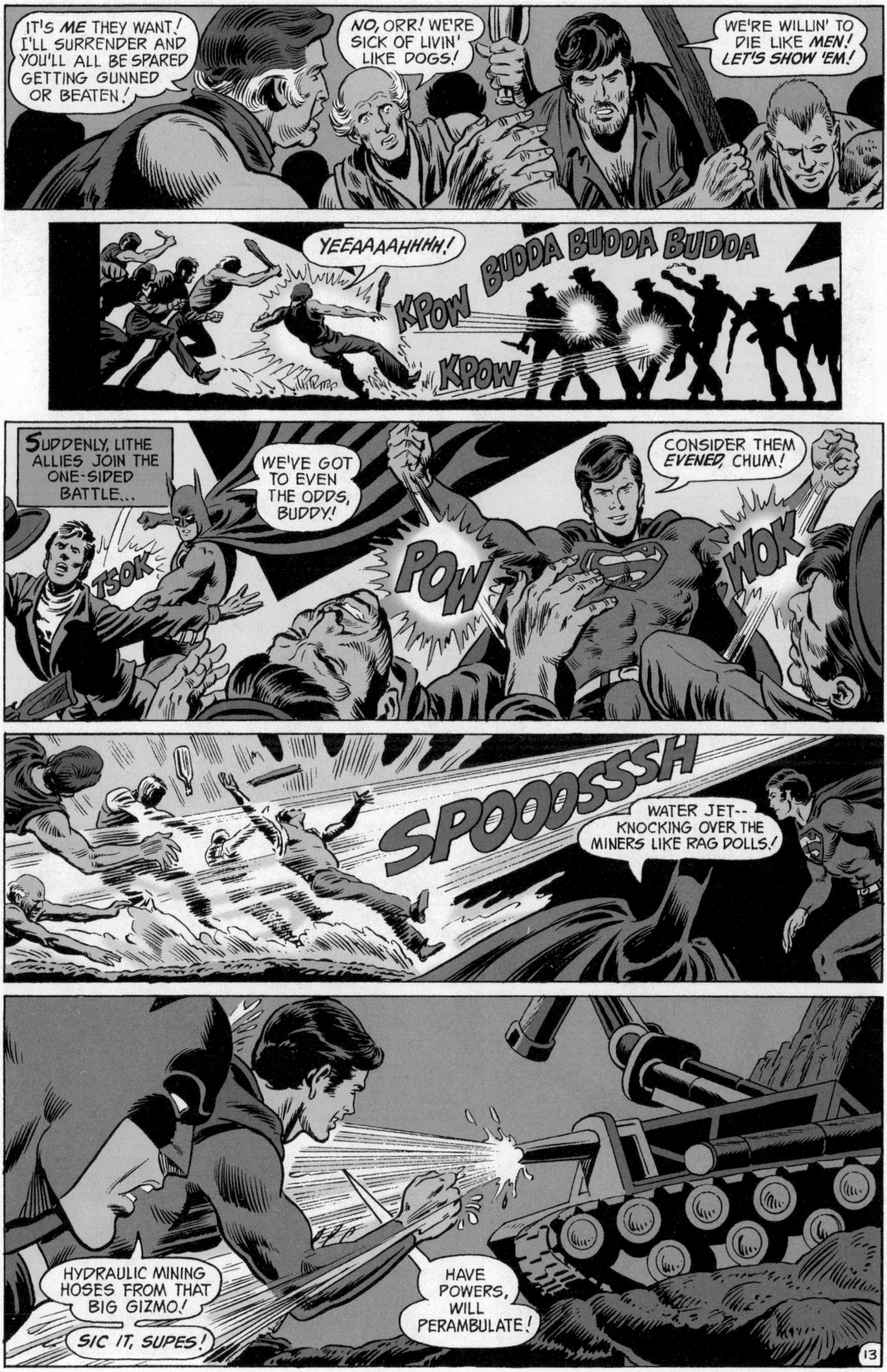
IT'S ME THEY WANT! I'LL SURRENDER AND YOU'LL ALL BE SPARED GETTING GUNNED OR BEATEN!
NO, ORR! WE'RE SICK OF LIVIN' LIKE DOGS!
WE'RE WILLIN' TO DIE LIKE MEN! LET'S SHOW 'EM!
YEEAAAAHHHH!
BUDDA BUDDA BUDDA
KPOW
KPOW
SUDDENLY, LITHE ALLIES JOIN THE ONE-SIDED BATTLE...
WE'VE GOT TO EVEN THE ODDS, BUDDY!
CONSIDER THEM EVENED, CHUM!
TSOK
POW
WOK
SPOOOSSSH
WATER JET-- KNOCKING OVER THE MINERS LIKE RAG DOLLS!
HYDRAULIC MINING HOSES FROM THAT BIG GIZMO!
SIC IT, SUPES!
HAVE POWERS, WILL PERAMBULATE!
13

THE NEXT MOMENT, A RED-AND-BLUE BLUR STREAKS FORWARD...

NOW I KNOW HOW AN EMERALD FEELS BEING BLASTED LOOSE FROM OLD MOTHER EARTH!

YOU JOKERS ARE WASTING WATER--AND THAT'S JUST NOT GOOD ECOLOGY!

KRUMMMK

THE NEXT INSTANT, THE TEN-TON ROCK CRUSHER PLUNGES...

WHRAANG

KRUMMMMAP

THEY REALLY WANT TO PLAY ROUGH!

MEANWHILE...

THE MINERS ARE DOING OKAY WITH *SUPES* HELPING!

DANNY! ORR! THEY MUST STILL BE IN THE BARRACKS!

BUT AS THE *CAPED CRUSADER* RE-ENTERS...

GONE, BOTH OF THEM!

THOSE FANCY SPANISH BOOT-PRINTS!

BRAZOS! HE WAS HERE AND GOT THEM!

14

QUICKLY, THE SON OF WAYNE SR. CRAWLS THROUGH THE TUNNEL--AND AFTER EMERGING FROM ITS OTHER END...

DANNY'S LOCKED IN HIS QUARTERS! THAT DOOR LOOKS TOUGH --BUT I'VE GOT TO BE *TOUGHER!*

BRAZOS LOCKED ME IN AND TOOK JACK ORR AWAY! SAID IT WAS FOR MY OWN PROTECTION!

BAD NEWS! HE MUST KNOW HIS REAL IDENTITY! WE'VE GOT TO FIND THEM--*FAST!*

KWAAAM

SHORTLY...

NO ONE HERE....!

REPEATING EARLIER MESSAGE! GOVERNMENT FORCES ON WAY FROM MAINLAND TO PUT DOWN MINERS' REVOLT-- AS REQUESTED!

HEAR THAT!? BIG TROUBLE'S COMING!

THERE'S TRUCK TRACKS LEADING TO THE HILLS! *LET'S MOVE!*

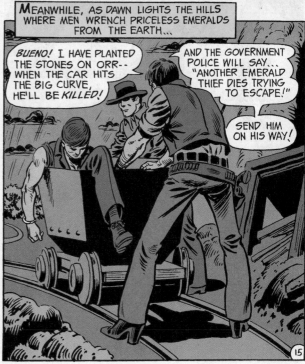

MEANWHILE, AS DAWN LIGHTS THE HILLS WHERE MEN WRENCH PRICELESS EMERALDS FROM THE EARTH...

BUENO! I HAVE PLANTED THE STONES ON ORR-- WHEN THE CAR HITS THE BIG CURVE, HE'LL BE *KILLED!*

AND THE GOVERNMENT POLICE WILL SAY... "ANOTHER EMERALD THIEF DIES TRYING TO ESCAPE!"

SEND HIM ON HIS WAY!

15

SOON...

IN THAT RUN-
AWAY CAR...
JACK ORR!
GOT TO SAVE
HIM!

DANNY! GRAB
THE WHEEL!

NOW AS A HARROW-
ING CHASE BEGINS...

FASTER!
FASTER!

THAT CURVE...
WE'LL NEVER
MAKE IT!

YOU WERE
FANTASTIC!
BUT I'M
AFRAID I
WRECKED THESE
WHEELS!

YOU DID
OKAY,
DANNY!

HOLD IT! I
HEAR A TRUCK!
BRAZOS--HE'S
COMING BACK
DOWN THE
ROAD!

16

POW POW POW

BWEEEE

TZINNNG

RUN, DANNY! BEING MARK KING'S SON WON'T STOP SLUGS!

ZIING BWEEE-E

A *RIVER!* WE'LL HAVE TO USE IT! I CAN'T RUN FAST, LOADED LIKE THIS!

THEY CANNOT SURVIVE WHAT THE RIVER HOLDS IN STORE FOR THEM!

I WILL INFORM SEÑOR KING HIS SON DIED ...DEFYING MY EFFORTS TO PROTECT HIM!

AND SOON, AS THE TORRENT CARRIES THE TRIO ALONG LIKE HELPLESS CHIPS...

ROOUAWWAARRR

BUT CHIPS HAVE A WAY OF FLOATING WHEN OTHER THINGS SINK!

HEY! THAT PLUNGE SHOOK YOU AWAKE!

YEAH, JUST IN TIME TO BE SWEPT OUT TO SEA!

AND AS THE SWIFT CURRENT MERGES WITH THE TROPIC SEA...

WHERE AM I? WHAT'S HAPPENING?

WE'RE JUST ABOUT TO BECOME SHARK BAIT!

17

KEEP STILL -- DON'T MAKE ANY NOISE OR SUDDEN MOTIONS! THAT'S THE BOOK ON AVOIDING THEIR ATTACKS!

BUT... WHAT IF THESE KILLERS DIDN'T READ THE BOOK?!

BUT EVEN AS THE SHARKS SPEED IN FOR THE KILL...

BAM

WHAM

SUPES!! WHAT KEPT YOU?

HAD TO WAIT TILL THE NICK OF TIME, PAL!

WOK

WOK

I LEFT THE MINERS IN CONTROL OF THE CAMP-- AND CAME LOOKING FOR YOU, BUDDY!

MORE TROUBLE --THE LOCAL NAVY! BRAZOS SENT FOR THEM TO PUT DOWN THE MINERS!

YOU WILL COME ABOARD-- AT ONCE!

GLAD TO SEE YOU AGAIN, COLONEL!

HUH? YOU KNOW EACH OTHER?

SI, SEÑOR ORR WAS WORKING FOR OUR GOVERNMENT, INFIL-TRATING THE MINE CAMP TO GATHER EVIDENCE!

BUT WE HEARD THE RADIO SAYING TROOPS WERE COMING TO PUT DOWN THE MINERS!

A LITTLE LIE, MUCHACHO --TO KEEP BRAZOS AND HIS THUGS THINKING THEY HAD NOTHING TO FEAR! NOW WE SHALL ROUND THEM UP TO FACE JUSTICE!

14

18

WELL, DANNY-- WERE WE *LYING* ABOUT WHAT WENT ON AT THE MINES?

NO...BUT I STILL CAN'T BELIEVE MY DAD-- MARK KING-- REALLY KNEW OR ORDERED IT ALL! I'VE GOT TO MAKE *SURE!*

SOME DAYS LATER, WHERE GOTHAM'S LATEST SKYSCRAPER GLITTERS AGAINST THE SKY...

HELLO, DAD, I'M *BACK!*

DANNY! I'M SORRY YOU RAN INTO SO MUCH TROUBLE ON MATANZAS ISLAND, KID!

KING BUILDI

IT WAS BRAZOS ...HE MESSED THINGS UP! AND THOSE TWO MEDDLING SUPER-PUNKS--

THOSE TWO ARE MY *FRIENDS,* DAD! AND BRAZOS COULD'VE BEEN FOLLOWING *YOUR* ORDERS!

WAS HE? OR *WASN'T* HE?

WHAT *IS* THIS? I DON'T NEED TO EXCUSE MYSELF TO YOU-- OR ANYBODY!

SURE, BRAZOS OBEYED MY ORDERS! SO THE MINE WAS CONFISCATED BY THE GOVERNMENT! SO WHAT?

I GOT PLENTY OF *OTHER* BUSINESSES AND PLENTY OF MONEY! I DON'T NEED IT!

JUST LIKE YOU DIDN'T NEED *ME!* ALL YOU EVER THOUGHT OF WAS *YOURSELF!!*

I THOUGHT YOU WERE *MY* KIND OF KID-- A CHIP OFF THE OLD KING-BLOCK,... BUT YOU'RE *NOT!* YOU'RE A *LOSER!*

AND *I'M* A WINNER--BECAUSE NOBODY CAN PROVE A THING AGAINST ME!

19

MAYBE THEY *CAN*... WITH THIS CABLE YOU SENT BRAZOS ORDERING JACK ORR'S "ACCIDENTAL" MURDER!

I THOUGHT IT MIGHT BE SOME KIND OF MISTAKE ...BUT NOW I KNOW *DIFFERENT*!

WHAT? GET THAT CABLE, MEN!

DON'T TRY-- UNLESS YOU WANT TO TANGLE WITH *US*!

PLUS A CHARGE OF OBSTRUCTING JUSTICE!

DANNY! DANNY-BOY! DON'T DO THIS...I'M YOUR *DAD*... YOU WOULDN'T...*PLEASE*!

OH, YES, I *WOULD*, BECAUSE I'M A CHIP OFF THE OLD BLOCK, REMEMBER?

COME ON, FELLAS!

SHORTLY OUTSIDE...

DANNY, THAT TOOK A LOT OF GUTS!

SURE--BUT I FEEL SO DOWN! NOW I'VE LOST *BOTH* MY FATHERS! TO THINK I BELIEVED JACK ORR WAS AN *ORDINARY* GUY!

HEROES ARE SOMETIMES ORDINARY PEOPLE LIVING ORDINARY LIVES--LIKE THE GUY *BEHIND* YOU!

JACK... I MEAN... *DAD*!!

HI, SON! HOW'S ABOUT PICKING UP WHERE WE LEFT OFF? YOU AND I'VE GOT A LOT OF LIVING LEFT TO DO!

KNOW SOMETHING, BUDDY--WE JUST LEARNED A VERY BIG LESSON! WHEN YOU THINK *YOU'VE* GOT IT TOUGH, SOMEBODY ELSE ALWAYS HAS IT *TOUGHER*!

"CHECK! OR "PEOPLE WRAPPED UP IN THEMSELVES MAKE PRETTY SMALL PACKAGES!"

SO LONG, *SUPER-SONS*, FOR NOW-- BUT YOU'LL BE BACK-- BECAUSE YOU, TOO, HAVE A LOT OF LIVING LEFT TO DO... RIGHT HERE IN *WORLD'S FINEST*!

THE END.

20

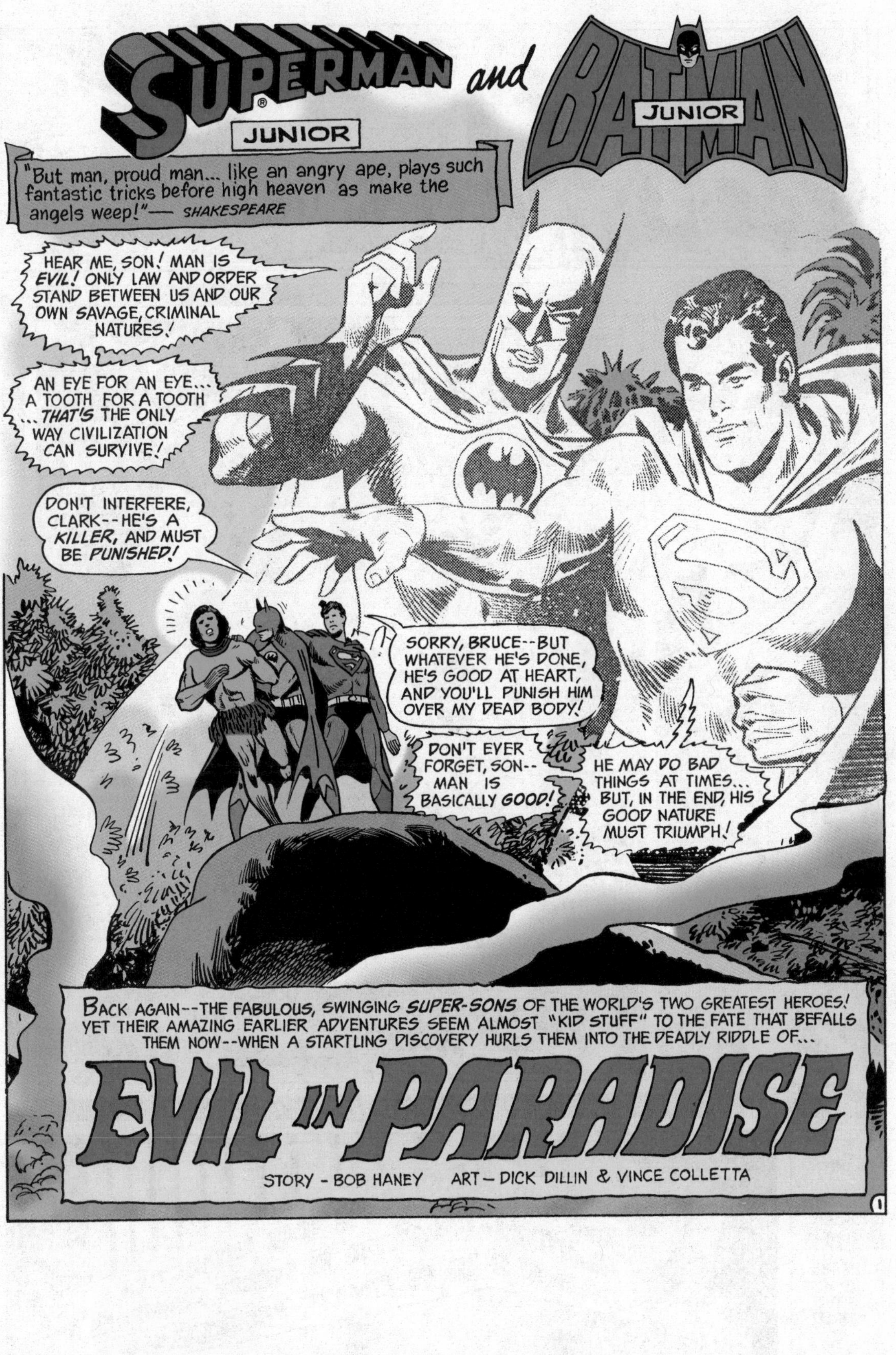
SUPERMAN JUNIOR and BATMAN JUNIOR
"But man, proud man... like an angry ape, plays such fantastic tricks before high heaven as make the angels weep!"— SHAKESPEARE
HEAR ME, SON! MAN IS EVIL! ONLY LAW AND ORDER STAND BETWEEN US AND OUR OWN SAVAGE, CRIMINAL NATURES!
AN EYE FOR AN EYE... A TOOTH FOR A TOOTH ...THAT'S THE ONLY WAY CIVILIZATION CAN SURVIVE!
DON'T INTERFERE, CLARK--HE'S A KILLER, AND MUST BE PUNISHED!
SORRY, BRUCE--BUT WHATEVER HE'S DONE, HE'S GOOD AT HEART, AND YOU'LL PUNISH HIM OVER MY DEAD BODY!
DON'T EVER FORGET, SON--MAN IS BASICALLY GOOD!
HE MAY DO BAD THINGS AT TIMES... BUT, IN THE END, HIS GOOD NATURE MUST TRIUMPH!
BACK AGAIN--THE FABULOUS, SWINGING SUPER-SONS OF THE WORLD'S TWO GREATEST HEROES! YET THEIR AMAZING EARLIER ADVENTURES SEEM ALMOST "KID STUFF" TO THE FATE THAT BEFALLS THEM NOW--WHEN A STARTLING DISCOVERY HURLS THEM INTO THE DEADLY RIDDLE OF...
EVIL IN PARADISE
STORY - BOB HANEY ART — DICK DILLIN & VINCE COLLETTA
1

IN THE VAST SEAS BETWEEN SOUTH AMERICA AND ANTARCTICA, AN INTERNATIONAL WEATHER PLANE PATROLS...

THERE IT IS--*DESOLATION ISLAND*-- ICE, PENGUINS, AND FRIGID FAHRENHEIT! BUT WHAT'S THAT *CLOUD* HOVERING OVER THE CENTRAL PEAKS?

THE CHART SAYS IT'S A PERMANENT LAYER OF MIST FROM VOLCANIC THERMAL SPRINGS! THE UNDERLYING TERRAIN IS *UNMAPPED!*

THEN NOBODY'S EVER SEEN WHAT'S BELOW? LET'S TAKE A LOOK!

WE'LL RACK UP ON A PEAK!!

NO--OUR ALTIMETER READS THERE'S PLENTY OF FREE FLYING SPACE BENEATH THIS SOUP!

THE CRAFT PLUNGES THROUGH THE STEAMING CLOUD-- AND THEN, SUDDENLY BREAKS INTO ...*CLEAR AIR*...

A LUSH VALLEY!!

ACTIVATE THE CAMERAS! THIS IS SOMETHING UTTERLY *FANTASTIC!*

THE DISCOVERY BURSTS LIKE A BOMB-SHELL ON THE REST OF THE WORLD...

TROPICAL VALLEY FOUND NEAR ANTARCTICA

PRIMITIVE TRIBE LIVING IN SECRET SHANGRI-LA

THERMAL SPRINGS CREATE POCKET CLIMATE

2

AND ON A LATE-NIGHT TV SHOW VIEWED BY MILLIONS...

AND YOU SAY, DR. FORBES, THIS *DESOLATION ISLAND* TRIBE IS UNIQUE?

YES, THESE BLOW-UP PHOTOS SHOW THEIR PRIMITIVE WAY OF LIFE IS UNCHANGED SINCE THE DAWN OF HISTORY, AND NEVER TOUCHED BY ANY OTHER "HIGHER" CIVILIZATION!

TO ME, MAN IS BASICALLY *GOOD*--IT IS CIVILIZATION AND ITS FALSE VALUES THAT *CORRUPT* HIM AND MAKE HIM ACT WICKED!

THIS IS A REAL HEAVY RAP FOR A TV SHOW!

YEAH, DOC FORBES IS A VERY COGENT THINKER!

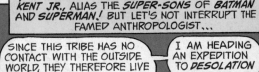

YOU RECOGNIZE *BRUCE WAYNE JR.* AND *CLARK KENT JR.*, ALIAS THE *SUPER-SONS* OF *BATMAN* AND *SUPERMAN*! BUT LET'S NOT INTERRUPT THE FAMED ANTHROPOLOGIST...

SINCE THIS TRIBE HAS NO CONTACT WITH THE OUTSIDE WORLD, THEY THEREFORE LIVE IN TOTAL GOODNESS...WITHOUT CRIME OR GREED!

I AM HEADING AN EXPEDITION TO *DESOLATION ISLAND* TO OBSERVE THEM AND PROVE MY THEORY!

WRONG! ABSOLUTELY WRONG!

I, OMAR BENSON, HEARTILY DISAGREE! MAN IS BASICALLY *BAD!* ONLY *FEAR OF PUNISHMENT* KEEPS MOST OF US FROM BEING CRIMINALS!

BENSON! YOU HAVE NO RIGHT!

THIS PROGRAM IS OPEN TO *ALL* OPINIONS! I CAN'T STOP MR. BENSON!

NOR MY IDEAS --WHICH IS WHY I HAVE THOUSANDS OF FOLLOWERS, OWN NEWSPAPERS AND TV STATIONS!

WE BENSONITES RECOGNIZE MAN FOR WHAT HE REALLY IS... A SAVAGE APE!

LOOK AT HISTORY-- FILLED WITH *WAR, CRIME, INJUSTICE* AND *HATRED!*

3

I AM LEADING MY *OWN* EXPEDITION TO *DESOLATION ISLAND* TO PROVE THAT TRIBE IS JUST LIKE THE REST OF US... *APES!*

NO! MAN IS GOOD ...A FALLEN ANGEL! MY EXPEDITION WILL PROVE IT!

AND AS THE SHOW ENDS IN A WHIRLWIND OF CONTROVERSY...

WOW! WHAT AN IDEA-- SETTLING THE BIGGEST QUESTION OF ALL...

BENSON'S *RIGHT*, NATCH!

HE'S JUST A NON-THINKING *CYNIC!*

NO WAY, CHUM! LET ME CLUE YOU IN--!

"I REMEMBER GROWING UP AND SEEING MY DAD TANGLE OFTEN WITH HUMAN NATURE.."

MY DARLING... YOU'RE HURT?!

ONLY A FLESH WOUND, DEAR! I'LL BE OKAY! BUT THAT CRIMINAL RAT WAS REALLY *TRYING*... I WAS JUST LUCKY!

MUST YOU GO OUT CRIME-FIGHTING *EVERY* NIGHT? YOUR FAMILY *NEEDS* YOU!

SORRY, HONEY-- BUT IT'S A JUNGLE OUT THERE THAT I'VE GOT TO KEEP FROM ENGULFING GOTHAM!

BRUCE, I CAN'T STOP YOU FROM BEING A SECOND *BATMAN*-- BUT ALWAYS REMEMBER, SON...

LAW AND ORDER ARE THE ONLY ANSWER TO MAN'S CRIMINAL INSTINCTS!

ALL HIS LIFE, MY DAD DEALT WITH *REALITY*-- NOT THEORIES!

HUMANS ARE APES, LIKE BENSON SAID!

WELL, MY FATHER DEALT WITH *SUPER-REALITY!* NOT JUST CRIME ON CITY STREETS!

4

"AS I GREW UP, HE SHOWED ME DOZENS OF EXAMPLES OF MAN'S BASIC GOODNESS..."

THAT FARM FAMILY'S SHARING THEIR LAST FOOD AND WATER WITH THOSE WAR REFUGEES! BURN THAT INTO YOUR MEMORY, SON!

DAD'S FLYING THAT TANK TO AFRICA FASTER THAN ANY JET--NOW THAT THESE DONORS GAVE THEIR BLOOD TO HELP OTHERS!

METROPOLIS BLOOD CAMPAIGN FOR PLAGUE VICTIMS!

CLARK, THOUGH YOUR POWERS ARE ONLY HALF OF MINE, THEY MUST SERVE MAN'S BASIC GOODNESS...

...AND HELP HIM WHEN HE STRAYS FROM THE RIGHT PATH!

A REAL SOB STORY, CLARK! BUT THOSE REFUGEES WOULD'VE TAKEN THAT FOOD BY FORCE ANYWAY! AND THEY MAKE YOU FEEL GUILTY IF YOU DON'T GIVE BLOOD!

ARE YOU EVER CYNICAL, BRUCE! YOU SOUND JUST LIKE A FOLLOWER OF BENSON!

MAYBE I AM! I NEVER REALIZED IT BEFORE!

WOW! WHAT AN IDEA! I'LL TRY TO JOIN BENSON'S EXPEDITION AND HELP HIM PROVE THE TRUTH ABOUT HUMAN NATURE!

OKAY, THEN I'LL JOIN DR. FORBES' TEAM AND PROVE THE REAL TRUTH... MAN'S A FALLEN ANGEL!

5

LOSER BUYS THE WINNER COKES AND HAMBURGERS FOR A MONTH! DEAL, BUDDY?

DEAL, CLARK, BABY-- YOU NAIVE BUT LOVABLE BOOB!

THUS, ON A GREAT BRIDGE SPANNING A MIGHTY RIVER, THE TWO *SUPER-SONS* CLASP HANDS ACROSS AN EVEN GREATER CHASM--THE TIMELESS DEBATE... *IS MAN GOOD OR EVIL?* LATER, IN THE COUNTRYSIDE...

DELIGHTED YOU SHOWED UP, *BATMAN JR.!* MY EXPERIMENTS TO PROVE MY BELIEFS ABOUT HUMAN NATURE USING PAID VOLUNTEERS...

BENSON FOUNDATION CAMP CAVE MAN DIVISION

...WERE NOT CONCLUSIVE SINCE THEY COULDN'T THROW OFF CIVILIZED HABITS --LIKE THAT KARATE CHOP!

BUT THAT *DESOLATION ISLAND* TRIBE IS THE PERFECT "TEST TUBE" TO SHOW MAN AS HE *REALLY* IS!

WHILE ALREADY LANDED ON *DESOLATION ISLAND*...

WE MUST SET UP CAMP *OUTSIDE* THE VALLEY, *SUPERMAN JR.*... SO THOSE TRIBESMEN HAVE *NO* CONTACT WITH US!

IN FACT, THEY MUSTN'T EVEN *KNOW* WE'RE HERE-- BUT HOW WILL WE PLANT THESE MICROPHONES AND TV CAMERAS IN THEIR MIDST?

LEAVE THAT TO ME, DR. FORBES!

6

TAKING THE SELF-CONTAINED DEVICES, THE *SON OF THE MAN OF STEEL* STREAKS FROM THE ICE-COATED MAIN PART OF THE ISLAND INTO THE LUSH VALLEY WHERE...

AT SUPER-SPEED, I CAN'T BE SEEN STASHING THESE THINGS RIGHT AMONG THEM!

AND SHORTLY...

GREAT WORK, LAD! WE'RE PICKING UP THEIR SPEECH... AND THE COMPUTER IS UNSCRAMBLING THEIR SIMPLE LANGUAGE, GIVING US ALMOST INSTANT TRANSLATION!

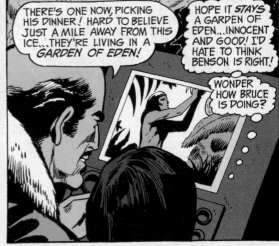

THERE'S ONE NOW, PICKING HIS DINNER! HARD TO BELIEVE JUST A MILE AWAY FROM THIS ICE...THEY'RE LIVING IN A *GARDEN OF EDEN!*

HOPE IT *STAYS* A GARDEN OF EDEN...INNOCENT AND GOOD! I'D HATE TO THINK BENSON IS RIGHT!

WONDER HOW BRUCE IS DOING?

AT THIS MOMENT, HIGH ABOVE THE SECRET VALLEY...

WHY ARE YOU DROPPING THESE GIZMOS, MR. BENSON?

THEY EMIT SOUND FREQUENCIES *ABOVE* THE LEVEL OF HUMAN HEARING...

...WHICH, UNKNOWN TO THEM, WILL IRRITATE THE TRIBES-MEN'S SUBCONSCIOUS MINDS, PUTTING THEM UNDER STRESS! IT IS THE ONLY WAY TO DIRECT OUR EXPERIMENT!

IF THEY ARE BASICALLY GOOD, THEY WILL NOT REACT AND SHOW BAD BEHAVIOR...

...BUT IF THEY ARE BASICALLY EVIL, THEY WILL BE *AT EACH OTHER'S THROATS* IN NO TIME!

SO THE GREAT EXPERIMENT-- *OPERATION HUMAN NATURE*-- IS INTO *PHASE 1!* WHAT WILL HAPPEN? FOR THE ANSWER, GO AT ONCE TO *PHASE 2!*

7

NOT LONG AFTER, AT THE BENSON EXPEDITION CAMP ALSO PERCHED ON THE ICY MAIN PART OF *DESOLATION ISLAND*...

MY BOY, SOMETHING'S *WRONG!* I'M NO LONGER PICKING UP SIGNALS FROM OUR HIGH-FREQUENCY SOUND-MAKERS!

THE NATIVES *COULDN'T* HAVE FOUND THEM... UNLESS THEY DEVELOPED SUPER-HEARING, LIVING SO ISOLATED IN THAT VALLEY!

NOT LIKELY, SIR! BUT YOU'VE GIVEN ME A HUNCH!

BE RIGHT BACK!

THERE'S ONLY *ONE* DUDE AROUND HERE WITH SUPER-HEARING, AND HE DOESN'T WEAR A FIG LEAF OR PICK FRUIT!

SOON, AS BATMAN'S OFF-SPRING LEAVES HIS SNOW-MOBILE WHERE THE THERMAL SPRINGS CREATE THE POCKET CLIMATE AROUND THE LOST VALLEY...

HOT AS BLAZES HERE!

SOMEONE... COMING --?

OKAY, CLARK, KIDDO! PUT 'EM BACK!

NO WAY, CHUM! LUCKY I PICKED ALL THESE UP USING MY SUPER-HEARING AND SPEED!

YOU AND BENSON ARE GUMMING UP THE EXPERIMENT! WE MUST OBSERVE THESE NATIVES WITHOUT INTERFERING IN THEIR UNSPOILED STATE!

8

YOU'RE *WRONG!* GOOD SCIENTIFIC METHOD SAYS THEY HAVE TO BE PUT UNDER *STRESS* TO TEST THEIR BASIC CHARACTER!

HAND 'EM OVER!

I'LL "HAND" 'EM, ALL RIGHT...

...*LIKE THIS!*

KRUNNNCH

YOU MUSCLE-BOUND CLOWN!

OWWWW! OWWWW!

SEE? YOUR PUNCH SHOWS THAT DESPITE BEING BASICALLY *GOOD*, SOMETIMES YOUR ADOLESCENT *TEMPER* GETS THE BETTER OF YOU!

AND SINCE I'M ALSO BASICALLY GOOD, I WON'T HIT YOU BACK! IT WOULD MERELY HALF KILL YOU!

AND YOU'RE *HALF A FREAK* 'CAUSE YOUR OLD MAN'S A CRAZY KRYPTONIAN -- SO WHAT WOULD *YOU* KNOW ABOUT *HUMAN* NATURE!?

*T*WO OLD FRIENDS FEELING THE PRESSURE OF THEIR WORK...AND SHORTLY...

SO FAR, ALL OUR OBSERVATIONS OF THOSE NATIVES SHOW THEM TO BE PEACEFUL, INNOCENT, AND LOVING BEINGS!

ESPECIALLY SINCE WE GOT RID OF BENSON'S LITTLE SONIC IRRITATORS!

WHAT'S *THIS?* A HORDE OF *INSECTS* DEVOURING THE VALLEY'S MAIN FOOD CROP... THOSE BREADFRUIT TREES!

THAT'S BAD NEWS, SIR! I'VE GOT TO DO SOMETHING!

*I*N SECONDS, THE *MAN OF TOMORROW'S* SON IS STREAKING SKYWARD...

THOSE BIRDS IN THAT CLIFF ROOKERY... COULD BE THE ANSWER!

IMMEDIATELY, THE JUNIOR *SUPERMAN* CREATES A FUNNELING WIND...

I'LL JUST DRAW ALL THESE FEATHERED FREELOADERS BACK TO THE VALLEY FOR A BUG LUNCH!

AND SHORTLY...

THAT WAS *BRILLIANT* OF YOU, YOUNG MAN! BUT *WHERE* DID THOSE INSECTS COME FROM? THEY'RE NOT NATIVE TO THIS ISLAND!

WHILE NOT FAR AWAY, ALSO PICKING UP THE TV TRANSMISSION...

MY PAL GOT RID OF THE INSECTS YOU INTRODUCED INTO THE EXPERIMENT, MR. BENSON!

AH, YES, BUT NOT BEFORE THEY ATE MOST OF THE BREADFRUIT CROP!

LET'S SEE WHAT HAPPENS TO THESE GOOD TRIBESMEN UNDER STRESS OF A *FOOD SHORTAGE!*

NICE OF DR. FORBES TO PROVIDE US WITH TV COVERAGE!

AND BY THE FOLLOWING DAY...

THEIR HUNGER PANGS ARE GROWING *ACUTE!* THEY SHAKE THE TREES ANGRILY FOR WHAT'S LEFT!

NOW, SURELY, GREED, FRICTION, EVEN *VIOLENCE* WILL FOLLOW!

10

WHAT'S THIS? THEY'RE SHARING THE REMAINING FRUIT *EQUALLY* AMONG ALL THE TRIBE?

LOOKS LIKE MAYBE THESE PEOPLE *ARE* DIFFERENT FROM THE REST OF THE WORLD, SIR, AND *DON'T* HAVE BAD IN THEM!

NONSENSE! THEY SIMPLY HAVEN'T BEEN PUT UNDER ENOUGH PRESSURE YET!

THE BEAST IN MAN WILL *ALWAYS* SURFACE, GIVEN ENOUGH URGENCY!

THAT ONE SEEMS TO BE THE *LEADER!* HE'S THE KEY TO THE NEXT PHASE OF MY EXPERIMENT!

COME, WE'RE GOING HUNTING!

SOON...

MY LIFELONG RESEARCH HAS SHOWN THAT A HERO IN THEIR MIDST WILL MAKE PEOPLE ACT *"ABOVE"* THEMSELVES...

...STIFLING THEIR BAD INSTINCTS AS THEY IMITATE THE MAN THEY ADMIRE!

IF WE *REMOVE* HIM, THE PEOPLE WILL THEN REVERT TO THEIR *"NORMAL"* BEHAVIOR... THAT IS, THE *"BAD"* WILL COME OUT!

CAPTURE THEIR LEADER!

11

BUT AS THE JUNIOR SUPER-HERO FROM OUR OWN CULTURE APPROACHES THE PUZZLED NATIVE...

OONAK! OONAK!

OKAY, I GUESS THAT'S YOUR NAME! NOW I'M NOT GOING TO HURT YOU, OONAK-- JUST COME ALONG QUIETLY!

HUHHH?

THIS DUDE KNOWS SOME KIND OF PRIMITIVE JUDO-- AND THINKS THIS IS ALL A FUN GAME! HAVE TO CONVINCE HIM OTHERWISE!

NOW AS THE HEIR OF MIGHTY *BATMAN* LEAPS TO SUBDUE HIS QUARRY...

HA HA

HA HA HA

SUDDENLY...

AIIIII...

OONAK! OONAK!

SINCE YOU WERE UNABLE TO SUBDUE HIM, I USED A HARMLESS TRANQUILIZER DART!

BRING HIM ALONG!

12

ARE WE DOING RIGHT, MR. BENSON? HIS WIFE OR GIRL-FRIEND...SHE'S SURE FREAKING OUT!

HE WON'T BE HURT-- JUST REMOVED FROM THEIR MIDST!

BUT AS THE COPTER LOFTS SKYWARD...

WE'RE VIBRATING LIKE *CRAZY!* WHAT'S *WRONG?*

SUPES!?

DR. FORBES AND I SAW EVERYTHING ON THE TV MONITOR!

LET OONAK GO!

I CAN'T MAKE HEADWAY--!

I'LL DISSUADE YOUR SUPER-ZEALOUS FRIEND-- JUST KEEP US ON AN EVEN KEEL!

WE'RE SHOOTING *UP!* HE MUST'VE LET GO!

HE HAD NO CHOICE AGAINST THOSE GRENADES I BROUGHT ALONG IN CASE OF POSSIBLE ATTACK FROM THE NATIVES!

BLAAMM

BLAAM BLAAM

BLAAAM

ENOUGH *TNT* TO KILL 10 MEN BLASTING THE *SON OF STEEL* WHILE THE *JUNIOR CAPED CRUSADER* FLIES OFF CALLOUSLY! BUT MORE SHOCKS AWAIT IN *PART 3--NEXT!*

13

IT IS ONLY A FEW MINUTES LATER, AND AS THE SOUNDS OF THE COPTER'S ROTORS DIMINISH INTO THE MIST ABOVE THE LOST VALLEY...

WHEW! THOSE GRENADES CAN'T KILL ME, OF COURSE, BUT THEY SURE DO BRUISE AND SHAKE A GUY!

BRUCE IS HELPING BENSON *RUIN* THE WHOLE EXPERIMENT! DR. FORBES' WAY IS THE ONLY WAY! GOT TO FOLLOW THEM AND RESCUE OONAK!

MY WRIST RADIO... A MESSAGE FROM CAMP!

DR. FORBES MISSING! RETURN AT ONCE!

AND VERY SOON, ON THE ICE FIELDS SURROUNDING THE VALLEY...

DR. FORBES WENT TO LOOK FOR YOU! WE FOUND HIS ABANDONED SNOW-MOBILE AT THE EDGE OF THIS CREVASSE!

FORBES EXPEDITION

BAD NEWS! BENSON AND *BATMAN JR.* WILL HAVE TO WAIT!

WHILE THE SON OF *SUPERMAN* SEARCHES FOR HIS MENTOR-- NOT TOO FAR AWAY...

IS...IS THAT "TIGER CAGE" NECESSARY, MR. BENSON?

IT WON'T HARM OONAK, LAD-- ONLY PUT HIM UNDER STRESS AS WILL THIS ULTRASONIC HORN BOMBARDING HIS BRAIN NIGHT AND DAY!

MEANTIME THE TRIBE MUST GET ALONG WITHOUT ITS LEADER!

AT THE RIGHT TIME, WE'LL RETURN HIM TO HIS PEOPLE AND OBSERVE HIS *AND* THEIR REACTION!

14

AND AS THE CONDITIONING PROCESS GOES ON...

THAT PHOTO...?

YES, IT SHOWS HER BEING EMBRACED BY ANOTHER MAN! I MADE A BLOW-UP FROM THE TV TAPES! THIS WILL STIMULATE HIS *JEALOUSY!*

AND THIS PHOTO OF OTHERS EATING OONAK'S OWN SUPPLY OF FOOD WHILE WE STARVE HIM A BIT HERE... THAT WILL ADD *STILL* MORE STRESS!

SEE? WITHOUT HIM, THE TRIBE IS ALREADY SHOWING IGNOBLE BEHAVIOR!

AREN'T WE OVERDOING IT? AREN'T WE INFLUENCING THE EXPERIMENT'S OUTCOME?

IF OONAK IS TRULY *GOOD* AT HEART, HE WILL *RESIST* THE CONDITIONING!

IF HE IS *BAD* AT HEART, THEN IT CANNOT CHANGE HIM INTO WHAT HE ALREADY IS!

SO WE SHALL SOON PROVE IF OONAK--OR ANY *OTHER* HUMAN --IS TRULY ANGEL--OR APE!

MR. BENSON, YOU *ARE* A HEAVY HEAD!

MEANTIME, IN A VAST LABYRINTH OF CREVASSES UNDERLYING THE ISLAND'S ICE FIELDS...

THIS PLACE IS A REGULAR MAZE! AND IT'S GETTING WARMER THE FARTHER I GO! THE ICE IS MELTING AND--

HELP!

DR. FORBES!

THANK HEAVENS YOU FOUND ME! MY LEG'S BROKEN... I COULD *NEVER* HAVE CRAWLED OUT OF HERE!

15

BUT HOW'D YOU GET DOWN *HERE?*

I SAW SOME OF BENSON'S MEN DESCENDING INTO THE CREVASSE VIA ROPES!

I FOLLOWED AND THEY AMBUSHED ME! MY LEG WAS BROKEN IN THE STRUGGLE!

THEY LEFT ME HERE TO DIE... AND CLIMBED BACK OUT! I NEVER DID FIND OUT WHAT THEY WERE UP TO!

GOT TO GET YOU BACK TO CAMP AND HAVE THAT LEG FIXED! YOU COULD GO INTO SHOCK FROM EXPOSURE IF YOU STAYED HERE MUCH LONGER!

MEANWHILE...

NOW WE RETURN OUR HUMAN GUINEA PIG TO HIS TRIBE AND OBSERVE THE RESULTS!

SOON...

THE GREAT EXPERIMENT REACHES ITS *CLIMAX!*

COME OUT, OONAK! COME OUT, YOU POOR APE!

HE ADVANCES ON THEM! NOW THE VIOLENT, JEALOUS APE WILL EMERGE!

WHAT? THEY'RE SHAKING HANDS? SMILING AND LAUGHING?

16

HE...HE'S EMBRACING HER?! I... I CAN'T BELIEVE IT!

COULD THE WHOLE EXPERIMENT BE WRONG--?

YOU PRIMITIVE BRUTE!

YOU CAN'T SHRUG OFF MY CONDITIONING!

YOU CAN'T MAKE A FOOL OF OMAR BENSON.!!

POW

YAAAAAYAAAAAWN

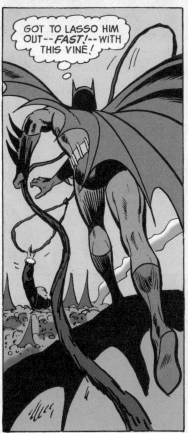

GOT TO LASSO HIM OUT--FAST!--WITH THIS VINE!

DESPERATELY, THE HEIR TO THE MASKED MANHUNTER HAULS ON THE VINE, AND...

HE'S NOT MOVING ...OR BREATHING!

DEAD... NOBODY COULD LIVE EVEN A FEW MOMENTS IN THAT BOILING GLOP!

17

YOU *MURDERER!* HOW ABOUT IF I SHOVE *YOU* IN? AN EYE FOR AN EYE--

--*HOLD IT!* WE SAW EVERYTHING ON THE HOOKUP!

STAY OUT OF THIS, *SUPIE!* HE KILLED BENSON AND MUST BE PUNISHED!

WE ARE OUTSIDERS, AND HAVE NO AUTHORITY HERE!

THEN HIS *OWN* PEOPLE MUST RETALIATE!

IMPOSSIBLE! THEY HAVE NO IDEA OF "PUNISHMENT" BECAUSE THEY NEVER HAD ANY CRIME HERE!

NOT UNTIL *NOW!*

BUT ANY JURY WOULD SAY OONAK WAS DRIVEN TO REACT ANGRILY BY BENSON'S INHUMAN CONDITIONING ...AND THAT HE ONLY MEANT TO *SHOVE* BENSON--NOT *KILL* HIM!

IF THE CONDITIONING DID IT, WHY DIDN'T HE GET VIOLENT AGAINST *HER* OR THAT RIVAL?

IF BENSON HAD *UNDERSTOOD* THEIR LANGUAGE, AS I NOW DO, HE'D HAVE KNOWN THAT "RIVAL" WAS HER *BROTHER*, SHARING WITH HER THE LOVE AND COMFORT ALL THESE PEOPLE GIVE EACH OTHER!

IRONIC, ISN'T IT?

I....I WON'T LET YOU CONFUSE ME! HE MUST'VE HAD EVIL IN HIS HEART ALL ALONG!

LET HIM GO, BUDDY, OR I'LL BE FORCED TO RESTRAIN YOU, *SUPER-STYLE!*

18

JUST TRY, YOU MUSCLE-BOUND BOOB--

WHAT'S THAT??!!

WHA-ROOOOM

SOUNDS LIKE *TNT*... SOMEWHERE UNDERGROUND!

THE THERMAL SPRINGS-- THEY'RE *CAVING IN!* NOW I REMEMBER... THEY MUST CONNECT WITH THE ICE CREVASSES!

BENSON'S MEN MUST HAVE SET THOSE EXPLOSIVES!

WHOOOOOOOSH

HISSSSSS

KWOK

WITHOUT THE HOT SPRINGS, THE "GREENHOUSE EFFECT" OF THE CLOUD COVER WILL BE GONE! THE VALLEY CLIMATE WILL TURN *ICE-COLD!*

JUST WHAT BENSON HAD IN MIND... TO PUT THESE PEOPLE UNDER MORE STRESS!

KRUUUNNKK

KRUNNNNK

HUH?

19

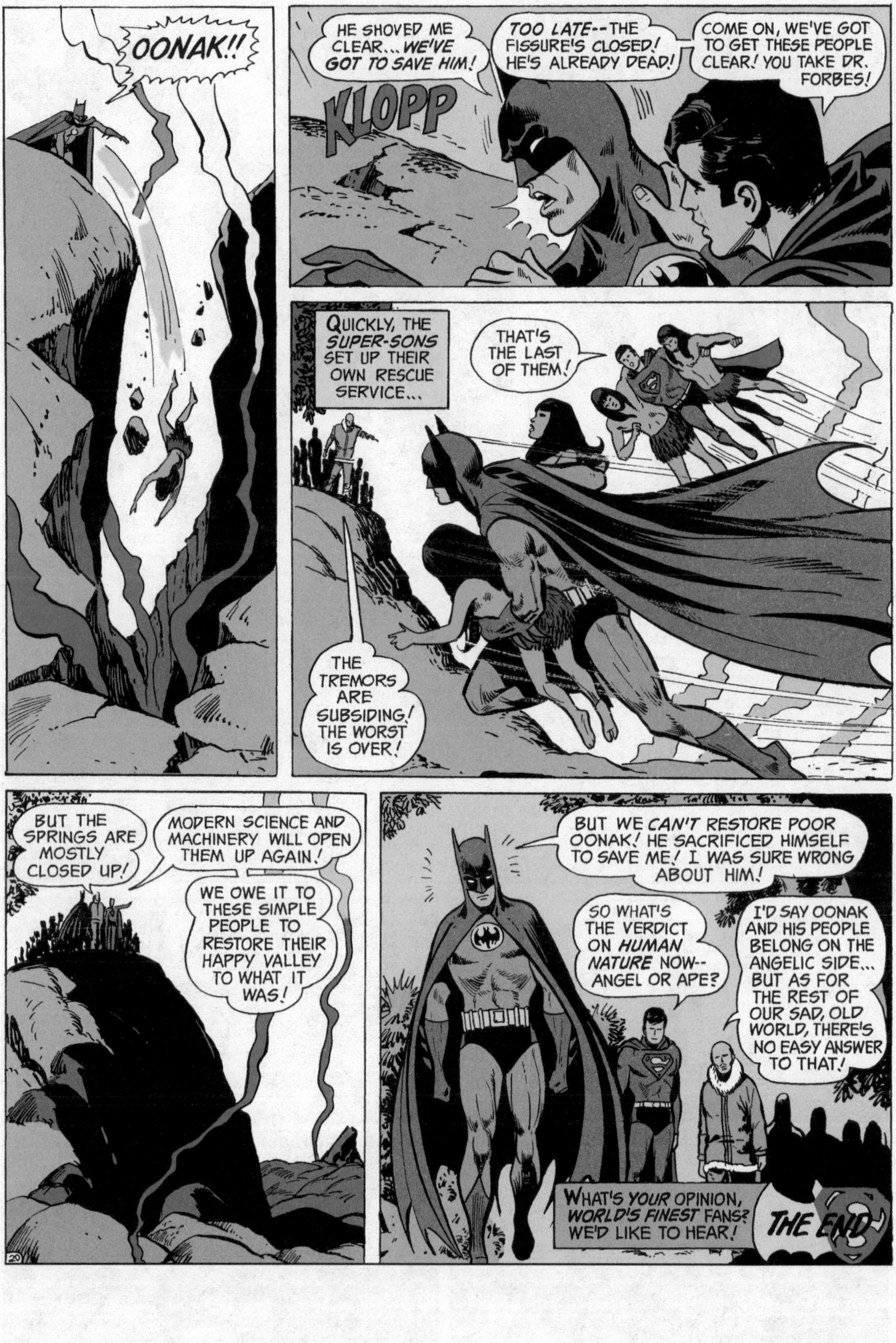
OONAK!!
HE SHOVED ME CLEAR... WE'VE GOT TO SAVE HIM!
KLOPP
TOO LATE--THE FISSURE'S CLOSED! HE'S ALREADY DEAD!
COME ON, WE'VE GOT TO GET THESE PEOPLE CLEAR! YOU TAKE DR. FORBES!
QUICKLY, THE SUPER-SONS SET UP THEIR OWN RESCUE SERVICE...
THAT'S THE LAST OF THEM!
THE TREMORS ARE SUBSIDING! THE WORST IS OVER!
BUT THE SPRINGS ARE MOSTLY CLOSED UP!
MODERN SCIENCE AND MACHINERY WILL OPEN THEM UP AGAIN!
WE OWE IT TO THESE SIMPLE PEOPLE TO RESTORE THEIR HAPPY VALLEY TO WHAT IT WAS!
20
BUT WE CAN'T RESTORE POOR OONAK! HE SACRIFICED HIMSELF TO SAVE ME! I WAS SURE WRONG ABOUT HIM!
SO WHAT'S THE VERDICT ON HUMAN NATURE NOW--ANGEL OR APE?
I'D SAY OONAK AND HIS PEOPLE BELONG ON THE ANGELIC SIDE... BUT AS FOR THE REST OF OUR SAD, OLD WORLD, THERE'S NO EASY ANSWER TO THAT!
WHAT'S YOUR OPINION, WORLD'S FINEST FANS? WE'D LIKE TO HEAR!
THE END

SUPERMAN and BATMAN

METROPOLIS, U.S.A., AND A FAMED, TITANIC FIGURE STREAKS DOWN FROM AN UPPER STORY OF AN OLD, DILAPIDATED BUILDING IN A DINGY PART OF TOWN...

SUPERMAN'S GOT THE LAST OF 'EM! THE ENTIRE PLACE IS EVACUATED! THAT OLD WRECK CAN COLLAPSE ANY TIME IT WANTS...NOW!

AMONG THE TENSE AND AWED SPECTATORS, A YOUNG MAN WHO LOOKS MORE THAN FAINTLY FAMILIAR...!

HOTEL

HOTEL

ROOMS FOR RENT $2.00

DAD'S DONE HIS BIG RESCUE ACT...BUT JUST TO MAKE SURE, I'LL USE MY X-RAY VISION--

WHAT'S THAT? I SEE A DOG...TIED AND LEFT BEHIND!

TROUBLE IN THE BIG CITY--BUT IT KICKS OFF YET ANOTHER CHAPTER IN THE CONTINUING SAGA OF THE OFFSPRING OF SUPERMAN AND BATMAN--WHEREIN THE WORLD SEEMS TURNED UPSIDE DOWN BY...

The SHOCKING SWITCH of the SUPER-SONS

ART BY: DICK DILLIN & VINCE COLLETTA - STORY BY: BOB HANEY

PART 1 A CHASM SO WIDE...!

HEY, THAT CRAZY KID'S RUNNING INTO THE HOTEL!

HE'LL BE KILLED!

IT'S MY OWN SON... CLARK JR.--!

AND AN EYE-BLURRING INSTANT AFTERWARD...

SUPERMAN'S AFTER HIM... BUT THE PLACE IS COLLAPSING!

THEN, THROUGH A CASCADING TORRENT OF TIMBERS, BRICKS, AND SMOTHERING DUST...

RAFF! ARFF!

SUPERMAN DID IT! HE SAVED 'EM BOTH!

BUT AS THE MAN OF STEEL SPEEDS OUT OF THE AREA...

YOU CAN PUT US DOWN, DAD! WE'RE CLEAR NOW!

I COULD'VE SHAKEN OFF THAT COLLAPSING BUILDING AS EASY AS THIS PUP SHAKES OFF FLEAS!

EXACTLY WHY, YOU YOUNG FOOL, I'M TAKING YOU OUT OF EARSHOT OF THAT CROWD OF WITNESSES!

I HAD TO "RESCUE" YOU TO PROTECT YOUR SECRET SUPER IDENTITY! YOU DIDN'T THINK OF THAT! AND WHY WERE YOU HANGING AROUND ANYWAY?

EASY, DAD! I JUST WANTED TO BE NEAR YOU! I HARDLY EVER SEE YOU... YOU'RE ALWAYS OFF ON SOME WORLD-SHAKING PROBLEM OR CRISIS!

2

WELL, YOU PICKED A *FINE* TIME AND PLACE FOR "TOGETHERNESS"! TROUBLE WITH YOU IS, YOU'RE STILL *IMMATURE* AND *SELF-CENTERED*!

TROUBLE WITH *YOU* IS, YOU SHOULD NEVER HAVE HAD A SON WHO'S HALF-NORMAL *HUMAN* INSTEAD OF ALL-PERFECT *ALIEN* LIKE YOU!

COME ON, PUP!

MEANWHILE, THOUSANDS OF MILES AWAY, IN GOTHAM CITY, WHERE NIGHT HAS ALREADY FALLEN...

A MIDNIGHT MEETING WITH GOTHAM'S CRIME BOSS-- TO ARRANGE FOR A COP-KILLER'S SURRENDER! ALL PART OF A *BAT-MAN'S* JOB!

WHO'S THAT, UP AHEAD...?

JUST A DERELICT, SLEEPING IT OFF...

BUT EVEN AS THE MASKED MANHUNTER STRIDES BEYOND THE SLUMPED FIGURE...

DAD! LOOK OUT!

KWOK

BRUCE...? MY BOY... BRUCE?

BLAM

THWACK

WE'RE *SOME* TEAM, POP!

OH-OH, HERE COMES THE FUZZ!

AND HERE *WE* GO, YOU YOUNG HOTHEAD!

3

WHY'D WE SPLIT THAT SCENE?

TO AVOID EXPLAINING TO THE POLICE HOW **YOU** "HAPPENED" TO BE AT **BATMAN'S** SECRET RENDEZVOUS!

SIMPLE! I HEARD YOU TELL MOM, AND FIGURED IT MIGHT REALLY BE AN AMBUSH AND YOU'D NEED HELP, WHICH WAS **RIGHT ON!**

BUT WHY DIDN'T YOU CLEAR IT WITH **ME** FIRST? YOU COULD'VE BEEN **KILLED!**

AND **YOU** DEFINITELY WOULD'VE BEEN KILLED IF I HADN'T DONE MY "BACK-UP BUM" BIT! COME ON, BE HONEST-- YOU'D NEVER HAVE OKAYED THE IDEA, ANYHOW!

YOU'RE SURE RIGHT ABOUT **THAT!** HOW LONG BEFORE YOU GROW UP AND START BEHAVING LIKE AN ADULT?

IF BEING ADULT MEANS ACTING THE WAY YOU ARE NOW, BIG DADDY... **NEVER!!**

YOU CAN'T TALK TO **ME** THAT WAY!

BRUCE! BRUCE!!

ALL OF WHICH IS WHY, TWO DAYS LATER, TWO STAUNCH FRIENDS MEET IN GOTHAM CITY FOR A "HEAVY RAP" SESSION...

THANKS FOR FLYING IN, CLARK BUDDY--BUT, MAN, I'M DOWN WITH THE SAME OLD PROBLEM... **GENERATION GAP, SUPER-STYLE!**

CHECK, BRUCE! ME, TOO!

YEAH, I'M READY TO GIVE UP EVER HAVING A ONE-TO-ONE RELATIONSHIP WITH MY OLD MAN!

HOLD IT, CHUM! **DIG THAT POSTER!**

④

AN ENCOUNTER CAMP! WHERE PEOPLE GET INTO THEIR OWN HEADS AND PROBLEMS! MAYBE *THAT'S* OUR ANSWER!

SURE, SURE-- BUT JUST IMAGINE *SUPERMAN* AND *BATMAN* GOING FOR A DEAL LIKE THAT! FORGET IT, PAL!

OUT OF TOUCH? MISUNDERSTOOD? try ENOYREVE AN ENCOUNTER CAMP IN THE GOLDEN WEST

*B*UT, ONE WEEK LATER, DEEP IN THE WESTERN ROCKIES...

CAN'T BELIEVE I'M HERE, BUT I'LL TRY *ANYTHING* ONCE!

SAME HERE, BUT *ENOYREVE* IS *EVERYONE* SPELLED BACKWARDS...

ENOYREVE

SO I GUESS EVEN FATHERS AS UNIQUE AS WE CAN'T ESCAPE HAVING PROBLEMS!

WELCOME! I AM *DR. ZAMM*, THE DIRECTOR AND YOUR GUIDE TO HEIGHTENED AWARENESS!

CLARK AND I ARE READY FOR ANY "TRIP" YOU SAY, DOC, AS LONG AS IT MAKES OUR DADS UNDERSTAND US!

IT WON'T BE EASY! WE REALLY HAD TO TWIST THEIR ARMS TO JOIN US HERE!

ENOUGH! YOUR FATHERS *DID* COME-- AND IT WAS MUCH HARDER FOR THEM THAN YOU TO MAKE THAT DECISION! SO I GIVE *THEM* MORE CREDIT!

SAY, I'M GOING TO *LIKE* THIS PLACE, AFTER ALL!

NO, MR. KENT, YOU ARE GOING TO *DISLIKE* IT, BECAUSE HERE YOU WILL ENCOUNTER *TRUTH*...ABOUT YOURSELF AND YOUR EMOTIONS!

IT TAKES EVER MORE COURAGE TO *STAY* HERE!

BEHOLD OUR OTHER GUESTS ENCOUNTERING THEIR TRUE SELVES VIA VARIOUS EXERCISES DESIGNED TO BREAK DOWN THE BARRIERS BETWEEN HUMAN BEINGS!

HEAVY STUFF, MAN! WHAT ABOUT THAT GUY, DOC?

UH...MR. BELL... MY MOST *DIFFICULT* GUEST! IMPOSSIBLE TO GET THROUGH TO HIM-- HE JUST SITS AND BROODS FOR HOURS!

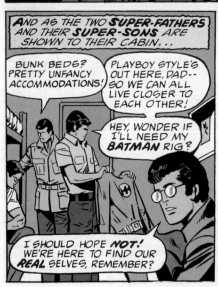

AND AS THE TWO *SUPER-FATHERS* AND THEIR *SUPER-SONS* ARE SHOWN TO THEIR CABIN...

BUNK BEDS? PRETTY UNFANCY ACCOMMODATIONS!

PLAYBOY STYLE'S OUT HERE, DAD-- SO WE CAN ALL LIVE CLOSER TO EACH OTHER!

HEY, WONDER IF I'LL NEED MY *BATMAN* RIG?

I SHOULD HOPE *NOT!* WE'RE HERE TO FIND OUR *REAL* SELVES, REMEMBER?

AT THIS MOMENT, NOT FAR AWAY...

A DEAD GRIZZLY... HALF TORN TO PIECES! BUT THE HUNTING SEASON'S OVER...

...AND NO *NATURAL* ENEMY'S BIG ENOUGH TO DO *THAT* TO A GRIZZLY!

A MYSTERY IN THE MOUNTAINS-- WHAT POSSIBLE CONNECTION COULD IT HAVE TO OUR FOUR HEROES? READ RIGHT ON...IN *PART 2 -- NEXT!*

6

A LITTLE LATER, FOUR PEOPLE BEGIN PERHAPS THE STRANGEST EXPERIENCE OF THEIR UNIQUE LIVES...

THAT'S IT... **TOUCH** EACH OTHER! THE OTHER PERSON IS **THERE!** HE'S...**REAL!**

OWWWW! TAKE IT EASY, DAD!

REMEMBER, I'M ONLY **HALF** SUPER, SO YOUR PINCHES HURT!

HMMM, THE KENTS SHOW DEEP, HIDDEN HOSTILITY TOWARD EACH OTHER...

...WHILE THE WAYNES CAN'T EVEN MANAGE TO TOUCH... WHICH IS EQUALLY BAD!

NOW, MR. KENT, **SCREAM** AS LOUD AS YOU **CAN!** GET THAT HOSTILITY **OUT** OF YOU!

HUH? I'LL TRY!

AHHHW

NOT GOOD ENOUGH! **REALLY** LET GO! **SCREAM!**

HOWWWLLL WHOOOOOOOOUSSH

THAT TREE...? I MUST'VE **IMAGINED** IT!

DAD'S HOWL BLEW OVER THIS SAPLING--BUT DR. ZAMM CAN'T SEE ME RE-ROOTING IT AT SUPER-SPEED!

NOW YOU WAYNES-- **LAUGH!**

BUT THERE'S NOTHING FUNNY!

THINK OF SOMETHING FUNNY ABOUT EACH OTHER! SHOW SOME INTEREST IN EACH OTHER! **TRY!**

7

WELL, I REMEMBER MY SON USING MY AFTER-SHAVE LOTION ON HIS FIRST DATE SO THE GIRL WOULD THINK HE WAS OLD ENOUGH TO SHAVE! *HA! HA! HA!*

DAD... THAT'S NOT FAIR!

HA! HA! HAR! HA! HO!

CUT IT, DAD!

OBVIOUSLY, YOUR FATHER LIKES TO THINK YOU'RE TOO YOUNG TO BE A MAN-- BUT, THEN, BY SHOWING ANGER OVER A PROBLEM HE HASN'T SOLVED, YOU DEMONSTRATE YOU *ARE* YOUNG AND IMMATURE!

NOW, I WANT *BOTH* FATHERS TO DANCE WITH THEIR SON!

D-DANCE? MEN... DANCING TOGETHER?

OF COURSE! MANY EUROPEAN MALES, AMONG THEM GREEK MOUNTAIN TROOPS-- SOME OF THE WORLD'S MOST MASCULINE MEN -- DANCE TOGETHER IN JOY AND COMRADESHIP! *DANCE!*

COME ON, DAD, GET WITH IT!

YOU, TOO, DAD...HOW ABOUT THE "FUNKY ROBOT"?

SUDDENLY!

SHERIFF LATIMER..!?

≷WHEW≷ A WELCOME INTERRUPTION!

SORRY TO BARGE IN, DOCTOR ZAMM-- BUT THERE'S SOMETHING LOOSE IN THE AREA...

...A SAVAGE KILLER WITH THE STRENGTH OF 10 MEN!

IT'S BEEN SLAYING ANIMALS AND TEARING APART ABANDONED CABINS AND FENCES!

YOU BEST KEEP YOUR GUESTS STICKING CLOSE TO CAMP!

CERTAINLY WILL! THANKS FOR THE WARNING, SHERIFF!

SHORTLY...

ENCOUNTER CAMP'S VERY INTERESTING... BUT I NEED A CHANGE OF PACE--LIKE CHECKING ON THIS MYSTERIOUS MARAUDER!

I'M WITH YOU! COME ON, BOYS! WE'LL **ALL** GO!

SOON...

COOL IDEA, DAD--US PATROLLING TOGETHER!

BUT WE'D COVER **TWICE** THE TERRITORY, SON, IF WE SPLIT UP!

OKAY, OKAY, YOU JUST DON'T WANT ME **WITH** YOU!

THAT'S **NOT** WHAT I MEANT, CLARK, BUT IF YOU FEEL THAT WAY...

THIS IS A DRAG, DAD, CHECKING UNDER ROCK AND CACTUS!

GOOD DETECTIVE WORK'S 99 PERCENT A DRAG, BRUCE! THERE ARE NO SHORTCUTS! IF YOU DON'T LIKE MY METHODS, GO DO IT YOUR **OWN** WAY!

OH, SURE! HOW MUCH GROUND COULD I COVER WITHOUT WHEELS?

GOTCHA, BUDDY! I OVERHEARD YOU VIA MY SUPER-HEARING! BEST WE KIDS WORK ON OUR OWN!

SHORTLY...

FOUND ANYTHING, **BATMAN?**

NOT YET--BUT WHATEVER'S ROAMING AND WRECKING AROUND HERE **IS** SOMETHING OF IMMENSE POWER AND DANGER!

9

SUDDENLY...!

WH--?? A NET?!

I'LL SMASH US FREE!

LOOK! A GOVERNMENT COPTER!

WE KNOW YOU CAN BREAK THE TITANIUM NET, SUPERMAN, BUT WE REQUEST YOU TO ALLOW US TO TAKE YOU ALL AWAY!

HI, DADS--FANCY MEETING YOU HERE!

CUT THE COMEDY, CLARK! WHAT'S GOING ON?

UNCLE SAM WILL SOON LET US KNOW! MEANTIME, EN-JOY THE SCENERY...AND LEAVE THE DRIVING TO THEM!

SHORTLY, AT A SECRET COMPOUND DEEP IN THE MOUNTAINS...

GENTLEMEN, THIS IS A UNIQUE CRISIS! THAT TRAIN IS LOADED WITH DEADLY NERVE GAS-- ENOUGH TO WIPE OUT MILLIONS!

IT MUST BE TRANSPORTED TO THE COAST! USING UNUSUAL PRECAUTIONS, WE CAN PREVENT ACCIDENTS--BUT SABOTEURS ARE ANOTHER MATTER!

GENERAL, PUT ENOUGH GUARDS ON THAT CHOO-CHOO, AND NO ENEMY AGENTS WOULD DARE INTERFERE WITH IT!

IT'S NOT ENEMY AGENTS WE FEAR-- BUT ONE OF OUR OWN!

10

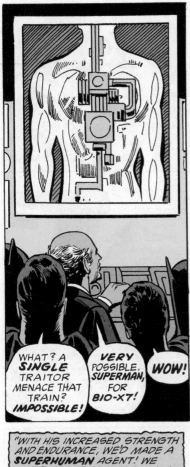

"**BIO-X7** WAS OUR TOP AGENT, UNTIL HE WAS BROUGHT IN CLINICALLY 'DEAD' AFTER A CAR ACCIDENT..."

HIS BRAIN'S INTACT--BUT HIS BODY ORGANS ARE DESTROYED!

HMMM, A PERFECT CHANCE TO TRY... **OPERATION SUPER-AGENT!**

"IT WAS AN EXPERIMENT WE'D LONG PLANNED! THE CORPSE'S ORGANS AND TENDONS WERE REPLACED WITH DUPLICATES MADE OF **SPECIAL METAL ALLOYS AND PLASTIC**..."

HIS BIO-CHEMICAL SYSTEM WILL BE FUELED VIA A TINY NUCLEAR POWER-PACK! HE'LL NEVER NEED FOOD..., OR SLEEP!

WHAT? A **SINGLE** TRAITOR MENACE THAT TRAIN? **IMPOSSIBLE!**

VERY POSSIBLE, **SUPERMAN,** FOR **BIO-X7!**

WOW!

"WITH HIS INCREASED STRENGTH AND ENDURANCE, WE'D MADE A **SUPERHUMAN** AGENT! WE WERE ABOUT TO INFORM HIM OF HIS NEW 'LIFE' WHEN..."

THE NUCLEAR POWER-PACK-- IT'S GOT A MALFUNCTION WE MISSED CHECKING! WE MUST OPERATE AGAIN TO **FIX** IT!

BUT **BIO-X7** HAD VANISHED FROM HIS ISOLATED ROOM... WHICH LEADS US TO BELIEVE THAT **HE** IS THE THING WREAKING HAVOC IN THE AREA...

...A BERSERK FRANKENSTEIN UNAWARE HIS NEW INSIDES ARE INFLUENCING HIS HUMAN BRAIN!

THE NETS **YOU** FOUR STUMBLED INTO WERE TO TRAP **HIM**...

BECAUSE **BIO-X7** KNOWS THE NERVE GAS TRAIN LEAVES IN TWO DAYS--**AND** ITS ROUTE! HE MIGHT **ATTACK** IT!

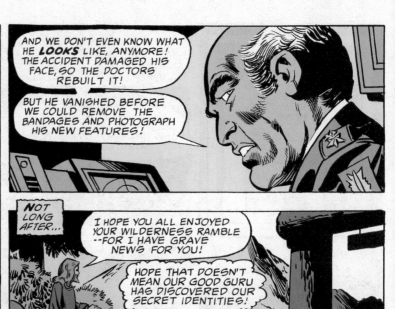

SINCE HIS POWERS ARE TOO MUCH FOR *ORDINARY* GUARDS, WE'RE ASKING *YOU FOUR* TO "RIDE SHOTGUN" ON THE SHIPMENT!

AND WE DON'T EVEN KNOW WHAT HE *LOOKS* LIKE, ANYMORE! THE ACCIDENT DAMAGED HIS FACE, SO THE DOCTORS REBUILT IT!

BUT HE VANISHED BEFORE WE COULD REMOVE THE BANDAGES AND PHOTOGRAPH HIS NEW FEATURES!

AGREED... BUT MAYBE WE CAN TRACK HIM DOWN BEFORE-HAND!

NOT LONG AFTER...

I HOPE YOU ALL ENJOYED YOUR WILDERNESS RAMBLE --FOR I HAVE GRAVE NEWS FOR YOU!

HOPE THAT DOESN'T MEAN OUR GOOD GURU HAS DISCOVERED OUR SECRET IDENTITIES!

NOT LIKELY! BEING A HIGHLY TRAINED AGENT, HE'S VERY WARY!

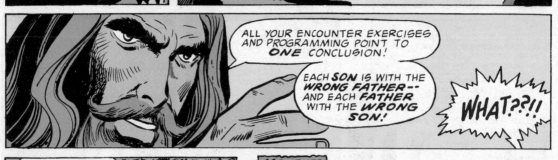

ALL YOUR ENCOUNTER EXERCISES AND PROGRAMMING POINT TO *ONE* CONCLUSION!

EACH *SON* IS WITH THE *WRONG FATHER*-- AND EACH *FATHER* WITH THE *WRONG SON!*

WHAT??!!

NO DOUBT OF IT. *YOUNG BRUCE* WOULD RELATE BETTER TO *KENT SR.,* AND *CLARK JR.* WOULD BE *HAPPIER* WITH *WAYNE SR.!*

FROM NOW ON-- YOU WILL ALL *SWITCH!*

AMAZING!

FLABBERGASTING!

MOMENTS LATER...

I *WON'T* DO IT! I'D RATHER *FIGHT* THAN SWITCH!

YOU'RE *RIGHT!* CLARK'S *MY* BOY...AND BRUCE IS *YOURS!* THAT'S A *FACT OF LIFE!*

12

BUT IT'S **ALSO** A FACT THAT ON OUR PATROL JUST NOW **NEITHER** OF US GOT ALONG WITH OUR REGULAR DADS--!

CHECK! DIDN'T BOTH YOU FATHERS PROMISE TO ABIDE BY THE RESULTS OF THE ENCOUNTER EXERCISES? YOU **CAN'T** GO BACK ON YOUR WORD!

OKAY, OKAY! BUT IT'S GOING TO BE DIFFICULT WITH US SLATED TO GUARD THAT NERVE GAS TRAIN IN LESS THAN 48 HOURS!

YOU SAID IT! IT'LL BE **ONE** SWITCH DR. ZAMM COULDN'T KNOW WOULD HAPPEN!

NOW AS THE NEW ARRANGEMENT BEGINS...

HA! HA! SAY, THAT'S A FUNNY STORY, MR. KENT! AND I ALWAYS THOUGHT YOU WERE A STRAIGHT, UPTIGHT GUY, LIKE CLARK SAID!

HMMM, HE **DID,** DID HE?

BRUCE MUST'VE BEEN JOKING WHEN HE SAID YOU NEVER HAD TIME TO TEACH A GUY ANYTHING, MR. WAYNE!

DID HE? WELL, I NEVER HAD SUCH A WILLING PUPIL, CLARK!

THAT EVENING...

WELL, BRUCIE-BOY, HOW DO YOU LIKE MY OLD MAN? YOURS IS AN OKAY GUY!

I DIG YOURS, TOO, CLARK, BUDDY! IT'S A REAL MIND-BLOWER TO THINK WE MAY WIND UP SWITCHING DADS **PERMANENTLY!**

YEAH, GUARDING THE NERVE GAS WILL BE THE ACID TEST!

HEY, THERE'S MR. BELL AGAIN... JUST WANDERING AROUND ALONE!

YEAH, POOR GUY'S NOT INTERESTED IN EATING! MUST HAVE A HEAVY PROBLEM! COME ON, I WANT TO "ENCOUNTER" A STEAK AND FRENCH FRIES!

WHILE OUR HEROES TAKE A DINNER BREAK--WE BREAK OUR STORY, BUT PART 3 IS ON THE GRIDDLE...NEXT!

13

PART 3 THE BREATH OF DEATH

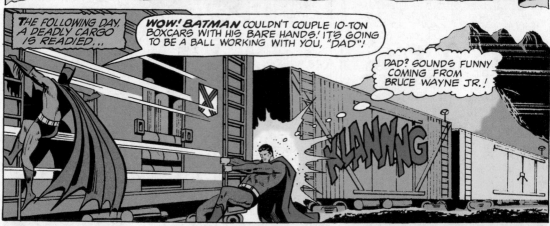

THE FOLLOWING DAY, A DEADLY CARGO IS READIED...

WOW! *BATMAN* COULDN'T COUPLE 10-TON BOXCARS WITH HIS BARE HANDS! IT'S GOING TO BE A BALL WORKING WITH YOU, "DAD"!

DAD? SOUNDS FUNNY COMING FROM BRUCE WAYNE JR.!

KLANNNG

MEANWHILE, ALREADY MOVING DOWN A NEARBY HIGHWAY...

THIS IS COOL, *BATMAN*-- YOU AND I TAKING THE *REAL* NERVE GAS, DISGUISED IN EACH VEHICLE'S COOKING TANK...

HAPPY DAYS CAMPER CARAVAN

...WHILE *SUPERMAN* AND *BATMAN JR.* ESCORT *EMPTY* TANKS ON THE TRAIN! GUESS THE GOVERNMENT FIGURES *WE'RE* THE TOP TEAM!

NO, CLARK, WE'RE REALLY *DECOYS!* 810-X7 ALSO KNEW THIS CAMPER CARAVAN WAS THE BACK-UP METHOD TO TRANSPORT THE GAS...

...SO THEY SWITCHED IT *BACK* TO THE TRAIN TO FOOL HIM!

WHAT? THEN THIS CANARY, USED FOR A SAFETY SNIFFER IN CASE OF GAS LEAKS, IS JUST ANOTHER DECOY FOOLER?

EXACTLY, LIKE THESE GOVERNMENT MEN PRETENDING TO BE TYPICAL TOURISTS! NOW STAY ALERT FOR ANY TROUBLE!

OKAY, BUT I CAN BEST PLAY GUARD FOR THIS CARAVAN UPSTAIRS!

SEE YA, BAT-DAD!

HAPPY CAMPER

14

NOW, AS THE INNOCENT-APPEARING CONVOY MOVES ALONG...

IN MY SIDE-VIEW MIRROR! A GUY DROPPING ONTO THE ROOF OF THE LAST VAN! IT'S GOT TO BE HIM-- BIO-X7!

THEN, WITH PRODIGIOUS STRENGTH...

WHERE'S SUPERMAN JR.? I CAN'T CALL HIM--HE DOESN'T WEAR A WRIST RADIO LIKE BATMAN JR.!

GIVE THAT TO ME! YOU DON'T KNOW WHAT YOU'RE DOING!

SSSSSS

SSS

OH, YES, I DO! I'M GIVING YOU A TASTE OF DEADLY NERVE GAS... LIKE THIS!

GOT TO PLAY DEAD INSTANTLY LIKE IT REALLY AFFECTED ME!

THE OTHER DRIVERS ARE DOING LIKEWISE!

♪♪

THAT CANARY'S STILL SINGING? IT'S A FAKE! THEY DID A SWITCH ON THE SWITCH! THE REAL GAS IS ON THE TRAIN!

GOTCHA--!

YOU'RE MAKING A SERIOUS MISTAKE, TRYING TO INTERFERE WITH ME!

15

I DON'T KNOW *WHERE* I GOT SUCH STRENGTH-- BUT WHEN THE MOOD STRIKES... *I USE IT!*

THE IMPACT WOULD'VE INJURED AN ORDINARY MAN, BUT ONLY STUNS THE *CAPED CRUSADER...*

YOU OKAY, *BATMAN?* THAT CHARACTER TOOK OFF!

HE'S HEADING TO INTER-CEPT THE TRAIN! *SUPERMAN JR.* SHOULD HAVE STOPPED HIM! WHAT *HAPPENED* TO THAT BOY?

WELL, *BATMAN,* NOT FAR OFF, AT A SMALL RODEO...

THAT KID IN THE *SUPERMAN* OUTFIT'S A GREAT RIDER!

THIS IS REAL FUN, COMPETING IN A WILD BRONC-RIDING EVENT!

BESIDES, WHAT'S THE SENSE OF GUARDING A DECOY CARAVAN?

YAHOOO!

AND WHERE THE TRAIN RUMBLES THROUGH DUSTY CANYONS...

OKAY SO FAR!...WHAT'S *THAT?*

MY *TELESCOPIC VISION* SPOTS A BOULDER ON THE TRACK TWO MILES AHEAD!

IN A TWINKLING...

THIS'LL TAKE A SECOND! *BATMAN JR.'S* TO SIGNAL ME WITH A RAILROAD FLARE IN CASE OF TROUBLE!

BUT, AT THIS MOMENT, BACK AT THE TRAIN...

KWAAM

16

BUT WHAT IS *BATMAN JR.* DOING?

THANKS FOR LETTING ME HANDLE THE THROTTLE! I'VE BEEN A TRAIN BUFF SINCE I WAS A KID!

AM I SEEIN' THINGS, OR IS THAT--?

--*BIO-X7!* MUST SIGNAL *SUPERMAN*-- OH, *NO!* I LEFT THE FLARE BACK IN THE CABOOSE!

IT IS SOME TIME LATER, AND FOUR FAMILIAR FIGURES REGROUP...

GREAT WORK, *BATMAN JR.!* THE TRAIN GOT THROUGH, BUT *BIO-X7* IS LOOSE SOMEWHERE WITH A TANK OF NERVE GAS...

...ENOUGH TO WIPE OUT AN ENTIRE TOWN! ALL BECAUSE YOU WANTED TO PLAY "TRAINS"!

AND *YOU, SUPERMAN JR.,* BECAUSE YOU PLAYED RODEO HOTSHOT, *BIO-X7* WASN'T DELAYED LONG ENOUGH SO THE TRAIN COULD GET CLEAR!

YOU'RE *BOTH* IMMATURE FOUL-UPS!!

SEEMS I'VE HEARD *THAT* SONG BEFORE! LET'S SLIP BACK INTO *CAMP ENOYREVE!*

YEAH...TRADE FATHERS, AND YOU *STILL* GET THE SAME OLD JAZZ!

SHORTLY... ALL THE KENTS AND WAYNES ARE AVOIDING EACH OTHER AND BROODING...

COULD IT BE THEY'VE ENCOUNTERED THE HEART OF THEIR PROBLEMS?

17

WE'VE HAD **ENOUGH**, DR. ZAMM! IT WON'T **WORK**! MY SON BRUCE IS DIFFICULT, BUT HE'S BETTER FOR ME THAN CLARK JR.!

I'D RESENT THAT, FRIEND, EXCEPT THAT I AGREE ENTIRELY! CLARK'S A TRIAL SOMETIMES, BUT MUCH EASIER TO RELATE TO THAN YOUNG BRUCE!

WELL, HAVE WE GOT NEWS FOR YOU DADS--

WE FEEL THE **SAME** ABOUT YOU TWO!

YOU SEE? YOU'VE GOT TO **RE**-PROGRAM US ALL--BACK TO THE WAY WE **WERE**!

LOOKS LIKE YOU'VE **ALREADY** DONE THAT!

BESIDES, I "LIED" ABOUT THE NEED TO SWITCH! IT WAS A LITTLE EXPERIMENT...

...TO GET BOTH FATHERS AND SONS TO APPRECIATE EACH OTHER! PEACE!

HE'S A CLEVER FELLOW! AS CLARK KENT, I'M RELIEVED-- BUT, AS **SUPERMAN**, I'M WORRIED ABOUT **B10-X7** LOOSE SOMEWHERE WITH THAT GAS CANISTER!

WE HAVEN'T A CLUE! AND THE THOUGHT OF USING THE GAS MIGHT OCCUR TO HIM ANYTIME!

HOLD IT! HIS NORMAL HUMAN BRAIN GETS FREAKED OUT PERIODICALLY BY HIS FAULTY NUCLEAR POWER-PACK! RIGHT?

BUT HE DOESN'T KNOW HE'S BEEN TURNED INTO HALF A ROBOT! RIGHT?

SO HE'S LIKE ANY CAT WITH AN EMOTIONAL PROBLEM, AND BEING BASICALLY SMART, HE'D SEEK HELP!

RIGHT ON! AND MAYBE AT A PLACE LIKE **THIS**...WHERE HE'D SULK, AND FEEL GUILTY BETWEEN PERIODS OF GOING BERSERK...

18

...WHERE HE'D STICK TO HIMSELF... AND NOT EVEN EAT...

...LIKE A CERTAIN GUEST RIGHT HERE AT ENOYREVE!

BIO-X7 DOESN'T EAT BECAUSE HE DOESN'T HAVE TO!

SO BIO-X7 MUST BE OUR SILENT, FOODLESS FELLOW-GUEST WITH A HEAVY PROBLEM... MR. BELL! LET'S GO, DADS!

THAT'S MY BOY!

AND THAT'S MY BOY!

MOMENTS LATER...

SEE FOR YOURSELVES! MR. BELL CHECKED OUT AN HOUR AGO TO DRIVE TOWARD MESA SPRINGS! TOO BAD I COULDN'T SOLVE HIS PROBLEMS!

YOU DON'T KNOW HOW BAD!

COME ON, MEN!

MEANWHILE, IN THE QUIET LITTLE TOWN OF MESA SPRINGS...

WISH I COULD STOP MYSELF... BUT SOME TERRIBLE INNER URGE IS MAKING ME LET LOOSE THE GAS ON THIS HELPLESS TOWN!

QUICKLY, THE PRAIRIE BREEZE CARRIES THE DEADLY VAPOR DOWN THE MAIN STREET, AS...

MESA SPRINGS BELOW!

A BODY IN THE STREET! WE'RE TOO LATE!

19

IT'S...*HIM!* BIO-X7... ALIAS BELL?!

YOU *KNOW* HIM, *BATMAN?* CRAZY FELLER SUDDENLY RAN DOWN THE STREET...

MESA SPRIN

"...WARNING EVERYBODY TO STAY INSIDE! HE SEEMED TO BE GULPING IN ALL THE AIR IN CREATION!"

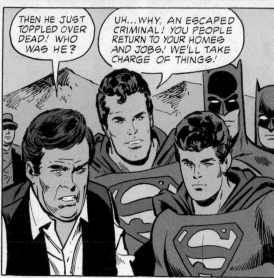

THEN HE JUST TOPPLED OVER DEAD! WHO WAS HE?

UH...WHY, AN ESCAPED CRIMINAL! YOU PEOPLE RETURN TO YOUR HOMES AND JOBS! WE'LL TAKE CHARGE OF THINGS!

BIO-X7 OBVIOUSLY INHALED ALL THE GAS HE HIMSELF HAD LET LOOSE-- BEFORE THESE PEOPLE COULD!

DESPITE HIS POWERS HE WAS STILL MORTAL! AND HIS HUMAN BRAIN AND WILL OVERCAME THE EVIL EFFECTS OF HIS MALFUNCTIONING ROBOT BODY...

TO SACRIFICE HIMSELF TO SAVE HIS INTENDED VICTIMS! AN IRONIC CLIMAX!

NOT LONG AFTER...

WELL, *SUPER-DADS*, WHAT'D YOU THINK OF ENCOUNTER CAMP?

A COOL TRIP, MAN! *HA! HA!*

A "GAS," MAN! *HA! HA! HA!*

THE WORLD'S MOST FABULOUS FATHERS AND THEIR SWINGING SONS WILL BE BACK--IN FUTURE SMASH ISSUES OF *WORLD'S FINEST!* MISS IT NEVER!

20.

THE END.

SUPERMAN & BATMAN
AND THEIR SONS
CO-STARRING ROBIN

WHAT IS IT, SUPERMAN?

OH, NO-- IT'S DAD!!

STAY BACK, BOTH OF YOU! NOTHING MUST BE TOUCHED-- CLARK AND BRUCE-- UNTIL THE POLICE COME!

I JUST ARRIVED FOR A VISIT... AND FOUND HIM LIKE THIS--!

BATMAN IS DEAD! THE KING OF CRIME-FIGHTERS IS NO MORE! AND WITH THIS STUNNING ANNOUNCEMENT BEGINS THE HISTORIC SAGA OF WHO SHALL SUCCEED TO A HERO'S THRONE... AS TWO SURPRISING RIVALS CONTEND AGAINST FATE AND UNPARALLEL ODDS TO WIN THE....

CROWN FOR A NEW BATMAN

CRY IT OUT, BRUCE-BUDDY! GET ALL THE GRIEF OUT OF YOU!

DEAD...? -SOB- BUT HE WAS ALWAYS SO ALIVE ...SEEMED SO INDESTRUCT-IBLE! HOW COULD HE -SOB- DIE...?

PENCILS BY: DICK DILLIN
INKS BY: TEX BLAISDELL
STORY BY: BOB HANEY

PART 1
AVENGE THY FATHER

I COULDN'T CARE FOR YOU MORE IF YOU WERE MY OWN SON, TOO, LIKE CLARK, HERE!

I LOST MY BEST FRIEND AND ALLY--YET THE WORLD'S LOSS IS GREATER THAN OURS...

...FOR THERE LIES THIS CRAZY, MIXED-UP PLANET'S GREATEST CRIME-FIGHTER AND STAUNCHEST GUARDIAN... THE BATMAN!!

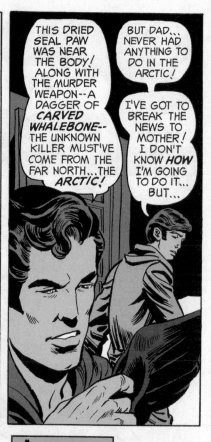

THIS DRIED SEAL PAW WAS NEAR THE BODY! ALONG WITH THE MURDER WEAPON-- A DAGGER OF CARVED WHALEBONE-- THE UNKNOWN KILLER MUST'VE COME FROM THE FAR NORTH...THE ARCTIC!

BUT DAD... NEVER HAD ANYTHING TO DO IN THE ARCTIC!

I'VE GOT TO BREAK THE NEWS TO MOTHER! I DON'T KNOW HOW I'M GOING TO DO IT... BUT...

SHORTLY, AN UNSUSPECTING WORLD LEARNS OF THE PASSING OF ONE MAN...

NEWSPA

BRUCE WAYNE DEAD; MILLIONAIRE MYSTERIOUSLY MURDERED

...BUT CANNOT KNOW THAT THIS IS A DOUBLE DEATH!

OH, THAT THIS DARK DAY HAD NEVER COME...! NOW I MUST LOCK THE MASTER'S COSTUME AWAY... FOREVER!

AND AS THE BUSINESS OF WRAPPING UP A LIFE GOES ON...

I'LL TAKE CARE OF YOU, MOTHER! I'M HEAD OF THE FAMILY NOW!

I GUESS THAT ALSO MAKES YOU THE NEW BATMAN!

HOLD ON! I HAVE SOMETHING TO SAY ABOUT THAT!!

2

DICK GRAYSON!

I HURRIED DOWN FROM COLLEGE SOON AS I GOT THE AWFUL NEWS FROM ALFRED!

AS BRUCE WAYNE'S LEGAL WARD, *I'M* THE LOGICAL HEIR TO THE *BATMAN* ROLE!

AND *I'M* HIS REAL HEIR-- *HIS OWN FLESH AND BLOOD!* I'M ALREADY KNOWN AS *BATMAN JR.* AROUND THE COUNTRY!

BUT I'M *WORLD-FAMOUS* FOR A LOT MORE YEARS AS *BATMAN'S* FIGHTING SIDEKICK-- *ROBIN!*

SO *WHAT?* YOU CAN KEEP ON BEING *ROBIN*, BIRD-BOY-- BUT NO WAY WILL YOU WEAR MY BELOVED DAD'S CAPE AND COWL!

YEAH? JUST TRY AND *STOP ME!* AND YOU DIDN'T LOVE HIM ANY MORE THAN I DID, *JUNIOR!*

STOP, *BOTH OF YOU!* WHAT A WAY TO BEHAVE, AT A TIME LIKE *THIS!* YOU DISHONOR HIS MEMORY!

NOW -- ACT LIKE *MEN!* IT'S TIME FOR THE FUNERAL...

AND SO, IN A QUIET GRAVEYARD, BESIDE HIS LONG-DEAD PARENTS, THE MAN WHO WAS A LIVING LEGEND IS LAID TO FINAL REST...

GOODBYE, DAD... I HOPE I'LL PROVE WORTHY OF YOU AS THE NEW *BATMAN!*

SO LONG, BRUCE WAYNE! TRUST ME TO CARRY ON AS ALWAYS AS... THE NEW *BATMAN!*

THOMAS AND MARTHA WAYNE

BRUCE WAYNE

3

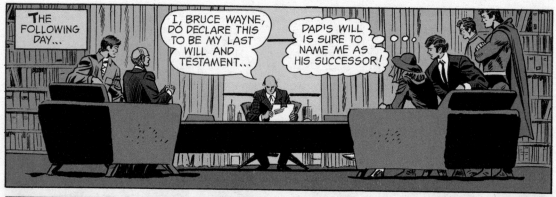

THE FOLLOWING DAY...

I, BRUCE WAYNE, DO DECLARE THIS TO BE MY LAST WILL AND TESTAMENT...

DAD'S WILL IS SURE TO NAME ME AS HIS SUCCESSOR!

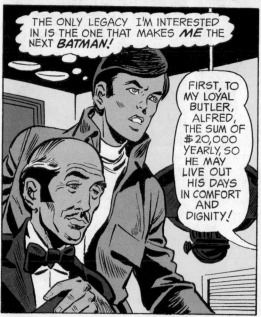

THE ONLY LEGACY I'M INTERESTED IN IS THE ONE THAT MAKES *ME* THE NEXT *BATMAN!*

FIRST, TO MY LOYAL BUTLER, ALFRED, THE SUM OF $20,000 YEARLY, SO HE MAY LIVE OUT HIS DAYS IN COMFORT AND DIGNITY!

TO MY WARD, DICK GRAYSON, I LEAVE THE SUM OF $1,000,000 SO HE CAN FOLLOW ANY LIFE-STYLE HE CHOOSES!

A MILLION--BUT NOT A WORD ABOUT ME BEING *BATMAN!*

AND AS THE FINAL BEQUESTS OF THE WORLD'S WEALTHIEST CRIMEFIGHTER GO ON...

TO MY BELOVED WIFE AND SON, I LEAVE THE BULK OF MY ESTATE SO THEY MAY CONTINUE THE WAYNE NAME AND CHARITIES AS BEFORE!

HUH? NOTHING ABOUT *MY* INHERITING THE *BATMAN* ROLE?!

AND NOW--MY FINAL REQUEST-- THE SUM OF $5,000,000, THE PROFITS FROM THE *SMOKE ISLAND CORPORATION...* TO BE PAID TO MY FORMER PARTNER, *SIMON LINK--IF* AND *WHEN* HE COMES FORWARD TO CLAIM SAME!

4

THUS ENDS THE READING OF THE WILL...

IT'S *CRAZY!* NO MENTION OF *WHO* IS *BATMAN*-- AND *$5,000,000* LEFT TO SOME MYSTERY MAN NAMED *SIMON LINK?!*

HMMM, WELL, *WHOEVER* HE IS, FIVE MILLION SHOULD BRING HIM FORWARD PRETTY QUICK!

ANYWAY, YOUR DAD'S LAST WISHES ARE *SACRED* ...NOTHING *WE* CAN DO ABOUT IT!

THAT NIGHT, A LITHE FIGURE SLIPS TOWARD A FRESHLY-COVERED GRAVE...

COULDN'T SLEEP ...SOME INNER DRIVE MADE ME PUT ON MY COSTUME AND COME HERE!

DAD... I SWEAR ON YOUR GRAVE, I'LL PROVE MYSELF WORTHY OF SUCCEEDING YOU!

YOU'LL HAVE TO CONVINCE *ME*-- FIRST!

ROBIN! WHAT ARE *YOU* DOING HERE?

I'VE AS MUCH RIGHT AS *YOU!* GUESS WE BOTH HAD THE SAME IDEA!

BUT LIKE WE WERE TOLD-- NO SENSE ACTING LIKE KIDS... I HAVE AN IDEA!

THERE'S ONLY *ONE* WAY TO PROVE WHO'S FIT TO FILL *BATMAN'S* BOOTS--

A COMPETITION BETWEEN US... TO SEE WHICH ONE CAN BRING HIS MURDERER TO JUSTICE!

HOW ABOUT IT, BRUCE...A *DEAL?*

IT'S A DEAL-- *WHAT?!*

WUSSSSHH

THUKKKK

5

A SOLEMN GRAVEYARD PACT HAS BEEN INTERRUPTED BY--

--A HARPOON?!

THERE'S THE BOZO WHO TOSSED IT!

I'LL GET HIM!

I CAN COLLAR THAT CHARACTER FASTER THAN JUNIOR BY VAULTING *OVER* THESE!

OUT OF MY WAY--*OUCCH!*

OUT OF MINE-- *UUJUFF!*

KHUMM

WHAMM

EACH OF US TRYING TO BEAT THE OTHER GAVE THAT GUY A CHANCE TO BUG OUT!

IT'S *YOUR* FAULT! IF YOU'D STAYED OUT OF IT, *I'D* HAVE NAILED HIM!

I'LL BET *HE'S* MY DAD'S KILLER!

SOME DEDUCTION, GENIUS! THE *REAL* DETECTIVE WORK WILL BE IDENTIFYING AND *CATCHING* THAT MURDERER!

WE'LL *BOTH* DO THE SLEUTHING, BUT *I'LL* DO THE HEAVY CATCHING... *ALONE!*

PROUD BOASTS IN A GRIM GRAVEYARD AS *PART 1* ENDS HERE! BUT *PART 2* OF *BATMAN'S* TANGLED LEGACY IS RIGHT *NEXT!*

6

THE RIDDLE OF SMOKE ISLAND

THE NEXT DAY, AS THE TWO BITTER RIVALS ANSWER AN URGENT SUMMONS...

BOYS... MEET *SIMON LINK!*

AS THE ESKIMOS SAY, LADS--MAY THE THIN BLUE ICE NEVER SHOW UNDER YOUR MUKLUKS!* GLAD TO MEET THE SONS OF MY LATE PARTNER!

* ESKIMO BOOTS MADE OF SEALSKIN OR REINDEER SKIN!

I'M MY DAD'S *ONLY* SON, MR. LINK! SO *YOU'RE* THE MYSTERIOUS GUY HE LEFT ALL THAT "BREAD" TO?

NOT SO MYSTERIOUS! YOUR FATHER INVESTED IN MY SEAL-HUNTING OPERATIONS YEARS AGO! I REGULARLY SENT HIM HIS SHARE OF THE PROFITS!

THOSE PROFITS GREW TO *FIVE MILLION* IN VALUE -- AND I GUESS YOUR DAD LEFT THAT MONEY TO ME FOR ALWAYS BEING SQUARE WITH HIM!

NOW I'M HERE TO CLAIM MY "INHERITANCE"!

ONE MOMENT, MR. LINK--!

THE WILL STIPULATES, YOU MUST TAKE *BRUCE WAYNE, JR.* TO *SMOKE ISLAND...*

...SHOW HIM THE TOUGH, CHARACTER-BUILDING LIFE OF THE ARCTIC SEAL HUNTER *BEFORE* YOU CAN CLAIM THE MONEY!

WHAT? BUT... UH... I'VE *RETIRED* FROM SEAL-HUNTING ...SPEND ALL MY TIME PROSPECTING FOR ORE! AND *SMOKE ISLAND'S* WAY OFF IN THE BERING SEA!

I'M AFRAID IT'S THE ONLY *LEGAL* WAY YOU CAN OBTAIN THE FIVE MILLION!

HOLD IT! ALL THE CLUES POINT TO DAD'S KILLER BEING FROM THE ARCTIC! DICK GRAYSON AND I SWORE TO TRACK HIM DOWN!

WHY DON'T WE JOIN FORCES, MR. LINK?

7

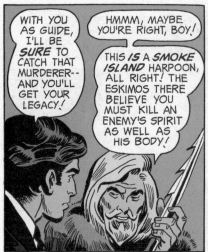

WITH YOU AS GUIDE, I'LL BE *SURE* TO CATCH THAT MURDERER-- AND YOU'LL GET YOUR LEGACY!

HMMM, MAYBE YOU'RE RIGHT, BOY!

THIS *IS* A *SMOKE ISLAND* HARPOON, ALL RIGHT! THE ESKIMOS THERE BELIEVE YOU MUST KILL AN ENEMY'S SPIRIT AS WELL AS HIS BODY!

THAT'S WHY THE KILLER HURLED IT INTO YOUR DAD'S GRAVE!

WELL, WE'LL HAUL HIM IN TO JUSTICE...OR MY NAME'S NOT SIMON LINK! *RIGHT, PARTNERS?*

RIGHT ON!

KK

THUK

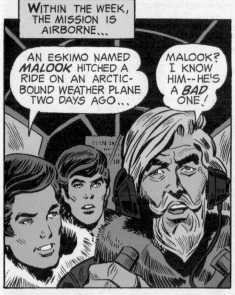

WITHIN THE WEEK, THE MISSION IS AIRBORNE...

AN ESKIMO NAMED *MALOOK* HITCHED A RIDE ON AN ARCTIC-BOUND WEATHER PLANE TWO DAYS AGO...

MALOOK? I KNOW HIM--HE'S A *BAD* ONE!

HE'S *GOT* TO BE THE KILLER!

LINK POLAR ENTERPRISES

BUT WHY WAS HE DAD'S *ENEMY?* GUESS WE'LL FIND THAT OUT ALL IN GOOD TIME!

TWO DAYS LATER, A CAMP ON THE FRIGID EDGE OF THE GREAT BERING SEA...

8

THAT'S SOME TOUGH CREW YOU HAVE, MR. LINK!

THEY *HAVE* TO BE TOUGH, LAD! IN THE ARCTIC, THE WEAK DON'T SURVIVE!

LET'S GET STARTED, LINK! MY SON AND I WILL FLY AHEAD--KEEP IN TOUCH VIA WRIST RADIO!

NOW THE SEARCH FOR A VERY *SPECIAL* KILLER BEGINS...AMIDST THE NORTHLANDS WONDERS!

MR. LINK! AREN'T THOSE SEALS BEHAVING AS IF SOMETHING'S AFTER THEM?

SOMETHING *IS* AFTER THEM, LAD... FOLLOWING THEIR SCAMPER-ING SHADOWS FROM *UNDER* THE ICE-- A *KILLER WHALE!*

KRAAA UNNNGGHHH

LIKE I SAID, THE ARCTIC'S A HARSH PLACE!

EMERGENCY RADIO CALL FROM *ICE STATION EASY,* BOSS! THEIR CAMP FLOE'S BREAKING UP-- *NEED HELP FAST!*

WE'D NEVER REACH THEM IN TIME! RADIO *SUPERMAN* AND HIS SON TO GO TO THEIR AID!

DON'T LIKE FACING THOSE *SMOKE ISLAND* RENEGADES WITHOUT THOSE TWO BACKING US UP...BUT WE'VE NO CHOICE!

9

HEY, I'D PREFER GOING INTO ACTION WITH MY PAL, CLARK, NEARBY--!

IF YOU WANT TO BE *BATMAN'S* SUCCESSOR, CHUM--YOU'VE GOT TO HAVE THE GUTS TO GO IT ALONE!

HOURS LATER, THE HOVERCRAFT SPEEDS ON ITS AIR CUSHION DEEPER INTO THE FROZEN SEAS WHEN...

SMOKE ISLAND AHEAD!

AND ESKIMOS ATTACKING!

KRAK *KRAKK* *KRAK* *KRAK*

I WARNED YOU, THESE NATIVE ISLANDERS ARE KILLERS--*RENEGADES!*

YOU LADS WILL BE SAFER BELOW!

BUT, MR. LINK--!

GO BELOW! THAT'S AN ORDER!

BLAAAM

KRAK KRAK

WHOOOMP

SOOSSSSSSSHHH

WE BROKE UP THEIR ATTACK! HEAD CLOSER TO THE ISLAND TO SHELL THEIR VILLAGE!

10

YET, AS THE SPEEDY MODERN CRAFT LEAVES THE AREA, TWO OF ITS PASSENGERS HAVE "ABANDONED SHIP"-- UNSEEN...

OUT OF MY WAY, *ROBIN!* I'M GOING TO FIND MALOOK *ALONE!*

NO WAY, *JUNIOR!* SEAL POWER WILL GET ME THERE...*FIRST!*

SOME MINUTES LATER ON THE ROCKY ISLAND...

THE NATIVE'S VILLAGE-- WRECKED BY LINK'S SHELLING!

AND AS *BATMAN JR.* CATCHES UP TO HIS "RIVAL"...

WHY, THERE'S NOTHING HERE BUT ONE OLD MAN...SOME SCARED WOMEN AND CHILDREN!

WHERE ARE THE MEN WHO ATTACKED THE HOVERCRAFT?

ODD, ISN'T IT? I'M GOING TO ASK THEM ABOUT MALOOK!

MALOOK! WHERE... IS... MALOOK?

MALOOK! MALOOK!

THE BOYS POINTING TO THOSE SNOW-SHOE TRACKS! MALOOK MUST'VE KNOWN WE'D BE AFTER HIM! AND HE'S SO *RIGHT!*

SHORTLY...

THESE ESKIMO SNOW-SHOES ARE GREAT!

SURE, THEY'RE JUST LIKE MALOOK'S SO WE'RE NOT GOING TO GAIN AN INCH ON HIM!

AND THIS ISLAND'S HIS TURF... HE COULD AMBUSH US FROM ANY ROCK!

11

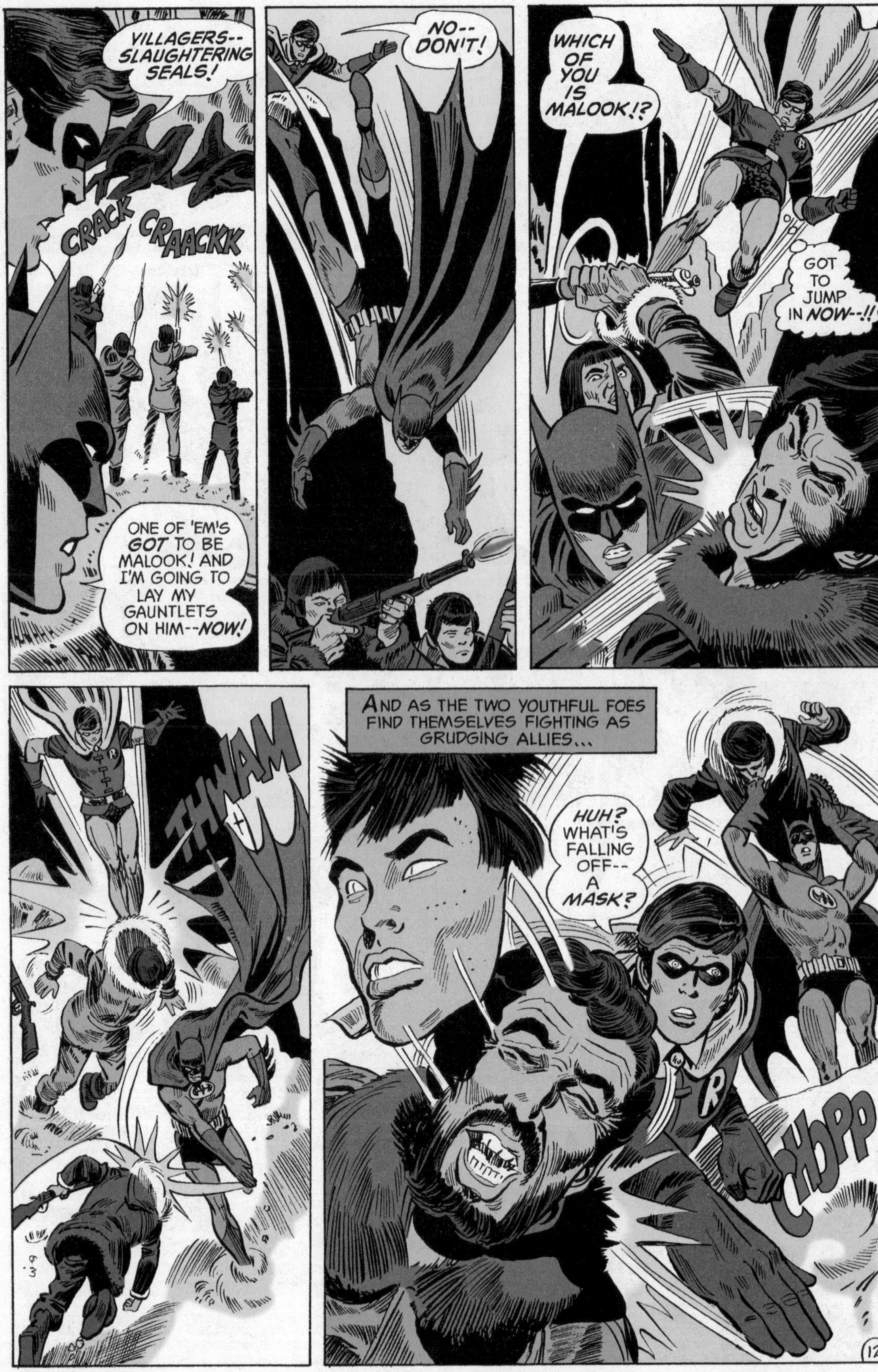
VILLAGERS-- SLAUGHTERING SEALS!
CRACK
CRAACKK
ONE OF 'EM'S GOT TO BE MALOOK! AND I'M GOING TO LAY MY GAUNTLETS ON HIM--NOW!
NO-- DON'T!
WHICH OF YOU IS MALOOK!?
GOT TO JUMP IN NOW--!!
THWAM
AND AS THE TWO YOUTHFUL FOES FIND THEMSELVES FIGHTING AS GRUDGING ALLIES...
HUH? WHAT'S FALLING OFF-- A MASK?
CHOPP
12

THEY'RE RUNNING AWAY! BUT WHICH ONE DO WE FOLLOW-- WHICH ONE IS *MALOOK*?

NONE OF 'EM, GENIUS!

THEY MUST *ALL* BE MASQUERADING AS ESKIMOS-- AS THIS MASK PROVES!

THE GUY WEARING THIS HAD A *BEARD*-- SOMETHING REAL ESKIMOS CAN'T GROW!

LISTEN-- YOU HEAR SOMETHING? ENGINES--?

COME ON--!

A FEW MINUTES LATER, ON THE SNOWFIELDS ABOVE THE COVE...

THOSE PHONY SEAL KILLERS HAD A COUPLE OF SNOWMOBILES STASHED UP HERE!

AND THEY PICKED UP THAT SNOWSHOE TRAIL WE WERE FOLLOWING! *MALOOK'S TRAIL!*

NO DOUBT ABOUT IT! THOSE TWO SNOWMOBILES ARE TRACKING MALOOK--!

MUST BE SOME OF LINK'S CREW! BUT WHY THE DISGUISES?

SHORTLY...

ANOTHER FAKE ESKIMO-- AND *DEAD!* MALOOK MUST'VE AMBUSHED HIM FROM THE ROCKS!

SOME TOUGH HOMBRE, THIS MALOOK! BUT THE OTHER SNOWMOBILE IS *STILL* FOLLOWING HIM!

I'M GOING TO USE THIS TO CATCH THAT ROTTEN KILLER!

WE'RE *BOTH* TAKING IT, CHUM! I'VE GOT TO LOOK OUT FOR YOU--

--BATMAN WOULD HAUNT ME IF I LET ANYTHING HAPPEN TO HIS PRECIOUS BOY!

AND AS THE YOUTHFUL AVENGERS OF THE DEAD *CAPED CRUSADER* RIDE ON DEEPER INTO MYSTERIOUS *SMOKE ISLAND*, WE END *PART 2! PART 3... NEXT!*

13

DEEPER INTO THE INTERIOR OF SINISTER *SMOKE ISLAND* MOVE THE TWO HEIRS TO *BATMAN'S* HEROIC LEGACY...UNTIL...

MALOOK GOT HIS SECOND PURSUER--ANOTHER MASQUERADER!

MAYBE I'VE GOT THE ANSWER! MR. LINK DISGUISED HIS MEN AS ESKIMOS SO THEY COULD MOVE AROUND THE ISLAND UNDETECTED AND CATCH MALOOK OFF-GUARD!

IF THAT'S TRUE, THEY CERTAINLY DIDN'T CATCH HIM OFF-GUARD! YOU SURE YOU WANT TO GO ON? HE'S A DEADLY OPERATOR!

TRY AND STOP ME, BIRD-BOY! WHOEVER GETS HIM WILL REALLY HAVE PROVED HE'S WORTHY OF *BATMAN'S* MANTLE! NAMELY... *YOURS TRULY!*

BUT AS THE TWO RESUME THE CHASE...

HEY! YOUR SNOW-MOBILE'S *FASTER* THAN MINE!

BRRRMMMMM

TOUGH LUCK, *JUNIOR!* NEXT WE MEET, I'LL HAVE MALOOK'S SCALP!

VVVRRRRMMM

HALF AN HOUR LATER...

BEE-OWW

VRRMIU

THEN SILENCE...BUT FOR THE CRUNCH OF SNOWSHOES ADVANCING OVER THE FROZEN CRUST...

CRUNCH

KRUNNCH

AND AS THE AMBUSHER AIMS AGAIN...

IF ONLY I'M IN TIME--!

BRRRRRMMM

14

KRAK

THUDD

I FAKED BEING HIT TO DRAW HIM FROM HIDING...!

CLEVER...BUT HIS SECOND SHOT WOULD'VE DRILLED YOU IF *I* HADN'T SHOWN UP IN THE NICK!

OKAY, MALOOK, *TALK!* WHY DID YOU MURDER BRUCE WAYNE? *WHY??*

MALOOK REALLY WANT TO KILL MY PEOPLE'S GREAT ENEMY-- SIMON LINK!

WHAT? MR. LINK? BUT... WHY?

LINK SLEW ALL YOUNG MEN OF MY VILLAGE-- WHEN WE TRY STOP HIM FROM KILLING TOO MANY SEALS!

WITHOUT SEAL MEAT... MY PEOPLE STARVE! THEN, AFTER MASSACRE...LINK DISAPPEAR!

BUT MALOOK KNOW LINK'S PARTNER-- BRUCE WAYNE-- LIVE IN UNITED STATES! MALOOK GO THERE TO KILL HIM...BE-CAUSE HE ALMOST AS EVIL AS LINK!

WITHOUT HIS MONEY, LINK NOT ABLE TO DO BAD THINGS!

WHY DIDN'T YOU GO TO THE AUTHORITIES?

NOBODY BELIEVE MALOOK! LAUGH AT CRAZY ESKIMO! MALOOK NOT HAVE WHITE MAN'S KIND OF PROOF!

ESKIMO'S WORD AND WHAT HE KNOW IS TRUE...BOTH NOT GOOD ENOUGH IN WHITE MAN'S WORLD!

SOME STORY! BUT IT COULD BE TRUE! IT HELPS EXPLAIN SOME OF THE STRANGE HAPPENINGS ON THIS ISLAND!

YOU BELIEVE THE MAN WHO KILLED BRUCE WAYNE? *NEVER!* HE'S LYING TO SAVE HIMSELF!

15

THERE IS *ONE* PROOF WHITE MAN MIGHT BELIEVE! ONE OF LINK'S OWN MEN--JUD TRENCH--REFUSE TO KILL SEALS AND ESKIMOS!

LINK THROW HIM INTO CREVASSE OF BIG ICEBERG THAT IS SHAPED LIKE POLAR BEAR!

TRENCH MY FRIEND-- HE TELL ME HE HAS PAPER WITH LINK'S WRITING, ORDERING-- KILL ESKIMOS!

HMMM, *THAT* PAPER WOULD CONFIRM YOUR STORY! IT'S "WHITE MAN'S PROOF"!

BUT TRENCH INSIDE ICEBERG! TAKE MANY YEARS FOR BERG TO GIVE BODY!

MAYBE WE CAN *TEST* YOUR STORY-- AND PROVE LINK'S GUILT OR INNOCENCE WITH A LITTLE LIE!

THIS IS *CRAZY!* MR. LINK'S GOT *NOTHING* TO PROVE! MALOOK'S THE CONFESSED ASSASSIN OF *BATMAN!*

MAYBE HE HAD REASONABLE CAUSE TO KILL HIM! WHILE WE TEST HIS STORY, HE'LL REMAIN A PRISONER IN THAT CAVE!

AND AFTER SECRETING THEIR COSTUMES...

MR. LINK-- WE CAME ASHORE LOOKING FOR MALOOK--BUT *FAILED!*

GET BACK *ABOARD!* THAT ROTTEN ESKIMO EVADED MY MEN, TOO!

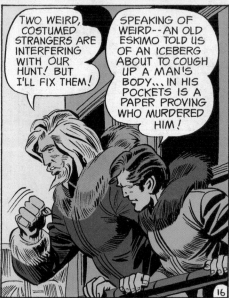

TWO WEIRD, COSTUMED STRANGERS ARE INTERFERING WITH OUR HUNT! BUT I'LL FIX THEM!

SPEAKING OF WEIRD--AN OLD ESKIMO TOLD US OF AN ICEBERG ABOUT TO COUGH UP A MAN'S BODY....IN HIS POCKETS IS A PAPER PROVING WHO MURDERED HIM!

16

THE ARCTIC'S FULL OF WILD STORIES, BOYS! PAY IT NO HEED!

NOW GET BELOW AND *STAY* THERE! I'M RESPONSIBLE FOR YOUR SAFETY!

NOT LONG AFTER, AS THE HOVERCRAFT SKIMS OVER FROSTY SEAS...

BRUCE, *LOOK!*

THAT ICEBERG... SHAPED LIKE A *POLAR BEAR!!*

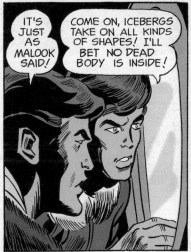

IT'S JUST AS MALOOK SAID!

COME ON, ICEBERGS TAKE ON ALL KINDS OF SHAPES! I'LL BET NO DEAD BODY IS INSIDE!

BUT A FEW MOMENTS LATER...

LINK'S *SHELLING* IT!

WHRUNNKK

BLAMM

LOOK... INSIDE THE ICE... A MAN'S BODY!!

MALOOK *WAS* RIGHT!!

BLAAM

CHUNNNK

17

GET THE BODY ABOARD--AND *FIND* THAT PAPER! THEN TOSS IT BACK INTO THE SEA!!

ONE MOMENT, LINK!

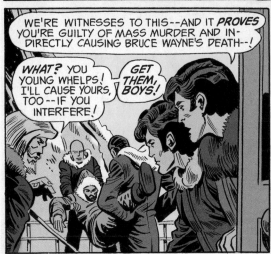

WE'RE WITNESSES TO THIS--AND IT *PROVES* YOU'RE GUILTY OF MASS MURDER AND INDIRECTLY CAUSING BRUCE WAYNE'S DEATH--!

WHAT? YOU YOUNG WHELPS! I'LL CAUSE YOURS, TOO--IF YOU INTERFERE!

GET THEM, BOYS!

WELL, CHUM, GUESS WE'LL *NEVER* KNOW WHO'S TO BE *BATMAN'S* HEIR NOW--!

CHECK--BUT IF I HAVE TO DIE THIS YOUNG...I'M PROUD TO BE IN YOUR COMPANY...CHUM!

SUDDENLY...

DROP YOUR GUNS, ALL OF YOU!

IMPOSSIBLE--! TRENCH... ALIVE?!

SUPERMAN!?

AND DON'T FORGET *JUNIOR!*

NICE JOB PLAYING CORPSE, POP!

I...DON'T-- --BELIEVE IT!

EXPLANATIONS LATER, BOYS... *WHERE'S LINK?*

HUH? HE SLIPPED AWAY!

HE WON'T GET FAR!

18

BUT AS THE YOUNG *ACTION ACE* ZOOMS UP AND OUT OVER THE PACK-ICE...

NOTHING.... JUST SOME SEALS! BUT LINK COULDN'T JUST *VANISH!*

MY PLANE'S PARKED BEYOND THE NEXT BERG! ONCE I REACH IT... I'LL BE OFF AND AWAY!

BUT FROM UNDER THE THIN BLUE ICE, COLD CRUEL EYES FOLLOW THE SCAMPERING PROGRESS OF WHAT APPEARS TO BE... *A SEAL!*

AND THE NEXT MOMENT...

KRAAAUNNNNC.CHHH

AIEEEEE

YES, WE KNEW LINK'S RADIO EMERGENCY FROM *ICE STATION EASY* WAS A FAKE—WE PRETENDED TO GO THERE WHILE WE SET UP THIS TRAP FOR HIM!

I DON'T GET IT—

SUDDENLY, AS A PLANE SKIMS DOWN ONTO THE ICE...

MY GOD... DAD!?

BATMAN!?

19

YES, BOYS, I'M ALIVE AND WELL!

SORRY I HAD TO PLAY DEAD TO BRING LINK TO JUSTICE-- BUT IT WAS NECESSARY!

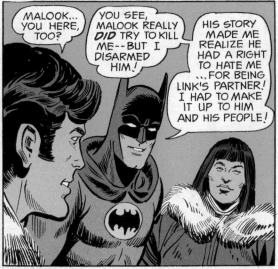

MALOOK... YOU HERE, TOO?

YOU SEE, MALOOK REALLY *DID* TRY TO KILL ME--BUT I DISARMED HIM!

HIS STORY MADE ME REALIZE HE HAD A RIGHT TO HATE ME ...FOR BEING LINK'S PARTNER! I HAD TO MAKE IT UP TO HIM AND HIS PEOPLE!

SO *SUPERMAN* AND I ARRANGED MY "MURDER" AND THE FAKE WILL REQUIRING LINK TO RETURN TO *SMOKE ISLAND* TO GET THE FIVE MILLION!

OUT HERE, WE FIGURED WE COULD GET PROOF OF HIS CRIMES!

CLARK AND I RETRIEVED POOR TRENCH'S BODY TWO DAYS AGO, AND *I* TOOK HIS PLACE IN THE ICE!

BUT THERE *NEVER* WAS ANY PAPER IN HIS POCKET...THAT WAS PART OF THE *BAIT* TO TRAP LINK!

WE COULDN'T TELL YOU FELLERS THE TRUTH--YOU HAD TO BELIEVE I WAS *REALLY* DEAD TO PLAY YOUR PARTS CONVINCINGLY AND FOOL LINK!

I'M TRULY SORRY FOR WHAT I PUT YOU BOTH THROUGH!

IT'S OKAY, DAD! IT MADE ME GROW UP A BIT MORE-- AND REALIZE I'M NOT YET READY TO FILL YOUR BOOTS!

THAT GOES FOR ME TOO, "BROTHER"!

THE END

20

SUPERMAN and BATMAN and THEIR SONS

On its eternal orbit hundreds of miles above Earth, a weather satellite sends back from space an endless series of photos...

THIS IS *FANTASTIC*!

WE MUST INFORM PROFESSOR HANSON AT ONCE!

MEANTIME, IN GOTHAM CITY, A LITHE FIGURE LEAPS INTO ACTION!!

THIS GUY STALKING THE OLD LADY'S *GOT* TO BE THE MURDERING MUGGER TERRORIZING THE NEIGHBORHOOD!

BACK AGAIN (BECAUSE OF SUPER SALES) THE TWO AND ONLY SONS OF *BATMAN* AND *SUPERMAN* SWING THROUGH THEIR LATEST SAGA... A SENSATIONAL SAFARI TO A LOST CITY... AS MAN'S INHUMANITY TO MAN LEAPS THE GENERATION GAP, PITTING THE JUNIOR HEROES AGAINST...

END OF THE LINE, LOUSE!

THE GIRL WHOM TIME FORGOT

STORY BY: BOB HANEY

ART BY: SWAN & BLAISDELL

BATMAN, JR.? I'M A *POLICE OFFICER!* THERE GOES THE *REAL* MUGGER!

SHORTLY...

B-BUT, *DAD*-- HOW COULD *I* KNOW OFFICER FORST, HERE, WAS A POLICE DECOY!? WHY WASN'T *I* TOLD?

BECAUSE IT ISN'T *YOUR* BUSINESS TO PLAY CRIMEFIGHTER! THAT'S *MY* JOB-- AND THE POLICE DEPARTMENT'S!

NOW THAT MUGGER'S ESCAPED, AND ALERTED TO ANY FUTURE TRAPS... THANKS TO *YOU!*

YES, IT'S *BATMAN* AND HIS SWINGING HEIR--AND LIKE ALL FATHERS AND SONS-- THEY'VE GOT THEIR PROBLEMS!

OKAY, I'M SORRY-- BUT I'M SO BORED WITH THE USUAL TEENAGE SCENE...

...AFTER DOING THE COSTUMED BIT, EVERYTHING ELSE IS NOWHERE!

HMMM, I WAS AFRAID OF THIS! GOT TO FIND A SOLUTION...

MEANWHILE, A THOUSAND MILES AWAY, OUTSIDE METROPOLIS...

THAT COMMUTER TRAIN'S STALLED... AND THE TRESTLE'S *COLLAPSING*--!

GNRRRRUNNK!

BUT THERE'S NOTHING TO WORRY ABOUT WHEN *I'M* AROUND!

GRUNNNCCHHH-- KRAAAASSSHH

2

DAD--?!

YOU IMPETUOUS *MEDDLER!* YOU JUST SPOILED THE BIGGEST DISASTER DRILL YET!

YES, IT'S *SUPERMAN AND SON*-- A NEW FIRM, BUT WITH PLENTY OF "BUSINESS" TROUBLES...

THAT TRAIN'S *OBSOLETE*... RETIRED FROM SERVICE!

THE PASSENGERS... ALL *DUMMIES!*

THE TRESTLE WAS CONDEMNED AS *UNSAFE*...

...AND WAS BEING *PURPOSELY* COLLAPSED TO GIVE THESE RESCUE UNITS *REALISTIC* TRAINING! NOW THE WHOLE EXERCISE IS *RUINED*... THANKS TO *YOU!*

GEE, DAD--HOW WAS *I* TO KNOW? I HAVEN'T MIND-READING POWERS, TOO!

I DIDN'T TELL YOU BECAUSE I FIGURED YOU'D BE BUSY DOING WHAT FELLERS YOUR AGE DO!

YOU MEAN, HANGING OUT, CRUISING CHICKS, AND ALL THAT?

NONE OF THAT'S A KICK AFTER DOING THE *SUPER-HERO* THING!

HMM, GUESS IT'S TIME I DID SOMETHING ABOUT *THAT!*

THAT NIGHT...

WE'VE GOT TO GET THOSE TWO BORED KIDS OUT OF OUR HAIR, *SUPES!*

AGREED! I THINK I'VE GOT THE *ANSWER*-- AN OLD FRIEND WHO'LL DO ME A FAVOR!

HAVE YOUNG BRUCE FLY TO METROPOLIS TOMORROW... *READY FOR ANYTHING!*

THE NEXT DAY, TWO LOYAL FRIENDS ARE REUNITED...

I CAN'T FIGURE WHAT OUR DADS COOKED UP, CLARK!

AND WHO IN BLAZES IS *PROFESSOR HANSON?*

JUST THE WORLD'S GREATEST AUTHORITY ON ANCIENT MAYAN CULTURE, BRUCE, MY *UN*-INFORMED BUDDY!

3

I'M PROFESSOR HANSON, BOYS, AND *THIS* IS MY OWN SON, *LANCE!*

THINK OF IT, LANCE, THE SONS OF A FAMOUS NEWSCASTER LIKE CLARK KENT AND A MILLIONAIRE LIKE BRUCE WAYNE...GOING WITH *US* TO FIND THE LOST CITY OF *MAYAN-75!*

HUH?

MAYAN-75...?

IT'S THE NAME I GAVE TO AN INCREDIBLE PLACE A SATELLITE DETECTED IN THE JUNGLE OF YUCATAN! MAINLY, ONLY THE *OUTLINE* SHOWS...

...BECAUSE IT SEEMS TO BE COVERED BY A VAST CAMOUFLAGE SYSTEM! THIS MIGHT MEAN IT'S STILL *INHABITED*-- THE ONLY *LIVING* EXAMPLE OF MAYAN CIVILIZATION *EVER FOUND!*

AND WHAT A CIVILIZATION! THOSE ANCIENT INDIANS WERE MASTER SCULPTORS AND ARCHITECTS--GENIUSES AT MATH AND ASTRONOMY!

YET THEY ALL *VANISHED MYSTERIOUSLY*... EXCEPT FOR SOME *RUINS!*

LIKE THE RUINS OF ITZLAN, WHICH YOU DISCOVERED, SIR?

YES, CLARK--FINDING ITZLAN YEARS AGO MADE ME FAMOUS! BUT I NEVER LOCATED THE CIPHER TO THE MAYAN HIEROGLYPHICS WHICH WOULD UNLOCK ALL THEIR SECRETS!

BUT PERHAPS *MAYAN-75* CONTAINS THAT CIPHER! IF IT *DOES*, WE'LL FIND IT....*TOGETHER!!*

HOW ABOUT IT, BOYS??

RIGHT ON, PROF!

4

LATER, PREPARING FOR THE EXPEDITION...

WHY PACK *THAT?* NO CHANCE OF USING IT IN A DUSTY, LOST CITY!

PROBABLY WHAT OUR DADS HAD IN MIND... BUT WE BETTER TAKE OUR UNIFORMS, CHUM...

...'CAUSE YOU NEVER KNOW!

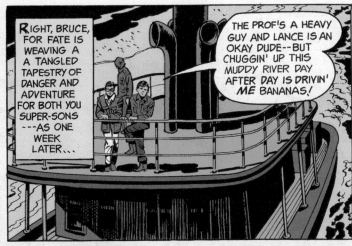

RIGHT, BRUCE, FOR FATE IS WEAVING A TANGLED TAPESTRY OF DANGER AND ADVENTURE FOR BOTH YOU SUPER-SONS ---AS ONE WEEK LATER...

THE PROF'S A HEAVY GUY AND LANCE IS AN OKAY DUDE--BUT CHUGGIN' UP THIS MUDDY RIVER DAY AFTER DAY IS DRIVIN' *ME* BANANAS!

THEN, AS THE LITTLE STEAMER ROUNDS ONE MORE BEND...

A GIANT WATERFALL!!

CHUGG
CHUGG
CHUGGG

CAPTAIN *DIEGO!* HEAD FOR SHORE AND WE'LL UNLOAD! THEN YOU CAN START BACK DOWN-RIVER!

SI, SEÑOR PROFESSOR! I WILL BE HAPPY TO GET AWAY FROM *THAT!* IT IS THE GRANDFATHER OF *ALL* WATERFALLS!

CLARK, FOR A GUY WITH GLASSES, YOU SURE SEEM TO SEE BETTER THAN ANYONE ELSE! WHAT'S IT THIS TIME?

UP THERE, LANCE... ON THAT *LEDGE!*

AND IN THE THUNDERING MIST NEAR THE FALLS' SUMMIT...

A *BEAUTIFUL GIRL!* SHE'S GESTURING... DOWN AT US?!

5

THE NEXT MOMENT...

MADRE DE DIOS! WHIRPOOL!

THE PEACEFUL RIVER SUDDENLY BECOMES A SPINNING, CLUTCHING NIGHTMARE!

CLARK! SAVE THE SUPPLIES!

LANCE AND THE PROF WERE SWEPT DOWNSTREAM! *I'LL* HELP THEM!

UNSEEN, THE SON OF *SUPERMAN* QUICKLY SALVAGES THE HEAVY CRATES IN HIS OWN, UNIQUE WAY...

I'LL JUST CARRY THESE INTO THE SHALLOWS AND UP ONTO DRY LAND WHERE NOBODY WILL SEE ME!

WHILE A WAYS DOWNSTREAM...

THANKS, BOYS-- NOT AS YOUNG AS I WAS ON THE EXPEDITION THAT FOUND ITZLAN!

THE STEAMER'S GONE... *SUNK!* BUT WHERE'S CAPTAIN DIEGO?

HE'S DEAD... *DROWNED!* THE SUPPLIES ARE SAFE ...THE WHIRLPOOL TOSSED THEM ONTO THE RIVER BANK!

GOOD LORD! POOR DIEGO! COME, LADS, WE MUST DO HIM PROPER HONOR!

AN OMINOUS BEGINNING-- AND AFTER A SOLEMN CEREMONY...

I KNOW YOU GUYS THINK THAT *GIRL* MADE THAT WHIRLPOOL-- THAT'S *IMPOSSIBLE!*

BUT SHE SEEMED TO CONJURE IT UP WITH THE MAYAN SYMBOL OF MAGICAL POWER, THE PLUMED SERPENT SCEPTER! AND SHE WAS SO *BEAUTIFUL*, LIKE A *DREAM!*

HEY, LANCE, YOU FLIP OVER THAT CHICK? YOU BETTER HOPE SHE'S *JUST* A DREAM-- OR WE'RE *REALLY* IN HEAVY TROUBLE!

6

PART 2 THE SILENT CITY

IT IS LATER, AND BY THE LONELY GRAVE ON THE RIVER BANK, A STRANGE "BIRD" THE JUNGLE HAS NEVER SEEN SITS READY...

THE COPTER'S SET TO FLY, BOYS! OUR BAD LUCK'S *BEHIND* US!

NEXT STOP... *THE LOST CITY!*

SHORTLY, AS THE "CHOPPER" LOFTS ABOVE GREEN-CARPETED PLATEAUS AND RIDGES...

WE'RE YAWING!

LANCE... HE'S GOING OUT!

DOWN THERE... IT'S HER!?

AND AS THE WHIRLYBIRD IS DRAWN DOWNWARDS BY SOME IRRESISTIBLE FORCE...

I'LL GRAB LANCE... AFTER I FAKE FALLING OUT TO SAVE BRUCE AND THE PROFESSOR!

WHAT'S THIS? SHE'S *STEADYING!* I'LL SET HER DOWN IN THAT TINY CLEARING!

BUT LANCE... AND CLARK--?!

CLARK--?

WHEW! LUCKY THIS TREE HAD A LIMB STUCK OUT MY WAY! I'M SHOOK UP... BUT OKAY!

QUICK THINKING, SUPER-BUDDY!

7

139

BUT LANCE IS *GONE!* HE FELL FROM MUCH HIGHER UP-- BACK ABOVE THOSE CRAGS!

DON'T GIVE UP HOPE! CLARK AND I WILL GO BACK TO SEARCH FOR HIM! MAYBE HE HAD A LUCKY BREAK LIKE CLARK!

GOOD IDEA! THE COPTER'S PROVEN TOO RISKY! I'LL HEAD TOWARD THE CITY, WHICH SHOULD BE OVER THIS NEXT RIDGE, AND AWAIT YOU THERE!

CHUM, IT'S TIME TO STOP PLAYING ARCHAEOLOGISTS --AND START DOING OUR COSTUMED HERO BIT!

SOON, TWO FAMILIAR FIGURES FLY BACK ALONG THE COPTER'S COURSE...

LANCE DROPPED OUT OF SIGHT BEFORE I COULD GRAB HIM!

BUT NO SIGN OF HIM IN THE JUNGLE BELOW-- OR OF THAT INCREDIBLE GIRL ON THE CRAG!

BUT THEY COULDN'T BOTH JUST *VANISH!*

HOW'D SHE GET UP ON THAT STONE NEEDLE, UNLESS SHE'S PART BIRD?

OR *ALL WITCH!* ANYWAY, *TWICE* SHE WHAMMIED US...USING SOME KIND OF WEIRD POWER! OUR DULL EXPEDITION HAS SURE TURNED EXCITING!

RIGHT ON, *BATMAN, JR.,* FOR IN ONE OF THE JUNGLE'S DEEPEST POCKETS...

FIRST, YOU STOP MY FALL AND SAVE MY LIFE WITH THAT SCEPTER ...

NOW YOU EXPLORE MY FACE LIKE YOU NEVER SAW ANOTHER HUMAN BEING!

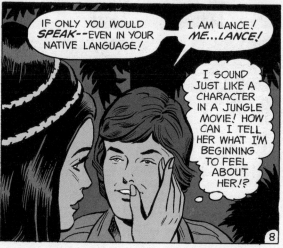

IF ONLY YOU WOULD *SPEAK*--EVEN IN YOUR NATIVE LANGUAGE!

I AM LANCE! *ME...LANCE!*

I SOUND JUST LIKE A CHARACTER IN A JUNGLE MOVIE! HOW CAN I TELL HER WHAT I'M BEGINNING TO FEEL ABOUT HER!?

8

MAYBE *THIS* WILL TELL YOU!

ARRRRRRRRRRR

SILENCE, *LINYA!*

YOU *DO* SPEAK-- AND IN *ENGLISH??*

ENGLISH? WHAT IS... THIS ENGLISH? I SPEAK WHAT MY FATHER, *HUNAB KU,* TAUGHT ME! HE IS THE *MASTER* OF ALL KNOWLEDGE AND MAGIC!

HUNAB KU? THAT'S THE NAME OF A GREAT ANCIENT MAYAN KING!

COME... I WILL TAKE YOU TO HIM! AND MY NAME IS... *MIMAYA!*

SOON, AFTER A SWIFT JOURNEY ACROSS A TREETOP ROUTE...

AMAZING! THIS IS THE *LOST CITY* DAD WAS SEEKING!

PERFECTLY *INTACT...* COVERED BY A WEB OF MAN-MADE CAMOUFLAGE!

BUT WHERE ARE THE *OTHER* INHABITANTS?

NOW AS THE MYSTERIOUS MIMAYA LEADS LANCE UP THE STEEP STEPS OF THE MAIN TEMPLE...

FATHER! I BROUGHT THIS ONE BACK! CAN I KEEP HIM FOR A PET, LIKE LINYA, MY JAGUAR?

YOU HAVE *DISOBEYED* ME, DAUGHTER! *RETURN THE SCEPTER!*

9

I **ORDERED** YOU TO USE THE SCEPTER'S SACRED POWER TO **DESTROY** THE INTRUDERS!

OOH!

BUT I HAD NEVER SEEN ANOTHER HUMAN-- EXCEPT **YOU!**

KWAK!

HE HAS A PLEASING FACE AND VOICE! HE MADE ME FEEL **GOOD** TO BE NEAR HIM!

HE IS **EVIL**-- LIKE **ALL** OUTSIDERS! I HAVE KEPT YOU APART FROM ALL OTHER HUMANS TO **PROTECT** YOU FROM THEM!

THEY **BETRAY** AND **DESTROY** ALL THEY TOUCH....AS THEY WILL THIS CITY **IF I DO NOT DESTROY THEM FIRST!**

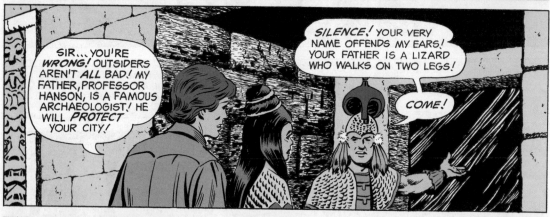

SIR....YOU'RE **WRONG!** OUTSIDERS AREN'T **ALL** BAD! MY FATHER, PROFESSOR HANSON, IS A FAMOUS ARCHAEOLOGIST! HE WILL **PROTECT** YOUR CITY!

SILENCE! YOUR VERY NAME OFFENDS MY EARS! YOUR FATHER IS A LIZARD WHO WALKS ON TWO LEGS!

COME!

AND INSIDE THE GREAT TEMPLE...

LOOK DOWN IN THE WELL CONSECRATED TO **AH PUCH,** THE GREAT **GOD OF DEATH!**

LOOK, AND **TREMBLE!**

OH, NO!!

DAD!?

HE CANNOT HEAR YOU! THOUGH HIS FLESH STILL LIVES, I HAVE ALREADY **DECREED** HIS DEATH TO PAY FOR HIS SINS!

10

FREE HIM! IF YOU'RE THE LAST OF THE MAYANS, IT'S A GOOD THING! **YOU'RE CRUEL ...AND MAD!**

STAY BACK, SON OF EVIL! YOUR ANGER IS THAT OF YOUTHFUL IGNORANCE! BUT MINE IS THE ANGER OF **JUSTICE!**

AND THE NEXT INSTANT, THE SERPENT SCEPTER'S STRANGE POWER FLASHES AGAIN...

PLEASE, FATHER! I...I...LOVE...HIM!

LOVE HIM!? NO! YOU **CANNOT!** ALREADY, HIS SINFUL PRESENCE HERE IS CORRUPTING YOUR HEART! BUT I WILL END ALL THAT... **SHORTLY!**

Yiiii!

NOT FAR AWAY, TWO AWED COMRADES WANDER THROUGH THE SPRAWLING CITY...

WE **FOUND** IT! AND LIKE THE PROF PREDICTED... IT'S **INTACT!** BUT I DON'T SEE ANY ANCIENT MAYAN TAXPAYERS!

WHAT ABOUT THAT GIRL? ANYWAY, WE'D BETTER FIND THE PROFESSOR-- AND GIVE HIM THE BAD NEWS ABOUT LANCE VANISHING!

AS THE **SUPER-SONS** MOVE THROUGH A PLAZA FILLED WITH STRANGE MONOLITHS...

IT'S LIKE A FOREST OF TOMBSTONES--

--YEAH, OURS! LOOK OUT!

KRUNNK

KRU-KRUNN

AND AS THE CRUSHING SLABS COLLAPSE LIKE SO MANY GIANT DOMINOES...

YEEOW! DON'T KNOW IF I SHOULD ZIG OR ZAG!

KLUNNK!

WHUNNKK!

KRUNNG!

11

A LITTLE SUPER SHOVE...

...AND THE NAME OF THE GAME'S... *REVERSE DOMINOES!*

WHUNK-WHUNK-WHUNK-WHUNK-WHUNKA

BRUCE--?

THOUGHT I WAS CRUSHED? NOT WITH A SNUG ROOF OVER MY HEAD! BUT SOMEBODY'S SURE TRYING TO *CLOBBER* US!

Now AS THE PAIR MOVE ONWARD...

MAYBE WE'LL FIND *SOME* SIGN OF THE PROFESSOR BEYOND THIS CAUSEWAY!

I'VE SEEN STONY-EYED STARES BEFORE--BUT *THIS* IS RIDICULOUS!

KWAM

SPLUUSSSHHH!

12

144

AS THE JUNIOR *MASKED MANHUNTER* VANISHES BENEATH THE DANK WATERS...

YOU GUYS ARE REAL *SWINGERS*-- BUT SO AM *I*!

MEANTIME...

WHAT'S *THAT* ON THE BOTTOM...?

CAYMAN!! AND I'M NUMBER ONE ON HIS TIDBIT PARADE!

CAN'T HOLD MY BREATH MUCH LONGER! THIS CHUNK OF STONE DEBRIS...

SUPES MUST BE DOING SOME DEMOLITION WORK ABOVE-- LUCKILY!

THE NEXT MOMENT, AS THE *CROCODILE* TORPEDOES TOWARDS THE TEENAGE *CAPED CRUSADER*...

AND SHORTLY...

ABOUT TIME!

FIGURED I'D HAVE TO DIVE FOR YOU!

THAT'LL BE THE DAY, TIGER! BUT I FOUND SOMETHING DOWN THERE...

...SOMETHING THAT MAY SOLVE THE MYSTERY OF THIS *SPOOKY LOST CITY*!

13

PART 3

SINS OF THE FATHERS

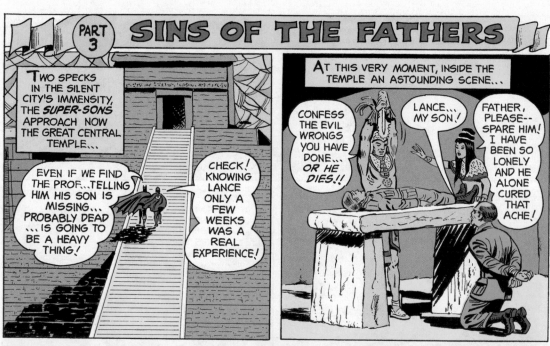

TWO SPECKS IN THE SILENT CITY'S IMMENSITY, THE *SUPER-SONS* APPROACH NOW THE GREAT CENTRAL TEMPLE...

EVEN IF WE FIND THE PROF...TELLING HIM HIS SON IS MISSING... PROBABLY DEAD ...IS GOING TO BE A HEAVY THING!

CHECK! KNOWING LANCE ONLY A FEW WEEKS WAS A REAL EXPERIENCE!

AT THIS VERY MOMENT, INSIDE THE TEMPLE AN ASTOUNDING SCENE...

CONFESS THE EVIL WRONGS YOU HAVE DONE... *OR HE DIES!!*

LANCE... MY SON!

FATHER-- PLEASE-- SPARE HIM! I HAVE BEEN SO LONELY AND HE ALONE CURED THAT ACHE!

I...I DON'T KNOW *WHY* YOU ACCUSE ME. I'VE DONE NOTHING BAD IN MY LIFE... EXCEPT STUDY THE ANCIENT MAYAN WAYS!

SURELY, YOU OF ALL PEOPLE, UNDERSTAND AND VALUE THAT!

I, OF ALL PEOPLE UNDERSTAND IT ONLY TOO WELL! YOU BUILT YOUR WHOLE LIFE ON A *LIE* ...A *BETRAYAL!*

BUT I AM DONE WITH YOUR DELAYS... YOUR SON BECOMES A SACRIFICE TO REDEEM YOUR SINS!

THE NAKED BLADE IS POISED ABOVE A DEFENSELESS YOUNG HEART-- BUT...

WHAT?

GONE--?

SUPERMAN, JR.? BATMAN, JR.? YOU...HERE?

SURE! WE'VE BEEN BACKING UP THE EXPEDITION SECRETLY SINCE THE BEGINNING! YOUR PALS, CLARK AND BRUCE, ARE OKAY...JUST TEMPORARILY LOST IN THE BUSH!

14.

LANCE!

HEY, LOOKS LIKE OUR PAL *DID* FIND HIS DREAM CHICK!

LINYA! ATTACK!

ARRRWWWW

ROORRRWW

SCHOOL'S OUT... AND HUMAN SACRIFICE IS DEFINITELY NOT *IN*-- SO NO MORE FUNKY MOVES!

THE SERPENT SCEPTER....ITS POWER WILL QUELL YOUR ARROGANCE!

YOU...*CRUSHED* IT TO FINE DUST? YOU ARE A SORCERER!

NO, I INHERITED MY POWERS FROM MY DAD, BORN ON A STRANGE PLANET ...NOW I'M LIABLE TO DO THE SAME TO *YOU* IF YOU DON'T BEHAVE!

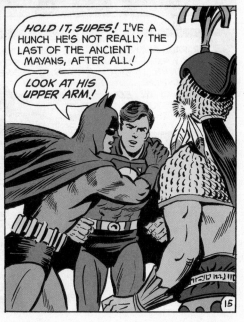

HOLD IT, SUPES! I'VE A HUNCH HE'S NOT REALLY THE LAST OF THE ANCIENT MAYANS, AFTER ALL!

LOOK AT HIS UPPER ARM!

15

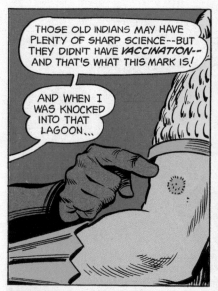

THOSE OLD INDIANS MAY HAVE PLENTY OF SHARP SCIENCE--BUT THEY DIDN'T HAVE *VACCINATION*-- AND THAT'S WHAT THIS MARK IS!

AND WHEN I WAS KNOCKED INTO THAT LAGOON...

"...I SAW SOMETHING WILD--A WRECKED PLANE... WITH SOME VERY SPECIAL WORDS LETTERED ON IT..."

ITZLAN EXP EDITION

ITZLAN EXPEDITION...?

ITZLAN EXPEDITION? CAN IT BE? HIS VOICE... SO FAMILIAR!

GOOD LORD! YOU... *HUNAB KU*... YOU'RE *HIM!* YOU'RE PAUL SOMERSET!

YES, HANSON, I AM THE FRIEND YOU BETRAYED!

THE MAN YOU *MURDERED*... ONLY I STILL LIVE FOR VENGEANCE!

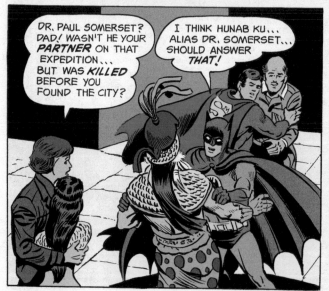

DR. PAUL SOMERSET? DAD! WASN'T HE YOUR *PARTNER* ON THAT EXPEDITION... BUT WAS *KILLED* BEFORE YOU FOUND THE CITY?

I THINK HUNAB KU... ALIAS DR. SOMERSET... SHOULD ANSWER *THAT!*

THE MASQUERADE IS OVER--THE *TRUTH* MUST NOW BE KNOWN!

YES, I WAS DR. PAUL SOMERSET, CHIEF OF THE PARTY SEARCHING FOR ITZLAN!

16

"ROGER HANSON WAS MY ASSISTANT-- AND TRUSTED FRIEND! TOGETHER, AFTER MUCH HARDSHIP, WE FOUND THE RUINS OF ITZLAN!"

"BUT MY WIFE, JANE, WAS EXPECTING A CHILD! AFTER WEEKS OF DIGGING IN THE RUINS..."

THIS WILL MAKE US BOTH FAMOUS, ROGER!

I MUST FLY JANE TO THE NEAREST HOSPITAL! YOU KEEP EXCAVATING, ROGER! WE'LL ANNOUNCE OUR GREAT FIND TO THE WORLD LATER!

"WE TOOK OFF--BUT, TWO HOURS LATER, AS WE HIT SOME TURBULENCE OVER THE JUNGLE..."

THE CONTROLS HAVE *SNAPPED!* WE'RE IN A *SPIN--!*

"SUDDENLY, BELOW, A GREAT CITY APPEARED BETWEEN TWO RIDGES! THE PLANE PLUNGED INTO ITS RESERVOIR..."

SPLASSSSHHH

"SOMEHOW, I MANAGED TO GET JANE AND MYSELF CLEAR OF THE SINKING WRECK..."

"BY ACCIDENT, WE HAD FOUND AN INTACT MAYAN METROPOLIS-- AN ARCHAEOLOGICAL DISCOVERY TEN TIMES GREATER THAN ITZLAN! YET A FEW DAYS LATER..."

MY BELOVED JANE IS DEAD... AFTER GIVING BIRTH TO MY NEW DAUGHTER!

17

"FATE HAD DEALT ME A CRUSHING BLOW--BUT LATER, ON INSPECTING THE SUNKEN PLANE..."

THE CABLES OF THE CONTROLS WERE PARTLY CUT THROUGH--*SABOTAGED!* ONLY *ONE* PERSON COULD'VE DONE IT-- *ROGER!*

"ROGER HANSON, MY FRIEND, HAD BETRAYED ME! AND FOR ONLY *ONE* REASON--SO HE COULD TAKE CREDIT FOR DISCOVERING ITZLAN ALONE-- AND THUS BECOME THE WORLD'S LEADING MAYAN EXPERT!"

FROM THIS TIME FORWARD, I SWEAR NEVER TO LIVE WITH EVIL MANKIND...

...TO REMAIN HERE AND RAISE MY DAUGHTER UNTAINTED BY HUMAN CONTACT!

JANE SOMERSET REST, BELOVED

"I DISCARDED MY OLD IDENTITY-- AND BECAME A *NEW* BEING: *HUNAB KU,* MAYAN PRIEST! FROM THE BEGINNING, I RAISED MY DAUGHTER AS A MAYAN..."

WE MUST HIDE OUR HOME FROM OUTSIDERS' SINFUL EYES, MIMAYA!

THEN FATE SENT YOU ALL HERE TO SPOIL OUR PURE AND BEAUTIFUL LIVES... AND CORRUPT MY DAUGHTER!

IF YOU MEAN SHE FELL IN LOVE WITH LANCE...THAT'S NATURAL AND HEALTHY, DR. SOMERSET!

THE SON OF THE MAN WHO BETRAYED ME?

NEVER!

I WILL *NOT* ALLOW IT!

BUT LANCE IS NOT EVIL-- HE IS GOOD, FATHER! PLEASE, I WANT TO BE WITH HIM... AND NOT BE LONELY ANYMORE!

I AM HEARTILY SORRY IF MY FATHER WRONGED YOU LONG AGO, SIR, BUT NOW YOUR BITTERNESS IS HARMING MIMAYA AND INNOCENT PEOPLE!

YOU DARE ACCUSE ME!?

I AM NOT THE GUILTY ONE!

18

HE IS! I'LL MAKE HIM *CONFESS!*

MURDERER OF MY WIFE! BETRAYER!

STAY AWAY! YOU'RE OUT OF YOUR MIND!

NO YOU DON'T!

HOLD IT!

LANCE AND MIMAYA!

THEY WERE HERE A MOMENT AGO!

WATCHING THEIR FATHERS HOWLING IN HATRED... HAD THEM REALLY SHOOK!

I DON'T LIKE WHAT I'M THINKING!

WE'VE GOT TO FIND THEM BEFORE--

WHERE COULD THEY HAVE GONE?

MIMAYA ALWAYS WENT TO ONE *SPECIAL* PLACE WHEN SHE WAS UPSET!

AND WHERE MIST RISES LIKE SMOKE FROM THUNDERING WATERS...

LANCE... MY LOVE! OUR FATHERS WILL NEVER LET US FIND HAPPINESS... THE PAST HAS CURSED OUR LIVES!

YES, MIMAYA... IT'S ALL SO BIZARRE, MY HEAD'S STILL IN A WHIRL!

THERE'S ONLY ONE WAY TO FIND PEACE... TOGETHER... AND JOIN THE GREAT SPIRITS OF THE MAYANS!

MIMAYA, WHAT ARE YOU GETTING AT?

19

SUDDENLY, AS THE END OF THE ROCK LEDGE CRUMBLES UNDERFOOT...

I'M THE ONLY FLY-GUY IN THIS NECK OF THE WOODS, PIGEONS!!

IT IS SOME TIME LATER, AND TWO MIDDLE-AGED MEN FACE EACH OTHER ACROSS A GULF OF BITTERNESS AND HATRED...

PAUL...THE TRAGEDY THAT ALMOST BEFELL OUR CHILDREN IS MY FAULT! YES, I DID SABOTAGE YOUR PLANE YEARS AGO!

IT WAS A MAD ACT--AN IMPULSE! YET ALL THESE YEARS, THERE WASN'T A NIGHT I WASN'T HAUNTED BY MY CONSCIENCE...

...AND ALWAYS I KNEW IT WAS YOU WHO FOUND ITZLAN ...NOT I!

I'LL FACE MY PUNISHMENT NOW BEFORE THE LAW-- ONLY DON'T TAKE OUT YOUR VENGEANCE ON LANCE AND MIMAYA!

YOUR WORDS, ROGER... ARE HEALING ONES! MY HEART HAS BEEN TOO OBSESSED WITH REVENGE AND BITTERNESS! I FORGIVE YOU!

THE PAST IS DEAD, AND NEW LIVES...AND NEW LOVES...MUST HAVE THEIR DAY!

HAPPY FADEOUT, CHUM--AND NOW WE BETTER FADE INTO THE BUSH AND RESUME BEING CLARK AND BRUCE, BORED SONS OF A COUPLE OF SQUARES!

END

⑳

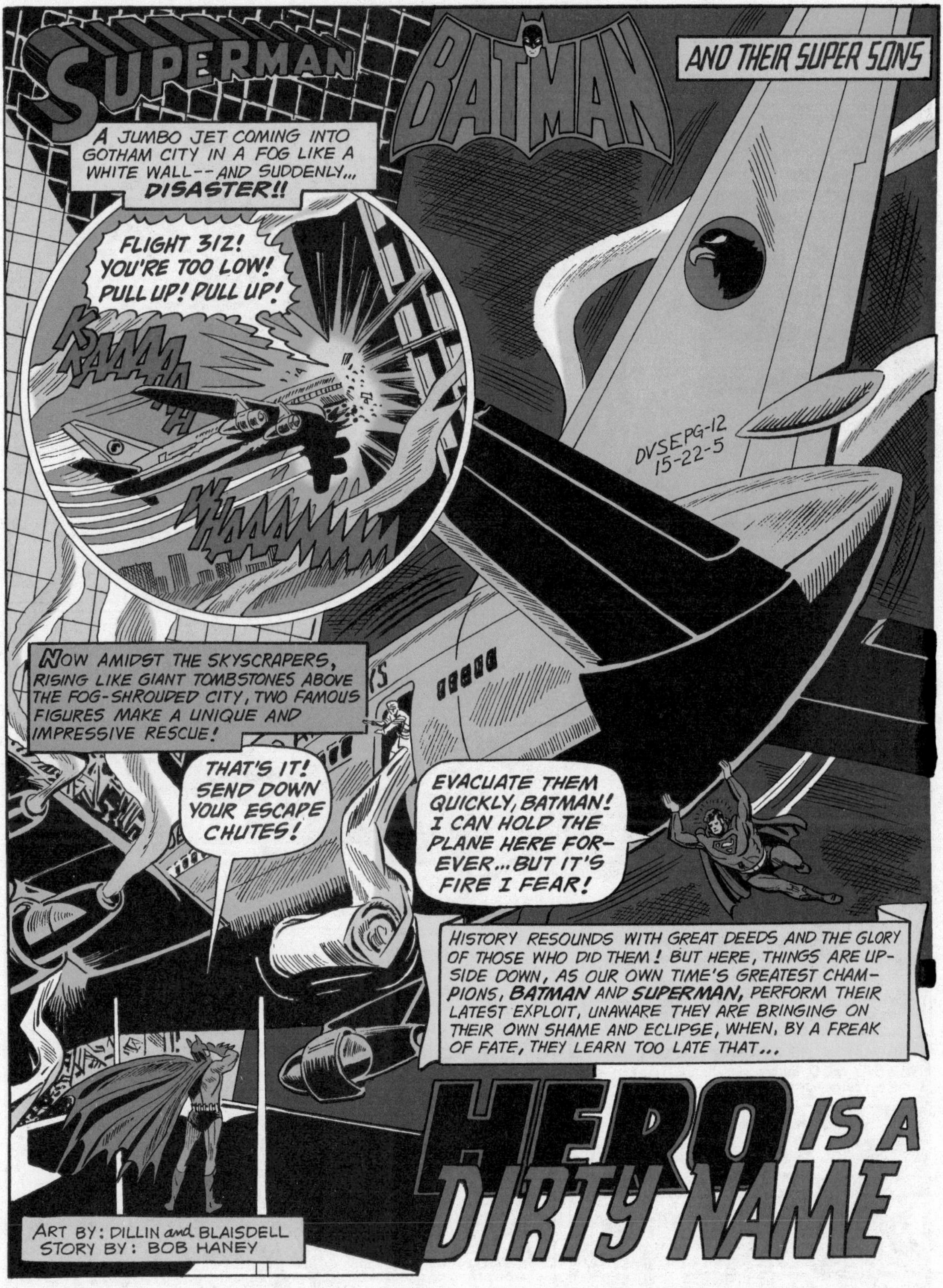
SUPERMAN
BATMAN
AND THEIR SUPER SONS
A JUMBO JET COMING INTO GOTHAM CITY IN A FOG LIKE A WHITE WALL--AND SUDDENLY... DISASTER!!
FLIGHT 312! YOU'RE TOO LOW! PULL UP! PULL UP!
KRAAAAAAH
WHAAAMMM
DVSEPG-12
15-22-5
NOW AMIDST THE SKYSCRAPERS, RISING LIKE GIANT TOMBSTONES ABOVE THE FOG-SHROUDED CITY, TWO FAMOUS FIGURES MAKE A UNIQUE AND IMPRESSIVE RESCUE!
THAT'S IT! SEND DOWN YOUR ESCAPE CHUTES!
EVACUATE THEM QUICKLY, BATMAN! I CAN HOLD THE PLANE HERE FOREVER...BUT IT'S FIRE I FEAR!
HISTORY RESOUNDS WITH GREAT DEEDS AND THE GLORY OF THOSE WHO DID THEM! BUT HERE, THINGS ARE UPSIDE DOWN, AS OUR OWN TIME'S GREATEST CHAMPIONS, BATMAN AND SUPERMAN, PERFORM THEIR LATEST EXPLOIT, UNAWARE THEY ARE BRINGING ON THEIR OWN SHAME AND ECLIPSE, WHEN, BY A FREAK OF FATE, THEY LEARN TOO LATE THAT...
HERO IS A DIRTY NAME
ART BY: DILLIN and BLAISDELL
STORY BY: BOB HANEY

THEN, THEIR PANIC QUELLED BY THE PRESENCE OF THE *WORLD'S FINEST* CHAMPIONS, THE JET'S SURVIVORS SLIDE TO SAFETY...

SHE'S AFIRE!

KEEP CALM! JUST...S-L-I-D-E!

AND WITHIN MOMENTS...

ALL OUT!

WHOOOOSSSHHHH

JUST IN TIME! MY SUPER BREATH WOULD HAVE BLOWN THE PASSENGERS AWAY... LIKE SO MANY FLIES IN A HURRICANE!

SOON, THE SCORCHED JET IS CARRIED TO ITS ORIGINAL DESTINATION...

FLIGHT 312 COMPLETED! NEVER THOUGHT A ROUTINE VISIT TO MY FRIEND *BATMAN* WOULD END UP WITH SOMETHING LIKE THIS!

NEITHER DID I, *SUPES!* GOOD THING THAT GLASS SKYSCRAPER KIND OF ABSORBED THE CRASH IMPACT-- KEEPING CASUALTIES LOW!

AND SO, AS THEY HAVE SO MANY TIMES BEFORE, THE *MAN OF STEEL* AND THE *CAPED CRUSADER* RECEIVE HUMANITY'S GRATEFUL THANKS ...

AS MAYOR OF GOTHAM, LET ME SAY GOD BLESS YOU BOTH ....AND WELL DONE!

OFFICE OF THE

GRAND-STANDERS!

STOP THIS! WHILE GIGANTIC PROBLEMS PLAGUE MANKIND, THESE TWO SPEND THEIR TIME DOING FANCY RESCUES!

RIGHT ON! PLAYING HERO IS A SMOKE SCREEN...BLIND-ING US TO THE WARS, POVERTY, HUNGER AND INJUSTICE ALL OVER THE WORLD!

SUPERMAN IS AN ESTABLISHMENT SYMBOL

BATMAN IS A FAKER FREAK

BLAZES! THEY'RE OUR OWN SONS-- BRUCE, JR. AND CLARK, JR.!

2

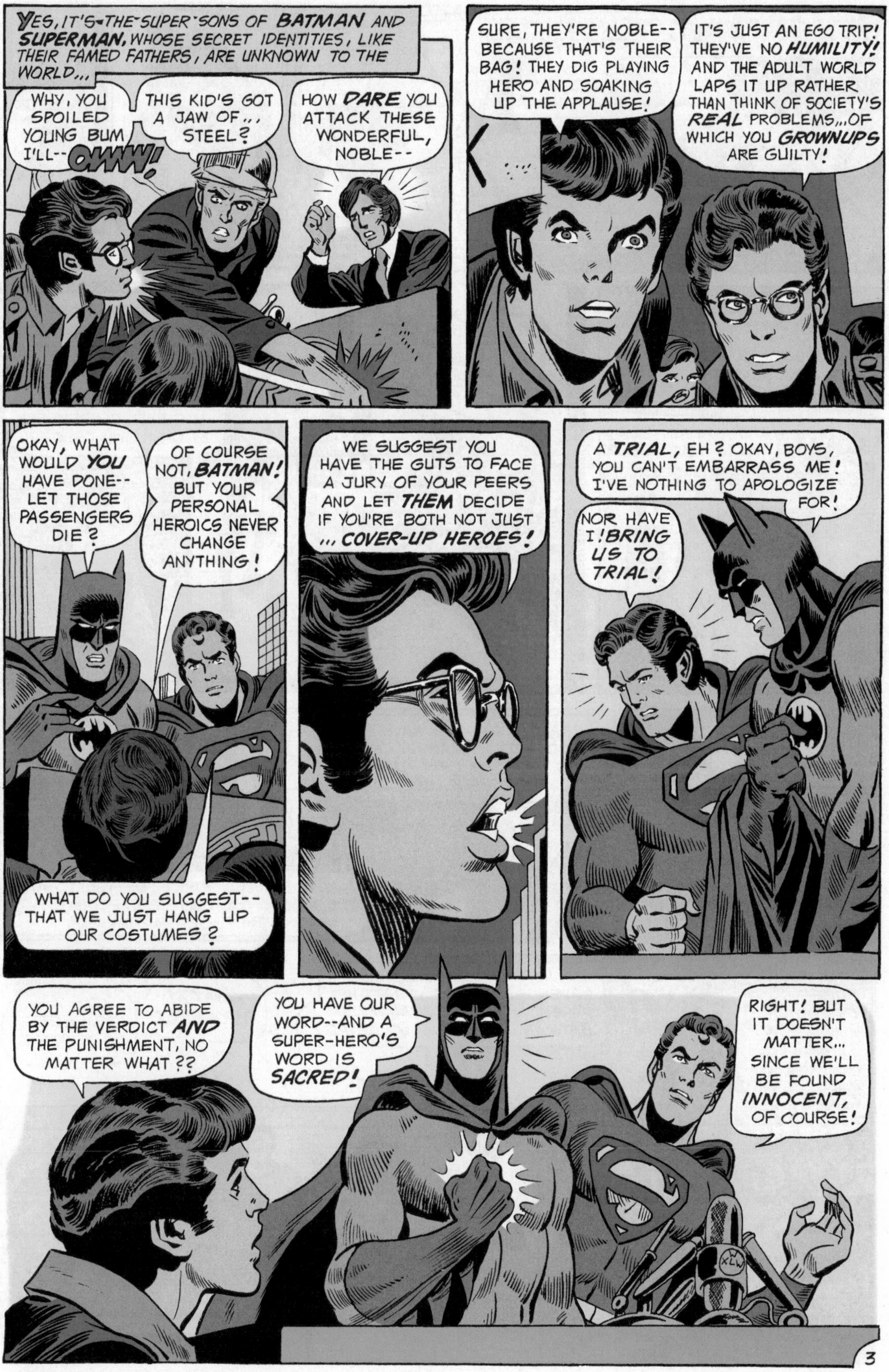
YES, IT'S THE SUPER SONS OF BATMAN AND SUPERMAN, WHOSE SECRET IDENTITIES, LIKE THEIR FAMED FATHERS, ARE UNKNOWN TO THE WORLD...
WHY, YOU SPOILED YOUNG BUM I'LL-- OWW!
THIS KID'S GOT A JAW OF... STEEL?
HOW DARE YOU ATTACK THESE WONDERFUL, NOBLE--
SURE, THEY'RE NOBLE-- BECAUSE THAT'S THEIR BAG! THEY DIG PLAYING HERO AND SOAKING UP THE APPLAUSE!
IT'S JUST AN EGO TRIP! THEY'VE NO HUMILITY! AND THE ADULT WORLD LAPS IT UP RATHER THAN THINK OF SOCIETY'S REAL PROBLEMS... OF WHICH YOU GROWNUPS ARE GUILTY!
OKAY, WHAT WOULD YOU HAVE DONE-- LET THOSE PASSENGERS DIE?
OF COURSE NOT, BATMAN! BUT YOUR PERSONAL HEROICS NEVER CHANGE ANYTHING!
WHAT DO YOU SUGGEST-- THAT WE JUST HANG UP OUR COSTUMES?
WE SUGGEST YOU HAVE THE GUTS TO FACE A JURY OF YOUR PEERS AND LET THEM DECIDE IF YOU'RE BOTH NOT JUST ... COVER-UP HEROES!
A TRIAL, EH? OKAY, BOYS, YOU CAN'T EMBARRASS ME! I'VE NOTHING TO APOLOGIZE FOR!
NOR HAVE I! BRING US TO TRIAL!
YOU AGREE TO ABIDE BY THE VERDICT AND THE PUNISHMENT, NO MATTER WHAT??
YOU HAVE OUR WORD--AND A SUPER-HERO'S WORD IS SACRED!
RIGHT! BUT IT DOESN'T MATTER... SINCE WE'LL BE FOUND INNOCENT, OF COURSE!
3

THUS, INCREDIBLY, A FEW DAYS LATER, A VERY SPECIAL COURT CONVENES...

OUR LAWYER'S JUST LETTING OUR DEEDS SPEAK FOR THEMSELVES!

OUR BOYS WERE FOOLS TO LET US PICK A JURY OF REAL, SOLID "ESTABLISHMENT" TYPES! THEY HAVEN'T A CHANCE OF PROVING THEIR CASE!

LATER, AS THE DEFENSE RESTS...

THIS SPECIAL COURT IS READY TO HEAR THE PROSECUTION'S CASE!

IT'S ALREADY BEEN HEARD, YOUR HONOR!

EXACTLY! THE CASE FOR THESE TWO HEROES IS ALSO THE CASE AGAINST THEM!

EVERY GRANDSTANDING RESCUE AND CRIMEBUSTING STUNT THE DEFENSE SHOWED ONLY PROVES OUR CASE BEYOND A DOUBT! SUPERMAN AND BATMAN HAVE BEEN CONDEMNED BY THEIR OWN DEEDS!

AS THE COURTROOM BUZZES WITH CONTROVERSY...

CRAZY! THE BOYS HAVE SURE GOOFED IT! IMAGINE TRYING TO USE OUR OWN CAREERS AGAINST US!

I ALMOST FEEL SORRY FOR THEM! BUT IT'S A GOOD GROWING-UP EXPERIENCE... MAKING THEIR OWN MISTAKES!

THINK SO, SUPER-DADS? A LITTLE LATER...

DUE TO THE OVERWHELMING EVIDENCE...WE...ER...FIND THE DEFENDANTS, SUPERMAN AND BATMAN...GUILTY AS CHARGED!

WHAT?! IMPOSSIBLE!

IT'S A TRAVESTY OF JUSTICE!

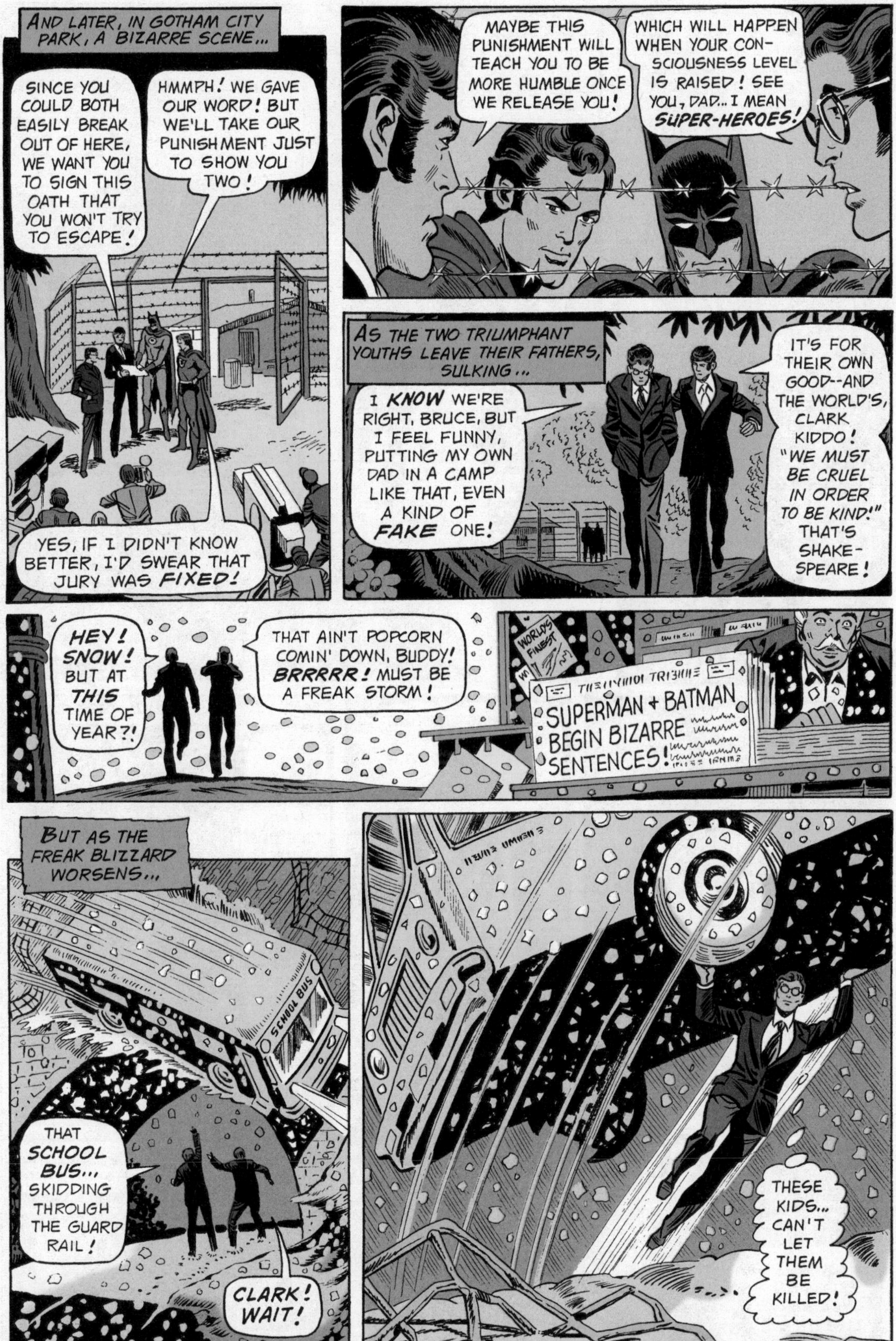

AND LATER, IN GOTHAM CITY PARK, A BIZARRE SCENE...
SINCE YOU COULD BOTH EASILY BREAK OUT OF HERE, WE WANT YOU TO SIGN THIS OATH THAT YOU WON'T TRY TO ESCAPE!
HMMPH! WE GAVE OUR WORD! BUT WE'LL TAKE OUR PUNISHMENT JUST TO SHOW YOU TWO!
YES, IF I DIDN'T KNOW BETTER, I'D SWEAR THAT JURY WAS FIXED!
MAYBE THIS PUNISHMENT WILL TEACH YOU TO BE MORE HUMBLE ONCE WE RELEASE YOU!
WHICH WILL HAPPEN WHEN YOUR CONSCIOUSNESS LEVEL IS RAISED! SEE YOU, DAD... I MEAN SUPER-HEROES!
AS THE TWO TRIUMPHANT YOUTHS LEAVE THEIR FATHERS, SULKING...
I KNOW WE'RE RIGHT, BRUCE, BUT I FEEL FUNNY, PUTTING MY OWN DAD IN A CAMP LIKE THAT, EVEN A KIND OF FAKE ONE!
IT'S FOR THEIR OWN GOOD--AND THE WORLD'S, CLARK KIDDO! "WE MUST BE CRUEL IN ORDER TO BE KIND!" THAT'S SHAKESPEARE!
HEY! SNOW! BUT AT THIS TIME OF YEAR?!
THAT AIN'T POPCORN COMIN' DOWN, BUDDY! BRRRRR! MUST BE A FREAK STORM!
WORLD'S FINEST
SUPERMAN + BATMAN BEGIN BIZARRE SENTENCES!
BUT AS THE FREAK BLIZZARD WORSENS...
SCHOOL BUS
THAT SCHOOL BUS... SKIDDING THROUGH THE GUARD RAIL!
CLARK! WAIT!
THESE KIDS... CAN'T LET THEM BE KILLED!
5

CLARK! THAT'S EXACTLY WHY WE PUT OUR DADS IN PUNISHMENT CAMP -- FOR PLAYING HERO!

WELL, SINCE THEY DIDN'T SEE US... I'M NOT ASKING FOR ANY THANKS! AND LIKE YOU AGREED WITH YOUR DAD, *BATMAN*...YOU JUST CAN'T LET PEOPLE DIE!

OKAY! OKAY! BUT DON'T LET IT HAPPEN AGAIN!

COME ON, THIS STORM'S GETTING WORSE! LET'S HITCH A RIDE ON THAT TRUCK!

BEAUTIFUL! LIKE WAS PROMISED, THE STORM'S SOCKING IN ALL ROADS TO THE CITY! WE'LL BE THE ONLY TRUCK TO MAKE IT... AND WE'LL QUADRUPLE OUR PRICE!

YEAH, *TEMPO UNLIMITED* SURE DELIVERED! BUT THEY TAKE A BIG CUT!

HEAR THAT? IT'S LIKE THEY *KNEW* THIS STORM WAS *ARRANGED!*

NOT LIKELY, CHUM!

BUT WHAT ELSE EXPLAINS WEATHER LIKE THIS?

⑥

SUNSPOTS? OR THE WEATHER GUY ON TV GOT OUT OF THE WRONG SIDE OF THE BED?

TERMINAL O

VERY FUNNY! I THINK WE'D BETTER CHECK THINGS OUT!

AS THE STORM SUDDENLY ABATES...

SAY, AREN'T YOU PLAYING HERO... LIKE OUR DADS!?

UH...NOT REALLY... JUST DOING A LITTLE DETECTIVE WORK LIKE ANY PUBLIC-SPIRITED CITIZEN! STAND BY!!!

AND STAND BY FOR *PART 2*...NEXT!

A MYSTERY BLIZZARD HITTING GOTHAM IN MID-SUMMER! TWO TRICKY DUDES TALKING ABOUT AN OUTFIT CALLED *TEMPO*! LET'S PICK UP THE BEAT...HERE!

PROFITS ARE UP A THOUSAND PERCENT IN ALL BRANCHES! *TEMPO'S* THE BEST PARTNER WE EVER HAD!

BUT WHO ARE THEY REALLY, BOSS? AND WHERE DO THEY OPERATE FROM?

I DON'T KNOW! WE JUST SEND THEIR CUT TO A SWISS BANK!

ALL I *DO* KNOW IS THEIR NEXT CAPER'S AT MIDWEST CITY-- SOMETHING TO DO WITH THE DROUGHT OUT THERE!

LOSING MY GRIP...I'M GONNA FALL!

CLARK! WE'VE STUMBLED ONTO A WILD CONSPIRACY TO FOOL WITH THE WEATHER! *TEMPO*... IT'S CLOSE TO THE WORD FOR WEATHER IN SEVERAL LANGUAGES ...*TEMPS...TIEMPO!*

NOW, IN AN ABANDONED BUILDING...

SO WE REALLY ARE BACK INTO PLAYING SUPER HERO--THE THING WE PUT OUR DADS IN PRISON FOR!

NO...BECAUSE BEING AWARE OF THAT WILL KEEP US FROM SEEKING APPLAUSE AND GRATITUDE LIKE THEM!

THESE ARE LITTLE FISH-- WE WANT THE CREEPS BEHIND IT ALL! NEXT STOP--*MIDWEST CITY!*

HOURS LATER, NEAR MIDWEST CITY, HUB OF A DROUGHT-STRICKEN FARM AREA...

WOW! THOSE CROPS DOWN THERE WILL BE DRY POWDER IF IT DOESN'T RAIN SOON!

WHICH IS WHAT THAT PLANE IS TRYING TO MAKE HAPPEN!

...BY SEEDING THESE CUMULUS CLOUDS WITH SILVER DIOXIDE CRYSTALS-- A TRIED AND TRUE METHOD!

HOLD IT! MY SUPER HEARING DETECTS ANOTHER PLANE UP HERE!

7

AND SLIGHTLY HIGHER IN THE SAME CLOUD...

THERE IT IS--! ODD, IT HAS NO LICENSE NUMBER... AND WHAT'S THAT LIQUID IT'S SHOWERING FROM THAT TANK?

YEEOW! I DON'T KNOW, BUT IT'S HOT!

IT'S ACID! IF I RECALL MY CHEM COURSES, CHUM, IT CAN WRECK SILVER COMPOUNDS...LIKE THOSE CLOUD-SEEDING CRYSTALS!

LET'S FOLLOW THAT PLANE!

SHORTLY...

IT'S LANDING IN THAT VALLEY! YOU NOTICE THAT ACID FOULED UP THE RAIN-MAKING? WE'RE ON TO SOMETHING, BUDDY MINE!

SOMETHING OUR DADS WOULD HAVE MADE INTO A GRANDSTAND PLAY--BUT NOT US!

BUT AS THE SUPER SONS DROP DOWN TOWARD THE DESOLATE AIRFIELD...

WE'RE SPOTTED!

MACHINE GUN! KEEP HIDDEN, BRUCE!

I WON'T EVEN STICK OUT A BAT-WHISKER!

RATA-TATATAT

IT'S GREAT, HAVING A PAL WHO'S ONLY TICKLED BY MG SLUGS...

MORE LIKE BEE STINGS, WISE GUY! I'M ONLY HALF SUPER ...UNLIKE MY OLD MAN!

OUCH!

WHUP

VIP

BEEEOW

WHUCK

VIIIP

8

SHOOTING AT PEOPLE'S ILLEGAL... UNHEALTHY,... AND FATTENING! IT GETS YOU A *FAT LIP!*

RUNNNCCCH

POW

TSOK

NOW TO SEE **WHO** AND **WHAT'S** BELOW THIS GUN NEST!

YOU KNOW, I'VE GOT A FEELING THINGS ARE ABOUT TO *REALLY* EXPLODE!

THWOK

VZZZZZZT

VZZZZZZT

HUH? AN ARROW KNOCKING A GRENADE AWAY?

I'M HIT!

BLA-AM

BRUCE--!

As the youthful *CAPED CRUSADER* collapses, wounded by a piece of *SHRAPNEL* ...

I...I'M OKAY,... ONLY ... A FLESH WOUND!

WOULD'VE BEEN MUCH WORSE IF I HADN'T KNOCKED THAT PINEAPPLE AWAY--!

GREEN ARROW!? YOU... HERE?!

THE PLANE TAKING OFF! GOT TO STOP IT!

NO NEED, YOUNG FELLA! MY BOON TRAVELING COMPANION WILL CANCEL THAT FLIGHT!

BRRRRUMM

9

AND AS THE CRAFT RACES FOR TAKE-OFF, A CRIMSON BLUR RANGES UP ALONGSIDE...

VRRRRRMMMM

THE FLASH--?

THE FLASH'S SLIPSTREAM HITS THE WHIRLING PROPS LIKE A MINI-TORNADO, SENDING THEM INTO COUNTER-ROTATION!

KRANNNG

BRRRMMMM

KRUNNCH

AND VERY SHORTLY...

QUITE A COINCIDENCE... THE FLASH... GREEN ARROW BOTH SHOWING UP HERE!

NOT SO COINCIDENTAL! WE'VE BEEN FOLLOWING CLUES ON TEMPO, UNLIMITED FOR SOME TIME! IT TRULY IS A CONSPIRACY TO CONTROL THE WORLD'S WEATHER!

OUR EMERALD ARCHER'S DEAD ON TARGET! BY CONTROLLING OR INTERFERING WITH THE WEATHER, TEMPO'S CLIENTS PROFIT...

... FROM ARTIFICIAL SHORTAGES, DELAYED SHIPMENTS, INSURANCE PAY-OFFS ON WRECKS, ACCIDENTS, AND SO ON!

CHECK! THESE BOZOS WERE BUSY FOULING UP RAIN-MAKING IN THIS DROUGHT AREA!

OF COURSE, THEY CLAIM THEY DON'T KNOW WHO THEY WORK FOR... IT'S ALL RUN SECRETLY FROM FAR AWAY!

WE FIGURED THAT OUT OUR-SELVES! AND WE DON'T NEED ANY ADULT SUPER HEROES HELPING US!

WHAT? YOU SURE NEEDED OUR HELP TODAY! YOU YOUNGSTERS THINK OLDER PEOPLE'S MOTIVES ARE ALL SHADY!

10

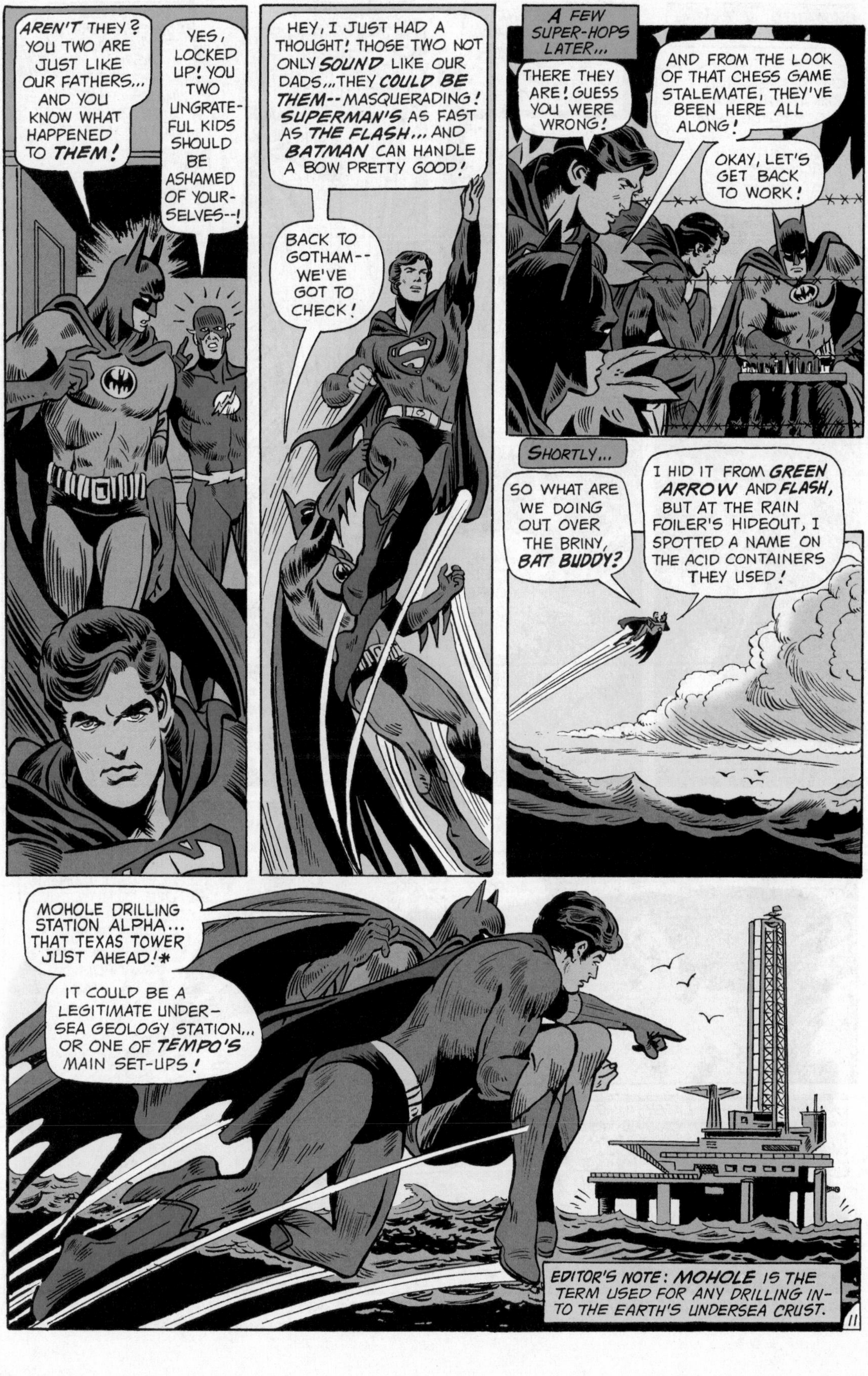
AREN'T THEY? YOU TWO ARE JUST LIKE OUR FATHERS... AND YOU KNOW WHAT HAPPENED TO THEM!
YES, LOCKED UP! YOU TWO UNGRATEFUL KIDS SHOULD BE ASHAMED OF YOURSELVES--!
HEY, I JUST HAD A THOUGHT! THOSE TWO NOT ONLY SOUND LIKE OUR DADS... THEY COULD BE THEM--MASQUERADING! SUPERMAN'S AS FAST AS THE FLASH... AND BATMAN CAN HANDLE A BOW PRETTY GOOD!
BACK TO GOTHAM-- WE'VE GOT TO CHECK!
A FEW SUPER-HOPS LATER...
THERE THEY ARE! GUESS YOU WERE WRONG!
AND FROM THE LOOK OF THAT CHESS GAME STALEMATE, THEY'VE BEEN HERE ALL ALONG!
OKAY, LET'S GET BACK TO WORK!
SHORTLY...
SO WHAT ARE WE DOING OUT OVER THE BRINY, BAT BUDDY?
I HID IT FROM GREEN ARROW AND FLASH, BUT AT THE RAIN FOILER'S HIDEOUT, I SPOTTED A NAME ON THE ACID CONTAINERS THEY USED!
MOHOLE DRILLING STATION ALPHA... THAT TEXAS TOWER JUST AHEAD!*
IT COULD BE A LEGITIMATE UNDERSEA GEOLOGY STATION... OR ONE OF TEMPO'S MAIN SET-UPS!
EDITOR'S NOTE: MOHOLE IS THE TERM USED FOR ANY DRILLING INTO THE EARTH'S UNDERSEA CRUST.
11

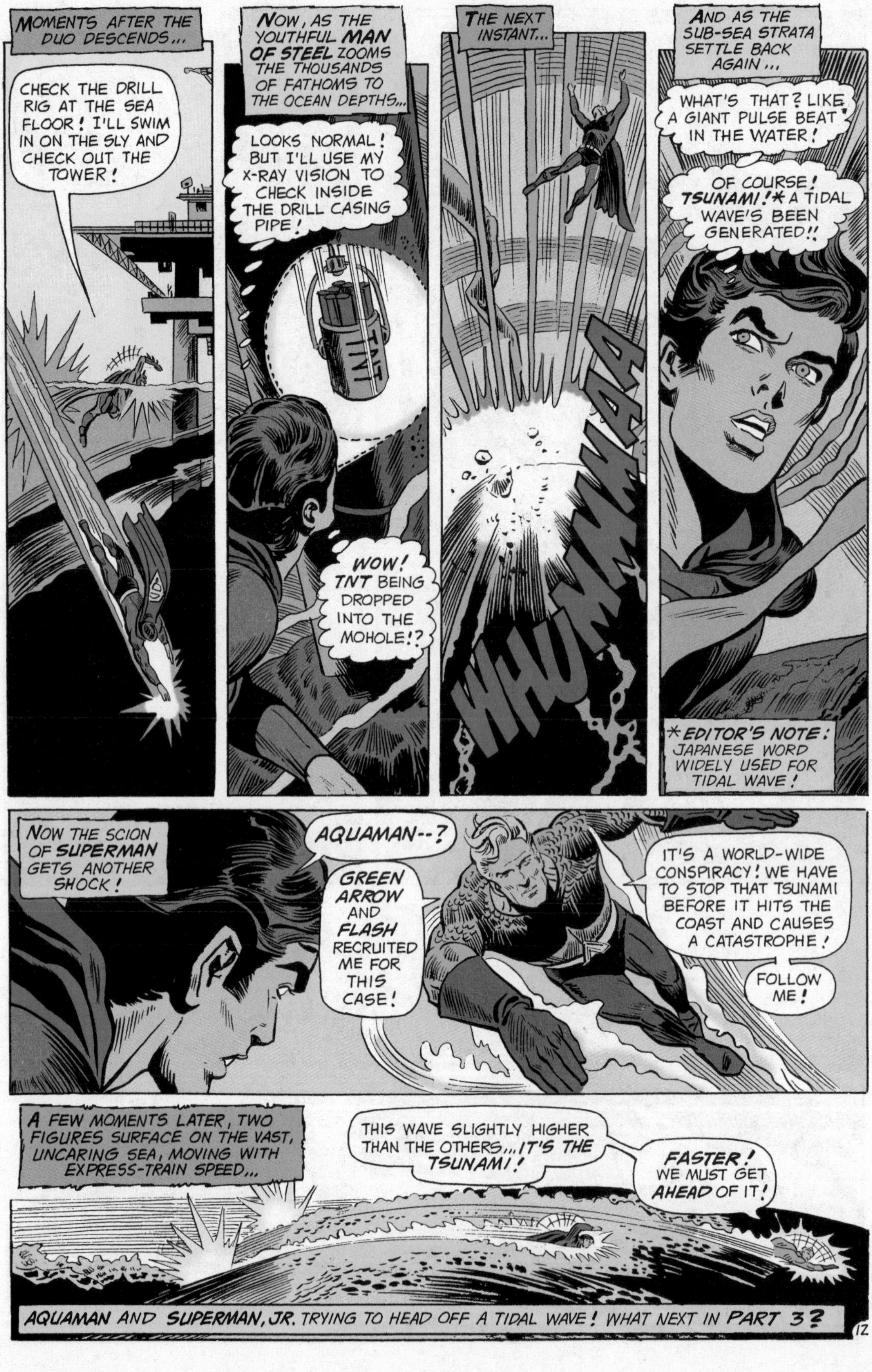

MOMENTS AFTER THE DUO DESCENDS...
CHECK THE DRILL RIG AT THE SEA FLOOR! I'LL SWIM IN ON THE SLY AND CHECK OUT THE TOWER!
NOW, AS THE YOUTHFUL MAN OF STEEL ZOOMS THE THOUSANDS OF FATHOMS TO THE OCEAN DEPTHS...
LOOKS NORMAL! BUT I'LL USE MY X-RAY VISION TO CHECK INSIDE THE DRILL CASING PIPE!
TNT
WOW! TNT BEING DROPPED INTO THE MOHOLE!?
THE NEXT INSTANT...
WHUMMMAA
AND AS THE SUB-SEA STRATA SETTLE BACK AGAIN...
WHAT'S THAT? LIKE A GIANT PULSE BEAT IN THE WATER!
OF COURSE! TSUNAMI!* A TIDAL WAVE'S BEEN GENERATED!!
*EDITOR'S NOTE: JAPANESE WORD WIDELY USED FOR TIDAL WAVE!
NOW THE SCION OF SUPERMAN GETS ANOTHER SHOCK!
AQUAMAN--?
GREEN ARROW AND FLASH RECRUITED ME FOR THIS CASE!
IT'S A WORLD-WIDE CONSPIRACY! WE HAVE TO STOP THAT TSUNAMI BEFORE IT HITS THE COAST AND CAUSES A CATASTROPHE!
FOLLOW ME!
A FEW MOMENTS LATER, TWO FIGURES SURFACE ON THE VAST, UNCARING SEA, MOVING WITH EXPRESS-TRAIN SPEED...
THIS WAVE SLIGHTLY HIGHER THAN THE OTHERS... IT'S THE TSUNAMI!
FASTER! WE MUST GET AHEAD OF IT!
AQUAMAN AND SUPERMAN, JR. TRYING TO HEAD OFF A TIDAL WAVE! WHAT NEXT IN PART 3?
12

HALF AN HOUR LATER, AT A DESOLATE ROCKY ATOLL CALLED "NEPTUNE'S PUNCH BOWL"...

YOU CAN'T STOP A TSUNAMI WITH YOUR BARE HANDS! YOU NEED *WATER* TO FIGHT WATER, LAD!

THIS LAKE'S FILLED *AND* DRAINED BY TIDAL ACTION... BUT THAT'S *TOO SLOW!*

THE WATER MUST BE RELEASED ALL AT ONCE! THAT'S IT-- BUST DOWN THE BOWL WALL!

THE TSUNAMI... *IT'S COMING!!*

PHOWW

KPOWW

AND AS THE TIDAL LAKE SUDDENLY EMPTIES INTO THE SURROUNDING SEA...

KHASPOOOOSSHHHH

IT *WORKED!* ONE WAVE'S CANCELLING THE OTHER!

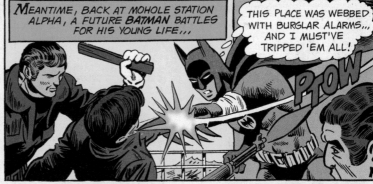

MEANTIME, BACK AT MOHOLE STATION ALPHA, A FUTURE *BATMAN* BATTLES FOR HIS YOUNG LIFE...

THIS PLACE WAS WEBBED WITH BURGLAR ALARMS... AND I MUST'VE TRIPPED 'EM ALL!

PTOW

BUT SUDDENLY, TWO WHISTLING SHAFTS FROM NOWHERE...

WZZZ'ZZZ

WZZZZ

THUNK

13

OKAY, ARCHER--YOU AND YOUR PAL GET A SLUG EACH IF YOU DON'T DROP THAT BOW...

CERTAINLY, CHURL, I'LL DROP MY BOW...

EXPLOSIVES

...IF YOU HOTSHOTS WILL SURRENDER YOUR THUNDER STICKS!

WHOOSSSSHHH!

LATER, A KIND OF REUNION TAKES PLACE...

YOU TWO AGAIN! DON'T TELL ME YOU NOTICED THAT SAME CLUE...?

SURE--BEFORE YOU HID IT, SONNY! AND WE TIPPED AQUAMAN TO SHOW UP, TOO! LUCKY WE DID--YOU NEEDED US OLD GAFFERS AGAIN!

ALWAYS GRABBING CREDIT, JUST LIKE OUR FATHERS!

WELL, WE DON'T NEED YOU TO FINISH THIS CASE!

MOMENTS LATER...

BACK TO GOTHAM? BUT WE ALREADY CHECKED ON OUR DADS DISGUISING THEMSELVES AS GA AND FLASH! AND WHAT ABOUT AQUAMAN?

YOU NEVER SAW AQUAMAN AND FLASH TOGETHER, DID YOU? SUPER-MAN COULD HOLD HIS BREATH EASILY AND IMPERSON-ATE HIM!

AND WE FORGOT ONE OTHER THING! ANDROIDS! BOTH OUR DADS HAVE ANDROID DOUBLES THEY COULD SUBSTITUTE FOR THEMSELVES!

14

GONE! THEY BROKE OUT!

SO THEN THEY **COULDN'T** HAVE BEEN **ANDROIDS!**

THIS PROVES THAT THEY WERE IMPERSONATING **GREEN ARROW, FLASH**...AND **AQUAMAN!** THEY BROKE THEIR WORD!

WHAT'S THAT SMOKE JUST BEYOND THE PARK? LET'S GO SEE--!

D-DAD?!

A SUBWAY FIRE TRAPPED THESE RIDERS, BOYS--BUT WE EVACUATED ALL OF THEM!

SOON...

AFRAID WE DID BREAK CAMP, SONS--BUT NOW WE'RE IMPRISONING OUR-SELVES AGAIN! SORRY!

HMMM, GUESS WE CAN FORGIVE THAT!

COME ON, CLARK-- WE'VE GOT A MISSION TO COMPLETE!

WELL, THEY SURE MADE US LOOK FOOLISH AND UNFAIR! AND NOW WE HAVEN'T A CLUE AS TO **TEMPO'S** NEXT CAPER!

I'LL FIND ONE BACK AT THE MOHOLE STATION! HEAD FOR IT!

AND ON THE NOW DESERTED TOWER...

NOTHING...I SEARCHED EVERY INCH!

YOU MISSED **THIS** MESSAGE CARVED ON THE SHAFT OF ONE OF **G.A.'S** ARROWS! *"COME TO VOLSUNG ISLAND! THE OLD GRANDSTANDERS!"*

15

AND AS ONCE MORE THE DUO TAKES TO THE SKIES...

GUESS WE *DID* NEED THEIR HELP TO PICK UP THE TRAIL--! AND I KIND OF DIG THOSE TWO BIG DADDIES!

DON'T WEAKEN, PAL! WE'LL ACCEPT THEIR HELP... BUT IT'S US WHO'LL COMPLETE THE MISSION... *WITHOUT* TAKING ANY CREDIT!

SOON, A VOLCANIC ISLAND IN THE ARCTIC...

YOU SURE THIS IS *TEMPO'S* NEXT SET-UP?

AND THE *BIGGEST!* WE SWEATED THE INFO OUT OF ONE OF THOSE TOWER THUGS BY THREATENING TO DROP HIM DOWN THE MOHOLE!

NOW, ALONG THE SEMI-ACTIVE VOLCANO'S CRATER RIM...

THE ROCKET'S LOADED WITH *FREON*-- THE GAS THAT IS USED AS A PROPELLANT IN AEROSOL PRODUCTS, LIKE IN SPRAY CANS!

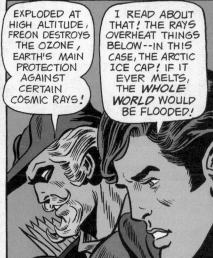

EXPLODED AT HIGH ALTITUDE, FREON DESTROYS THE OZONE, EARTH'S MAIN PROTECTION AGAINST CERTAIN COSMIC RAYS!

I READ ABOUT THAT! THE RAYS OVERHEAT THINGS BELOW--IN THIS CASE, THE ARCTIC ICE CAP! IF IT EVER MELTS, THE *WHOLE WORLD* WOULD BE FLOODED!

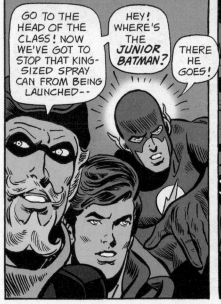

GO TO THE HEAD OF THE CLASS! NOW WE'VE GOT TO STOP THAT KING-SIZED SPRAY CAN FROM BEING LAUNCHED--

HEY! WHERE'S THE *JUNIOR BATMAN?*

THERE HE GOES!

HE'S TRYING TO TACKLE THOSE GOONS *ALONE!*

THEY SPOTTED HIM... AND ARE *FIRING THE ROCKET!*

ZOOOOCHHH

16

FLASH AND I'LL HANDLE THEM! CAN *YOU* STOP THAT ROCKET?

I'M ON MY WAY, G.A.!

AS THE *TEMPO* TERRORISTS FIRE AT THE SCAMPERING SON OF *BATMAN*, GREEN ARROW'S FLASH GRENADE EXPLODES IN THEIR MIDST!

KA-POWP

YIIIII!

CAN'T SEE--!

TSOK

PTOW

TSOK

PTOW

JUST LIKE *BLIND DUCKS* IN A SHOOTING GALLERY!

WHILE NEARBY...

THE ROCKET'S ALREADY EMITTING FREON... GOT TO MAKE A QUICK ANTI-MISSILE MISSILE!!

FREED BY THE *SON OF STEEL*, THE VOLCANIC FISSURE SENDS A SPOUT OF HOT LAVA ERUPTING UPWARDS...

SPOOOOOOSSSHHH

17

AND AS THE LAVA ALMOST INSTANTLY CONGEALS IN THE FRIGID AIR...

CONTAINED-- ONE *FREON* BOMB!

NICE WORK!

AS FOR YOU, *BATMAN, JR.* -- YOU ALMOST BLEW THE WHOLE DEAL!

YEAH, BUT I *STILL* THINK YOU'RE AS PHONY AS YOUR BEARD!

HUH? IT *DOESN'T* COME OFF!

OF *COURSE,* KIDDO! *FLASH* AND I ARE FOR *REAL!*

SOME TIME LATER...

THE *TEMPO* CONSPIRACY'S BROKEN...AND WE LEARNED OUR LESSON, DADS!

HEROES ARE NEEDED TO HELP PEOPLE....AND GRAND-STANDING'S REALLY ALLOWING *PEOPLE* TO SHOW THEIR GRATITUDE!

HEROES CAN'T SOLVE THE *BIG* PROBLEMS... ONLY SOCIETY AS A WHOLE CAN DO THAT! BUT THEY CAN INSPIRE MANKIND...AS *GREEN ARROW, FLASH* AND *AQUAMAN* DID US!

WELL SAID, BOYS! GUESS WE'RE FREE MEN AGAIN, *BATMAN!*

YOU KNOW WE *DID* BREAK OUR WORD TO THEM! EXCEPT FOR THAT LAST CAPER...

WHERE THE *REAL G.A.* AND *FLASH* APPEARED... IT WAS *US* MASQUERADING AS THEM AND *AQUAMAN!*

AND OF COURSE, THOSE *WERE* OUR ANDROID DOUBLES BOTH TIMES THE BOYS CAME BACK TO CHECK, AS WE ANTICIPATED!

I KNOW...BUT WE SIGNED THE PLEDGE AS *SUPERMAN* AND *BATMAN* -- BUT IT WAS AS *CLARK KENT* AND *BRUCE WAYNE* THAT WE BROKE OUT OF CAMP!

SO IT WAS ONLY A *WHITE LIE*...AND ONE THAT PRODUCED A HAPPY RESULT!!

WE, SUPERMAN and BATMAN, DO SOLEMNLY AGREE THAT WE ONLY STOP HEROING NEVER

Superman
Batman

THE END.

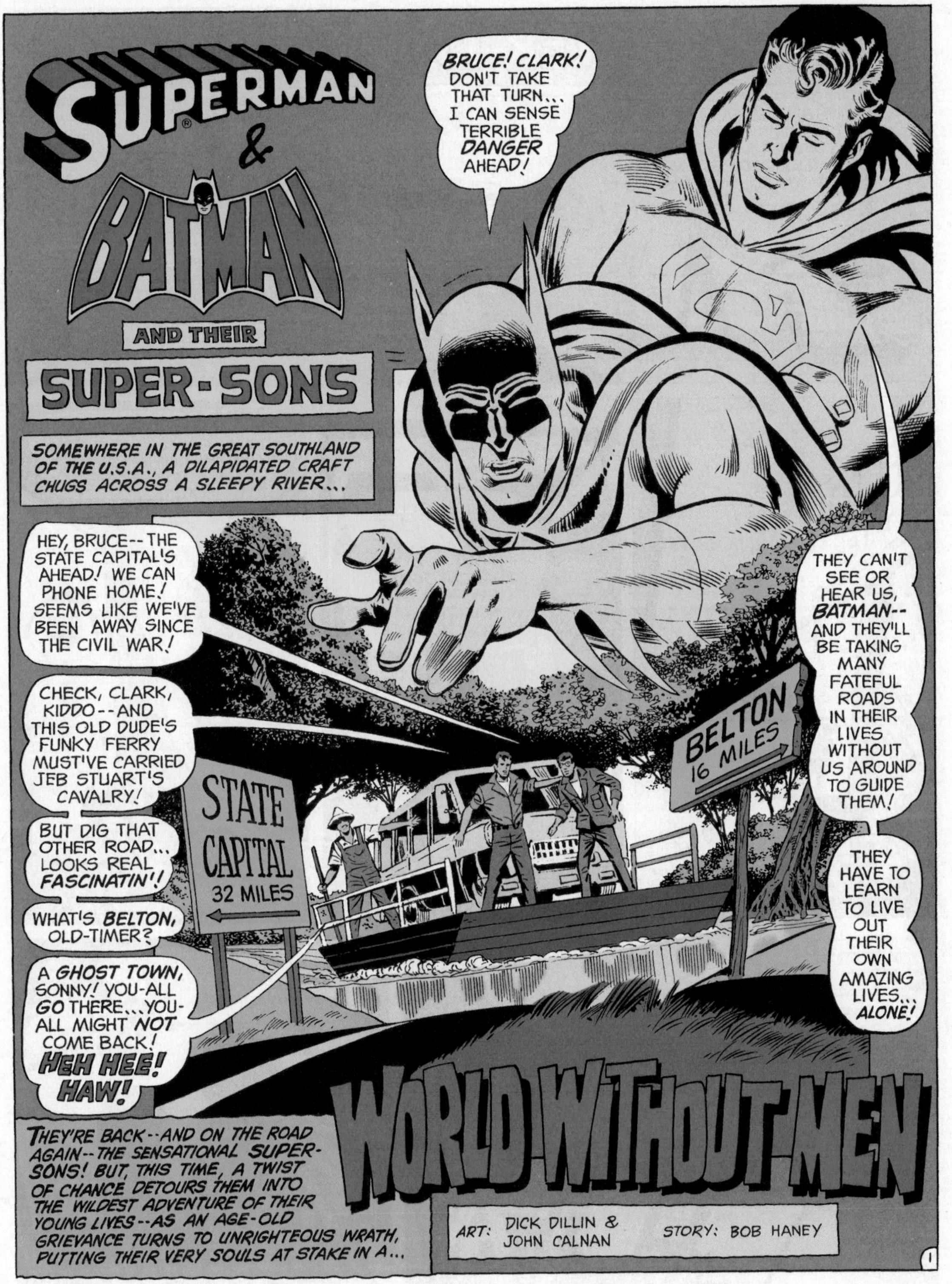
SUPERMAN & BATMAN
AND THEIR
SUPER-SONS
BRUCE! CLARK! DON'T TAKE THAT TURN... I CAN SENSE TERRIBLE DANGER AHEAD!
SOMEWHERE IN THE GREAT SOUTHLAND OF THE U.S.A., A DILAPIDATED CRAFT CHUGS ACROSS A SLEEPY RIVER...
HEY, BRUCE--THE STATE CAPITAL'S AHEAD! WE CAN PHONE HOME! SEEMS LIKE WE'VE BEEN AWAY SINCE THE CIVIL WAR!
CHECK, CLARK, KIDDO--AND THIS OLD DUDE'S FUNKY FERRY MUST'VE CARRIED JEB STUART'S CAVALRY!
BUT DIG THAT OTHER ROAD... LOOKS REAL FASCINATIN'!
WHAT'S BELTON, OLD-TIMER?
A GHOST TOWN, SONNY! YOU-ALL GO THERE... YOU-ALL MIGHT NOT COME BACK! HEH HEE! HAW!
STATE CAPITAL 32 MILES
BELTON 16 MILES
THEY CAN'T SEE OR HEAR US, BATMAN--AND THEY'LL BE TAKING MANY FATEFUL ROADS IN THEIR LIVES WITHOUT US AROUND TO GUIDE THEM!
THEY HAVE TO LEARN TO LIVE OUT THEIR OWN AMAZING LIVES... ALONE!
THEY'RE BACK--AND ON THE ROAD AGAIN--THE SENSATIONAL SUPER-SONS! BUT, THIS TIME, A TWIST OF CHANCE DETOURS THEM INTO THE WILDEST ADVENTURE OF THEIR YOUNG LIVES--AS AN AGE-OLD GRIEVANCE TURNS TO UNRIGHTEOUS WRATH, PUTTING THEIR VERY SOULS AT STAKE IN A...
WORLD WITHOUT MEN
ART: DICK DILLIN & JOHN CALNAN
STORY: BOB HANEY
1

BELTON'S AN OLD SWAMP LUMBER TOWN! WHEN THE SAWMILLS CLOSED DOWN, IT JEST DIED! YOU MIGHT, TOO, IF YOU-ALL TAKE THAT ROAD!

YOU-ALL TRYIN' TO *SCARE* US-ALL, POP? WELL, ONE THING MRS. WAYNE'S LITTLE BOY *BRUCE* CAN'T RESIST...

BELTON 16 MILES

...IS A *SCARY* DARE!!

VRRRRRMMMMMM

SHORTLY...

THIS IS ONE GLOOMY SWAMP, PAL!

THINK OF IT, CLARK-- *A REAL GHOST TOWN!* MAYBE WE CAN GET A BOWL OF *GHOST TOASTIES* ...I'M TIRED OF MONOXIDE-FLAVORED CHOCOLATE BARS!

VERY FUNNY, CLOWN!

HEY, THAT SIGN?! GUESS IT'S SOME KIND OF AD FOR EYE MAKE-UP!

MILES LATER...

A BLACKSMITH SHOP--HERE ON THE OUTSKIRTS OF BELTON!

LISTEN! SOME MUSCLE-BOUND *GHOSTLY GEEZER* POUNDING AWAY!

BLACKSMITH

KRUNNNG KRUNNNG

"OH, UNDER THE SPREADING SWAMP OAK, THE VILLAGE SMITHY STANDS..."

LET'S CHECK HIM OUT!

KRAANNG BLANNG KRUNNNG

2

YET AS THE TWO COMRADES ENTER THE DIM, OLD SHOP...

UH...MISS...LET ME HELP YOU...!

STAY BACK!!

YEEOW! A CHICK?! A GORGEOUS GIRL!?

KRANNNG

NO MAN TOUCHES ME...OR MY WORK!

WOWEE, IS SHE EVER HOSTILE! IF I DIDN'T HAVE SUPER EYE TISSUES, THAT HOT IRON WOULD'VE BLINDED ME!

YEAH, PAL! LET'S SPLIT THE SMITHY SCENE AND HEAD INTO TOWN! MAYBE THE PHANTOM CITIZENS ARE FRIENDLIER!

SHORTLY...

WELL, BELTON'S SURE NO GHOST TOWN! IT'S PRETTY POPULATED--

TOWN HALL

PRETTY IS THE WORD...THEY'RE ALL BEAUTIFUL CHICKS!

BUT NOT ONE MAN! IT'S A TOWN OF FEMALES ONLY!

3

173

BEING THE LOVER, I NOTICED IT FIRST--!

BEING THE BRAIN, I NOTICE THEY'RE ALL UNFRIENDLY LIKE THAT BLACKSMITH--AND THAT *SAME BIG EYE SIGN*-- IT'S *EVERYWHERE*-- WATCHING *EVERYTHING!*

EXACTLY! THE WATCHFUL EYE OF *BIG SISTER SYBIL,* OUR BELOVED LEADER AND GUIDE...

...AND YOUR BUS IS PARKED ILLEGALLY! THAT IS A $500 FINE!

HOLY--! A POLICE CHICK?? $500 FOR A PARKING FINE?? THAT'S CRAZY!

LISTEN, BEAUTIFUL, CAN'T WE WORK THIS OUT--?

A TYPICAL *MALE CHAUVINIST* REMARK! NO--*BIG SISTER SYBIL* SET SUCH A HIGH FINE TO DISCOURAGE MEN FROM STAYING IN BELTON!

HAVING TROUBLE, OFFICER DIANA? I AM *SISTER SARA,* BELTON'S MAYOR!

UH... MAYOR... DOLL... WE DIDN'T SEE ANY NO PARKING SIGNS! AND WE HAVEN'T GOT THAT KIND OF BREAD!

DON'T TOUCH ME! THAT'S ANOTHER OF *SYBIL'S* STRICT LAWS-- NO *MALE* MAY TOUCH A SISTER!

IF YOU CAN'T PAY THE FINE... YOU'LL BE *JAILED!*

JAILED? BUT THAT'S UNFAIR... ILLEGAL! WE HAVE OUR RIGHTS!

MEN HAVE FEW RIGHTS IN BELTON! *BIG SISTER* HAS SHOWN US OUR *FEMALE* RIGHTS TO LIVE IN DIGNITY WITHOUT MALES DOMINATING US!

REAL HEAVY *WOMEN'S LIB* STUFF! BUT, BABY, WITHOUT MEN HOW WILL YOU HAVE LOVERS... HUSBANDS... FAMILIES?

BIG SISTER SYBIL HAS PROMISED THAT WHEN MEN CHANGE THEIR DOMINEERING WAYS... WE SHALL ALLOW THEM TO TOUCH US... AGAIN!

4

MEANTIME, OUR STRENGTH IS IN LIVING *APART*... IN FREEDOM AND SISTER-HOOD!

DIANA-- TAKE THEM TO JAIL!

HELP!

THAT GIRL SHINGLING THE ROOF... SHE'S *FALLING!*

CLARK! WE'VE GOT TO *SAVE* HER!

STOP! TO SAVE HER, YOU MUST *TOUCH* HER--SYBIL *FORBIDS* THAT! OUR OWN RESCUE UNIT WILL DO IT!

I COULD LEAP UP THERE AND SAVE HER... BUT DIANA MIGHT SHOOT BRUCE! HOPE THAT RESCUE SQUAD IS IN TIME!

BUT A MOMENT LATER...

EEEEEK!

I CAN'T REACH HER!

SHE'S... *DEAD?!*

I SHOULD'VE MADE A TRY, ANYHOW...!

THIS IS VERY SAD... BUT CANNOT BE HELPED! SISTER JANE KNEW THAT IN DOING *MAN'S* WORK... SHE RAN THE SAME RISKS!

WHY, YOU COLD-BLOODED *WITCH!!* YOU...AND *BIG SISTER SYBIL* AND THIS WHOLE *WEIRDO* TOWN BELONG IN A *FREAK SHOW!*

TOUCH YOU? I OUGHT TO SLAP SOME SENSE INTO YOUR PRETTY FACES!

5

I'VE GOT **BOTH** OF THOSE MALE BULLIES, MAYOR SARA!

GOOD WORK, SISTER NORMA! **PUT THEM AWAY!**

CLARK! YOU **SUPER** BOOB, DO SOMETHING! WE'RE BEING DROPPED INTO A CHUTE!

BELTON TOWN JAIL

CRANNG

A **CELL!** WHY DIDN'T YOU STOP THIS FROM HAPPENING?

I'M NOT SURE...EXCEPT I'M BEGINNING TO FEEL THERE'S MORE THAN MEETS THE **BIG EYE** IN BELTON -- AND **NOT** PLAYING SUPER-HERO MAY BE THE WAY TO **SPY** IT OUT!

SO THOSE SHE-DEVILS GOT YOU TWO, EH? I DROVE MY TRUCK INTO TOWN MONTHS AGO... GOT JAILED ON A PHONY TRAFFIC TICKET!

THESE OTHER POOR SLOBS BEEN HERE EVEN **LONGER!** AND THERE'S BEEN SOME WHO VANISHED OUT OF THEIR CELLS!

MY HUNCH IS THOSE CRAZY DAMES **MURDERED 'EM!**

MURDER!? OKAY, FRIEND, WE'VE HEARD ENOUGH! WE'RE GONNA TAKE IT ALL UP WITH **SISTER SYBIL!**

THAT'S A LAUGH, SONNY! **NOBODY** EVER **SEES** HER-- NOT EVEN THOSE WACKY FOLLOWERS OF HERS!

SHE LIVES IN THE SWAMP... AND LIKE **NOBODY'S** EVER COME OUT WHO WENT IN TO FIND HER!

BELTON TOWN JAIL

6

As NIGHT ENVELOPS BELTON, THE *SONS* OF *SUPERMAN* AND *BATMAN* PONDER THE MOST BIZARRE DILEMMA OF THEIR YOUNG LIVES...

I'M ALL FOR GALS DOING THEIR OWN THING...BUT THESE BELTON BELLES ARE CARRYING IT DEFINITELY TOO FAR... LIKE MAYBE TO *MURDER!*

HOLD IT! MY SUPER HEARING'S PICKING UP AN INTERESTING RAP IN THE NEXT ROOM!

OH, SARA, I'M VERY UPSET! SISTER JANE'S DEATH WAS TERRIBLE...

...AND JAILING THOSE TWO YOUNG MEN... WHAT THEY SAID ABOUT US SHOOK ME BADLY!

I KNOW, SISTER DIANA, I FEEL THE SAME! THOSE TWO ARE DIFFERENT THAN THE CRUDE TYPES WHO BLUNDERED INTO BELTON!

BUT WE MUST BE STRONG! *BIG SISTER SYBIL* WARNED US THE WAY TO *FREEDOM* WOULD BE HARD!

WHEN WE RESTORED THIS GHOST TOWN UNDER HER INSPIRED GUIDANCE, WE FOREVER CAST OFF FEMININE WEAKNESS! OUR CAUSE IS JUST AND WILL *TRIUMPH!*

I KNOW-- BUT WE CAN'T KEEP THOSE MEN IN JAIL FOREVER!

WE SHALL ASK *BIG SISTER'S* WISHES ABOUT THEIR FATE... WHEN WE HOLD SISTER JANE'S FUNERAL BEFORE HER PRESENCE ON THE *SACRED SAVANNAH!*

AND AS CLARK RECOUNTS TO BRUCE WHAT HIS UNEARTHLY EARS OVERHEARD...

THAT'S *ONE* FUNERAL WE'RE GOING TO ATTEND! YOU GOTTA BUST US OUT OF HERE--BUT QUIET-LIKE!

THAT PRESENTS NO PROBLEM TO THE KENT MUSCLES!

7

ALL I NEED DO IS GRAB IT WITH MY FINGERNAILS-- AND *OPEN SESAME!*

I'D HATE TO BE YOUR *MANICURIST!*

LET'S GET OUT BEFORE OUR CELLMATES WAKE UP!

NOW TO BEND IT CLOSED SO THOSE GIRLS DON'T WONDER HOW TWO PUNY MALES COULD ESCAPE A STONE-AND-STEEL CELL!

BELTON TOWN JAIL

YEAH, I DIG GETTING THE FEMALE EYE--BUT NOT *BIG SISTER SYBIL'S!* SHE'S DOWNRIGHT *SPOOKY!*

SHORTLY...

IT'S *JUNIOR SUPER-HERO* TIME AGAIN! GOOD THING THEY DIDN'T SEARCH THE BUS--OR WE'D BE DOING OUR BIT IN T-SHIRTS!

QUIET, COMEDIAN! MY OTHER THAN MERELY MORTAL EARS AND EYES ARE PICKING UP SOMETHING AGAIN!

CRYING? MARCHING FEET--?

THE FUNERAL PROCESSION! WELL, IT'S GOING TO BE JOINED BY TWO *MALE* MOURNERS!

AND AS THE LARGE PIROGUE, OR SWAMP BOAT, BEARING ITS GRIM CARGO, IS SOON BEING PADDLED THROUGH THE DISMAL SWAMP...

AN ISLAND--OR SAVANNAH, AHEAD! MUST BE *BIG SISTER SYBIL'S* HANGOUT!

8

SHORTLY, A SOLEMN CEREMONY IN THE DEPTHS OF THE FOREST...

Hear me, women! Our sister Jane's death is a great loss! But better she died than have those two new intruders TOUCH her!

THAT MONOLITH ...IT *TALKS!* BUT *WHO*... AND *WHERE'S* BIG *SIS?*

For accepting male attention is a fate worse than death...

But sisters Sara and Diana are wavering! They have shown sympathy for those two young intruders! This weakness must *STOP!*

I...WE... ARE SORRY, *SYBIL!*

I see and know EVERY-THING! Those young men threaten our sacred cause!

Therefore, I command you to return to town... and EXECUTE them!

Bury your dead sister... and carry out my command!

BRRR! *BIG SIS* JUST SIGNED THE DEATH WARRANTS OF BRUCE WAYNE, JR., AND CLARK KENT, JR.!

GOOD THING "THEY" WON'T BE IN THAT JAIL CELL!

9

179

AND AS THE SIMPLE FUNERAL IS COMPLETED, AND BELTON'S FEMALE CITIZENS SWIFTLY PADDLE AWAY...

WHAT ARE YOU DOING? I'M GETTING BAD VIBES FROM THAT SLAB... THAT LOOKS LIKE A GIANT TOMBSTONE!

COME ON-- WE'RE GOING TO RAP WITH THAT GIZMO!

BIG SISTER SYBIL! WE MAY BE ONLY MERE MALES--BUT WE WANT ANSWERS TO SOME IMPORTANT QUESTIONS!

Ask them, costumed fools!

HMMM, STRANGE SHE DOESN'T RECOGNIZE US... BATMAN AND SUPERMAN ARE WORLD-FAMOUS!

WE DEMAND TO KNOW WHY YOU TURNED THESE GULLIBLE GIRLS AGAINST MEN... AND WHY YOU DON'T SHOW YOURSELF?

The enlightened females of Belton were already against men-- against men's domineering tyranny over all women!

I had no need to persuade them of what they knew was already true!

If you wonder why I remain hidden, it is because a leader who is familiar and seen by her followers loses authority!

She must inspire loyalty by remoteness... EVEN fear! But in a just cause... it can be excused!

EXCUSED? YOU GOTTA BE KIDDING! YOU AND THESE POOR MIXED-UP CHICKS ARE FREAKY... A MENACE TO MEN AND SOCIETY IN GENERAL!

I DARE YOU TO SHOW YOURSELF--!

TAKE IT EASY, PAL!

10

YEOW! WHAT'S GOT ME--?

A FORCE FIELD--?!

AS THE OLD SAYING GOES... YOU SHOULD ALWAYS MEET FORCE... WITH *MORE FORCE!*

ZAAAAAAP

POWWN

AS THE POWER OF *SUPERMAN'S* SON SENDS THE FORCE FIELD ENERGY CRACKLING AWAY AS A RANDOM BOLT...

GOT TO CLEAR YOU AWAY... BEFORE THE *BIG EYE* PUTS ANOTHER WHAMMY ON YOU!

I'VE GOT A HEADACHE LIKE A MULE KICKED ME!

THAT FORCE FIELD COULD'VE *KILLED* YOU... *CRUSHED* YOUR BONES... OR *CHOKED OFF* YOUR BREATHING!

WHERE DID THAT GIZMO GET SUCH POWER... UNLESS IT'S OLD SWAMP MAGIC?

HEY, YOU *HEAR* SOMETHING? HOUNDS BAYING--!?

ARRRUOOOOO

AWROOOOOOOOO

11

BLOODHOUNDS--! AND A POSSE OF BELTON'S SWEET PATOOTIES!

ARRUUOOW ARROOOOO

THEY'RE TRACKING US... USING MY SHIRT FROM THE BUS TO GIVE THOSE MUTTS OUR SCENT!

YOUR SCENT, BRUCE! BEING HALF KRYPTONIAN I DON'T HAVE A SCENT!

BAD SCENE! THE HOUNDS FOUND US!

ARROOOO ARROOOO

WHAT ARE WE WAITING FOR?

THOSE TWO FUGITIVES ARE UP THERE!

FIRE! KILL THEM! BIG SISTER MUST BE OBEYED!!

I...I CAN'T! IT'S... COLD-BLOODED MURDER!

I AGREE, DIANA! BETTER WE CAPTURE THEM! ALL OF US CAN EASILY TAKE JUST TWO ORDINARY MALES!

YOU'RE WEAK AND SOFT-HEARTED! WE'LL CARRY OUT SYBIL'S SACRED COMMANDS WITHOUT YOU!

SHOOT--!

POW POW POW KPOW KAPOW

A FUSILLADE OF DEADLY FIRE BURSTS INTO THE SHADOWY REACHES OF A SHELTERING TREE! WHAT HAPPENS TO ITS TWIN TARGETS IN PART 2...NEXT?

12

PART 2 THE GREATEST HATE

A HAIL OF METAL SLUGS RIPS THROUGH TANGLED BRANCHES AND DROOPING SPANISH MOSS, WHERE THE HEIRS OF *SUPERMAN* AND *BATMAN* PERCHED...

ZIIP

BEEEOW

BWEEEEE

WHILE ACROSS THE SWAMP MOON, A STRANGE, BIRD-LIKE SHAPE SOARS...

... A "BIRD" WHICH DESCENDS SOME DISTANCE AWAY!

EASY ENOUGH TO ESCAPE THAT POSSE OF BELTON'S BELLES, BRUCIE ... BUT IT'S SURE THOSE HOUNDS WILL PICK UP YOUR SCENT AGAIN!

SO IT'S *COSTUME-SWITCH* TIME!

BY WEARING *YOUR* CAPE AND COWL OUTFIT WITH THEIR TELLTALE SCENT, THE HOUNDS WILL FOLLOW ME! IT'LL BE A CINCH TO LEAD THEM BACK TO TOWN!

I DIG! AND WEARING *YOUR* SUPER THREADS, I CAN FADE INTO THE WOODWORK AND DO A LITTLE SLEUTHING!

MOMENTS LATER...

HERE THEY COME... BUT THEY'LL NEVER KNOW WHO THEY'RE TRACKING!

AROOOOO

ARROOOO

NOW I PLAY TARZAN AND GO THE OTHER WAY... KEEPING OUT OF SIGHT!

13

Sisters, you have betrayed the cause!

DIANA AND SARA... BEING HASSLED BY THE MONOLITH!

I cannot take any more chances with you both! Look into the eye of BIG SISTER!

LOOK... AND OBEY!

WOWW!! TH-THEY'RE HYPNOTIZED...AND WALKING...

...RIGHT INTO...

...THE MONOLITH!

YOU! STAY BACK!

YOU SAW MY SUPER POWERS BEFORE, BIG SIS! YOUR EYE AND YOUR FORCE FIELD CAN'T STOP ME LIKE IT DID MY BAT-BUDDY!

MY BLUFF WORKED! NEXT STOP...INSIDE!

BUT THE DISGUISED SON OF BATMAN SUDDENLY IS WHIRLED THROUGH A RINGING DARK VOID...

...TO EMERGE A MOMENT LATER...

I...I'M AT AN OLD SAWMILL IN THE THICKEST PART OF THE SWAMP?! BUT HOW--?

14

THEN AS HE ENTERS THE MOLDERING MILL...

ARRRRRRRR

GNNNNRRRRRRR

BEASTS-- OH, NO--!

CAN'T OUTRUN THEM! GOTTA FIND A PLACE ...TO HIDE!

RRRNNNRR

GAAAARRRRRK

QUICKSAND! I'M GOING DOWN... BUT SO ARE THEY!

AARRR

GNNNNRRR

THEIR HEAVY WEIGHT... MAKING THEM SINK FASTER!

AARRR

AIIIII

AND AS THE SUCKING, CLUTCHING MORASS CLOSES OVER THE NIGHTMARISH CREATURES...

I WANT TO LIVE!

BEFORE IT WENT UNDER... THAT THING... SPOKE?! ITS VOICE... I RECOGNIZED IT!

BUT IF I SINK ANY FURTHER... I'LL BE A SAND SLUG'S SUPPER!

15

NOW, AS EVEN THE BOLD HEART OF *BATMAN'S* SON FEELS PANIC...

SUPES! PULL ME OUT... QUICK!

WHY... ARE YOU... JUST *STANDING* THERE?

BECAUSE, LITTLE BUDDY, MY COSTUME DOESN'T ABSORB ANYTHING... THAT'S AS FAR AS IT WILL LET YOU SINK!

NOW YOU TELL ME! BUT WAIT'LL I TELL YOU WHAT HAPPENED!

SOON AS WE SWITCH, BRUCE! FLYING BACK FROM TOWN, A *REAL* BAT GOT INTERESTED IN ME!

BUT AS THE TWO COMRADES RESUME THEIR REGULAR ROLES...

...AND THAT'S THE INCREDIBLE STORY!

YEEOW! ANOTHER ONE!

THAT SINGLE EYE... LIKE *BIG SISTER SYBIL!?*

Yes, it is I, *SYBIL!*

I am from another world... the Monolith is both my spacecraft and remote identity in dealing with you mere Earthlings!

THAT'S WHY YOU DIDN'T KNOW WHO WE WERE?

Exactly! And I kept hidden so my disciples, those foolish Earth females, wouldn't guess I was changing them into ugly things... like *ME!*

THE BEAST WITH THE VOICE I RECOGNIZED-- IT WAS *DIANA*... AND THE OTHER *HAD* TO BE SARA!

Yes, a serum I put in the Belton water supply was slowly changing all the girls... but for those two wavering girls, I hastened the change, using the Monolith's special energy!

16

THEN THE WHOLE IDEA OF A MAN-HATING TOWN WAS TO KEEP THE GIRLS *ISOLATED* WHILE YOU DID YOUR HORRIBLE WORK?

Absolutely! The *ONLY* antidote to the serum was a *MALE'S* touch!

Hence my rigid rule against contact with men!

BUT.. BUT *WHY* DID YOU COME TO OUR WORLD AND DO *THIS?*

I was exiled from my own world for being *HIDEOUS!* Thus, I *HATE* all who are beautiful and must make them share my fate --*ETERNAL UGLINESS!*

I can't even stand looking at *MYSELF!*

Since you could warn my victims, I will give myself the added pleasure of destroying you!

YOU GOTTA BE KIDDING, GRUESOME! MY PAL, HERE, WILL *CLOBBER* YOU!

SUPES--?

HE'S... HE'S.... *GONE!?*

He may have formidable powers... but evidently lacks the courage to face me in combat!

STAY BACK, YOU GROTTY GOON!

KRAAAKK

THAT'S--

--*FAR*--

--*ENOUGH!*

17

NOW, AS A STRANGE GLOW SUFFUSES THE SWAMP SKY...

AS THE MONOLITH STREAKS AWAY LIKE A "RISING STAR"...

BUT HOW COULD EVEN *YOU* PICK IT UP WHEN IT WASN'T SOLID SUBSTANCE!

BY VIBRATING MY MOLECULES UNTIL THEY EQUALED THE OTHER-WORLD FREQUENCY OF THE MONOLITH'S OWN ATOMS...

...AND PRESTO, IT TURNED *SOLID!*

AND IN A SHORT TIME, LIGHT-YEARS FROM EARTH...

SYBIL, FOR YOUR CRIMES ON THAT POOR, PRIMITIVE PLANET, WE SENTENCE YOU TO THE ULTIMATE PUNISHMENT...

THE MONOLITH ...RISING INTO SPACE...?

MY HUNCH WAS SYBIL KEPT CLEAR OF THE MONOLITH BECAUSE BY RE-ENTERING IT, IT WOULD TRIGGER A RETURN TO HER HOME PLANET!

AND THERE SHE GOES!

...SEEING YOUR HIDEOUS SELF REFLECTED FOR ETERNITY!

OH, *NO!* ANYTHING BUT *THAT!*

LATER, IN THE VILLAGE OF BELTON...

SARA AND DIANA DEAD... AND *BIG SISTER SYBIL* A HORRIBLE ALIEN CREATURE WHO WAS DOOMING US INTO MONSTROSITIES! IT'S INCREDIBLE! AWFUL!

BUT THE *WORST* PART... THE ONLY ANTIDOTE TO *STOP* THE CHANGE...

...IS THIS!

LINE UP, GIRLS!

OH, BROTHER!

18

THE END

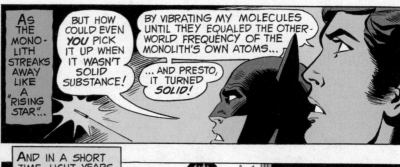

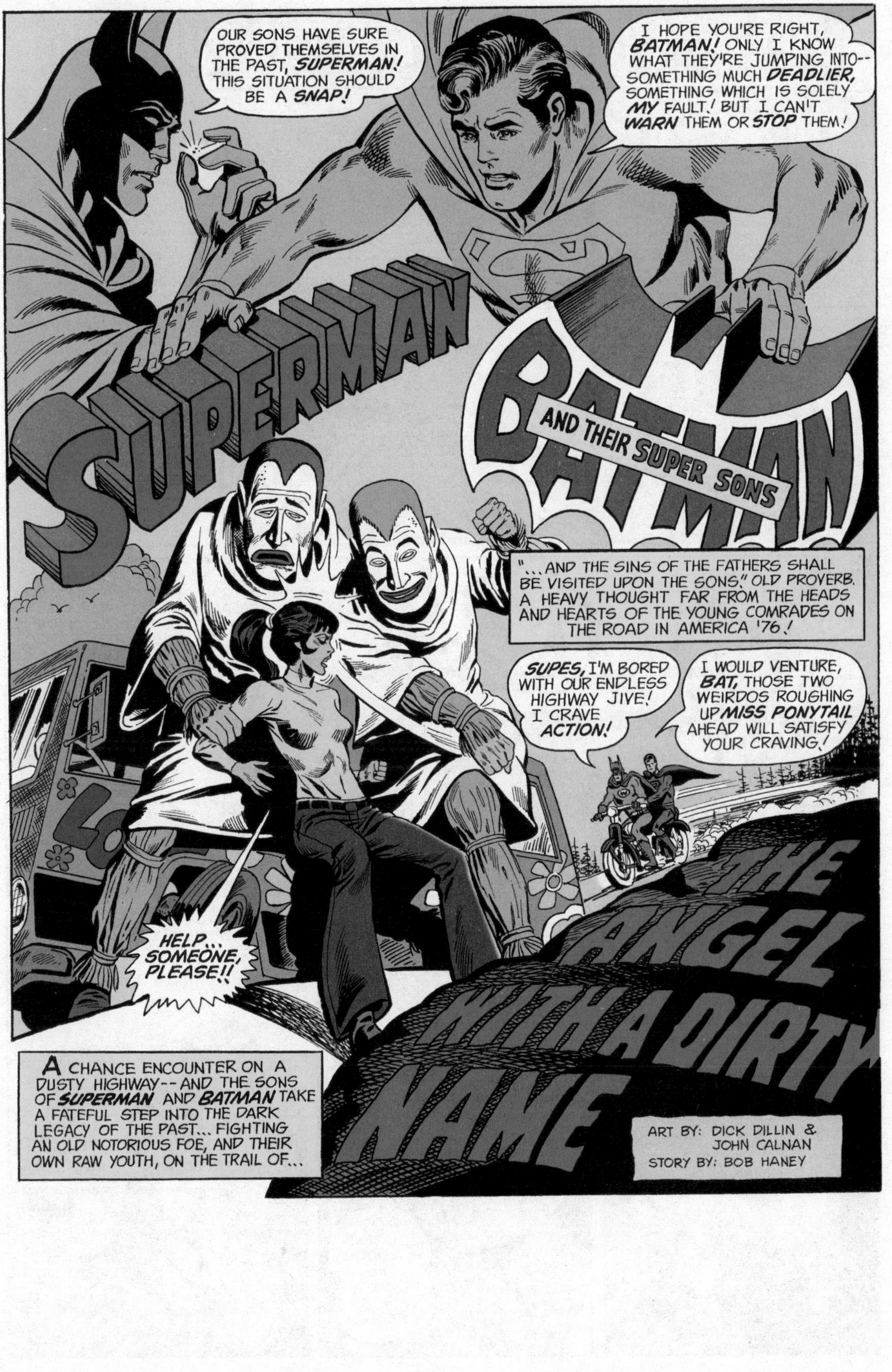

OUR SONS HAVE SURE PROVED THEMSELVES IN THE PAST, SUPERMAN! THIS SITUATION SHOULD BE A SNAP!
I HOPE YOU'RE RIGHT, BATMAN! ONLY I KNOW WHAT THEY'RE JUMPING INTO-- SOMETHING MUCH DEADLIER, SOMETHING WHICH IS SOLELY MY FAULT! BUT I CAN'T WARN THEM OR STOP THEM!
SUPERMAN
BATMAN
AND THEIR SUPER SONS
"...AND THE SINS OF THE FATHERS SHALL BE VISITED UPON THE SONS," OLD PROVERB. A HEAVY THOUGHT FAR FROM THE HEADS AND HEARTS OF THE YOUNG COMRADES ON THE ROAD IN AMERICA '76!
SUPES, I'M BORED WITH OUR ENDLESS HIGHWAY JIVE! I CRAVE ACTION!
I WOULD VENTURE, BAT, THOSE TWO WEIRDOS ROUGHING UP MISS PONYTAIL AHEAD WILL SATISFY YOUR CRAVING!
HELP... SOMEONE, PLEASE!!
THE ANGEL WITH A DIRTY NAME
A CHANCE ENCOUNTER ON A DUSTY HIGHWAY-- AND THE SONS OF SUPERMAN AND BATMAN TAKE A FATEFUL STEP INTO THE DARK LEGACY OF THE PAST... FIGHTING AN OLD NOTORIOUS FOE, AND THEIR OWN RAW YOUTH, ON THE TRAIL OF...
ART BY: DICK DILLIN & JOHN CALNAN
STORY BY: BOB HANEY

PART ONE THOSE WHO PLAY THE PUPPETS

THE "HOT HOG" SKIDS TO A HALT AND FAMOUS SONS OF FAMOUS FATHERS GO ON THE ATTACK!

CHIVALRY IS NOT DEAD! IT MERELY *SLEEPS*...

DORA'S MOBILE PUPPET THEATRE

...AND SO WILL *YOU*, BUSTER!

WHOK

HEY, MAN! WE GIVE UP!

KWAM

OKAY, GOONS--OFF WITH THOSE THREADS AND HIT THE MACADAM AWAY FROM HERE... *FAST*!

WE'RE *GOIN'*! WE'RE *GOIN'*! OF ALL OUR ROTTEN LUCK,...TO MEET UP WITH THE *SUPER SONS* OUT HERE!

WHY WERE THOSE CLOWNS SLAPPING YOU AROUND, DOLL?

I'M DORA REDSON! I GIVE SHOWS IN SCHOOLS, GHETTOS, MIGRANT LABOR CAMPS...EVERYWHERE AND ANYWHERE PEOPLE NEED ENTERTAINMENT!

DORA'S MOBILE PUPPET THEA

THOSE TWO WERE HITCHHIKERS I HIRED TO PLAY IN MY ENTERTAINMENTS!

WHEN MY VAN BROKE DOWN, THEY QUIT AND DEMANDED THEIR MONEY! I COULDN'T PAY THEM!

WELL, I'LL TAKE A SMOOCH FOR COMING TO YOUR RESCUE!

HE'S THE *SUPER* ONE, SO HE RATES A *SUPER* KISS!

OH, NO! ANOTHER CHICK WHO GOES FOR GOOD OLD NOBLE YOU!

THE WHEEL COLLAPSED... I'VE NOBODY TO PLAY THE PUPPET PARTS! AND I WAS TO GIVE A SHOW FOR THE CONVICTS AT KINGMAN PRISON!

NO PROBLEM, DORA!

TAKE ONLY A MINUTE TO REPAIR!

HE'S THE LIFTER... I'M THE LOVER!

SHE DOESN'T HEAR ME!

THE MASKED GIRLHUNTER AND I HAVEN'T ANYTHING BIG ON SO WE CAN BE YOUR PUPPETS-- IF YOU'LL HAVE US, DORA!

WILL I HAVE YOU? THAT CALLS FOR ANOTHER KISS!

A CERTAIN MONOTONY IS SETTING IN!

AND SO, THE SWASHBUCKLING OFFSPRING OF SUPERMAN AND BATMAN TAKE ANOTHER TURN IN THEIR UNIQUE YOUNG LIVES!

I'M WRITING NEW THINGS FOR THE SHOW TO SUIT BOTH OF YOU!

GREAT! HOW ABOUT GIVING ME THE LOVE SCENES-- SINCE OLD "STRAIGHT ARROW" GETS ALL THE REHEARSALS?

BRRRR, GRIM AS DRACULA'S CASTLE!

THAT'S WHY THE INMATES NEED CONTACT WITH THE OUTSIDE, TO PRESERVE THEIR SANITY AND HUMANITY!

KINGMAN MAXIMUM SECURITY PRISON
ALL VEHICLES STOP AT GUARD GATE

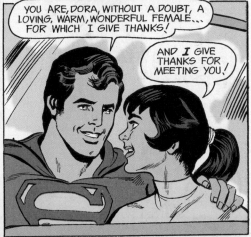

YOU ARE, DORA, WITHOUT A DOUBT, A LOVING, WARM, WONDERFUL FEMALE... FOR WHICH I GIVE THANKS!

AND I GIVE THANKS FOR MEETING YOU!

LATER...

WE'LL GIVE THEM AND DORA A GOOD PERFORMANCE!

SURE, I'VE LEARNED PLENTY ABOUT PLAY-ACTING, BEING THE WORLD'S NUMBER 2 BATMAN!

THE CURTAIN RISES, AND FOR A WHILE HARDENED, HOPELESS MEN FIND RELIEF FROM THEIR GRIM, DAILY LIVES...

OH, GOG, PLEASE HELP ME! IF THAT DEVILISH DEVICE GOES OFF, THE TOWN WILL BE DESTROYED AND MAGOG WILL CARRY ME AWAY!

BOMB

NEVER FEAR, DEAR GIRL! GOG WILL THROW IT FAR INTO THE SKY...

BOMB

BA-RROOM

...WHERE IT WILL EXPLODE HARMLESSLY!

AND AS FOR MAGOG, LET HIM TASTE THE MIGHT OF MY RIGHTEOUS RIGHT!

PTOW

AND AFTER THE CURTAIN FALLS...

THEY DUG IT, SUPES! BUT DID YOU HAVE TO BELT ME THAT HARD?

CLAP

SORRY, CHUM, I GUESS MY PART GOT AWAY FROM ME!

LET'S CHANGE! WE'RE TO MEET MY LOVIN' DORA IN THE WARDEN'S OFFICE!

CLAP

HI, WARDEN! DORA NOT HERE YET?

SHE'S *GONE!* AND SO IS OUR MOST DANGEROUS PRISONER-- *LEX LUTHOR!*

I'M HOLDING YOU TWO *FOR AIDING HIM* TO ESCAPE!

LEX LUTHOR?

YES, YOUR FEMALE ACCOMPLICE DROVE THROUGH THE GATES HALF AN HOUR AGO ....SHE SAID YOU TWO WOULD FOLLOW!

A CELL-CHECK LATER REVEALED *LUTHOR,* MISSING!

HE WASN'T IN HER TRUCK! THE GUARD GAVE IT A ROUTINE SEARCH!

I DON'T KNOW HOW YOU DID IT, BUT SOMEHOW, YOU TWO AND THAT GIRL SPRUNG HIM!

THAT'S SENSELESS! I HELP FREE MY FATHER'S *WORST ENEMY?*

WE DIDN'T EVEN KNOW *LUTHOR* WAS CONFINED HERE! AS FOR DORA, WE MET HER ONLY TODAY!

WE'RE GETTING NOWHERE HERE!

VEEOW

BEOEEOW

TZIIING

KPOW

KPOW

KPOW

STOP THEM! *FIRE!*

WHAT'S THIS? THE *SUPER SONS* FLEEING OFFICIAL CUSTODY? SHORTLY, A LONG, LONG LEAP BEYOND THE PRISON WALLS...

NOW YOU'VE TORN IT, *MUSCLES!* WHY THE BIG BUST-OUT ACT?

HOW COULD I FACE DAD AFTER HELPING HIS ARCH-FOE, *LUTHOR,* GET OUT?

BUT WE *DIDN'T!*

I'M NOT SO SURE! MY KRYPTONIAN HALF HAS A HUNCH DORA *DID* SPRING HIM-- USING US SOMEHOW!

COME ON, BUDDY... *LET'S FIND THEM!*

AGAIN, THE TWO SOUL BROTHERS TAKE TO THE AIR, AND SOON, ABOVE A HIDDEN RAVINE...

THERE IT IS-- DORA'S TRUCK AND A SPACE SHIP--? WONDER IF SHE'S INSIDE?

YOU CLAIM YOU ARE MY OWN DAUGHTER, ARDORA, FROM THE PLANET LEXOR? BUT I NEVER KNEW YOU EXISTED!

I WAS BORN YEARS AGO WHILE YOU WERE AWAY ON EARTH! MOTHER WAS SO ASHAMED I WAS NOT A SON...

...SHE HID MY EXISTENCE AND GROWING-UP YEARS FROM YOU! BUT NOW, BELOVED FATHER, I'M HERE TO PROVE MYSELF WORTHY TO BEAR THE NOBLE NAME OF LUTHOR!

DORA IS LUTHOR'S DAUGHTER!

THOUGH THE EVIL SUPERMAN IMPRISONED YOU UNJUSTLY ON EARTH, YOUR GREAT GENIUS IS NEEDED BACK ON LEXOR, NAMED IN HONOR OF ITS LEADING HERO!

BUT WE WASTE PRECIOUS TIME!

HATCH CLOSED! STAND BY FOR TAKE-OFF!

CLANNG

AND WITH A SUDDEN THRUST OF POWERFUL NUCLEAR ENGINES...

VROOOS SSSHHH

WHAT HAVE WE GOTTEN INTO? I NEVER LEFT MOMMA EARTH BEFORE!

TOO LATE NOW! GOT TO HANG IN AND BRING LUTHOR BACK!

THE SUPER SONS HEADING TOWARD THE FAR GALAXIES ...AND SHATTERING SURPRISES IN PART 2...NEXT!!

LEX LUTHOR HAS JUST MET A DAUGHTER HE NEVER KNEW EXISTED, AND WHILE TWO STOWAWAYS EAVESDROP, MORE AMAZING REVELATIONS UNFOLD...

SO, IT WAS *YOU* WHO SENT ME THAT CODED LETTER SETTING UP MY ESCAPE?

YES, MY TRAVELING PUPPET SHOW WAS A PERFECT COVER FOR GETTING INTO THE PRISON...

"...WHERE IT WAS SO SIMPLE FOR YOU TO DROP OUT OF THE AUDIENCE AND BE CONCEALED IN MY STAGE PROP BOMB..."

"AND EASY FOR YOU TO BE EJECTED, ONCE *SUPERMAN, JR.* TOSSED THE BOMB INTO THE SKY, WHERE THE FIREWORKS FLASH HID YOU FROM VIEW..."

BA-ROOOOMM

BUMB

MY BROKEN-DOWN VAN AND BEING ATTACKED WERE PART OF THE PLOT TO GET THE *SUPER SONS'* HELP! I KNEW THEY WERE TRAVELING THAT WAY!

YOU'RE A BEAUTIFUL CHIP OFF THE OLD BLOCK! WHAT SWEET REVENGE ON *SUPERMAN*, HIS OWN SON FOOLED INTO HELPING ME! HA-HA-HA!

SORRY, PAL! YOU WERE RIGHT AS RAIN WITH THAT HUNCH!

I REALLY FELT A WARM THING FOR ARDORA! I STILL DO!

AFTER ALL, HER FATHER IS A HERO TO HER, AND HIS ESCAPE JUSTIFIED!

AND AS THE SLEEK CRAFT HURTLES FURTHER INTO SPACE....

YOU SAY, ARDORA, I'M *NEEDED* BACK ON LEXOR....?

A MYSTERIOUS PLAGUE HAS STRUCK OUR PEOPLE! MANY HAVE GROWN INTO PONDEROUS GIANTS...

"...THEIR BODIES GROTESQUELY BLOATED! THEY BLUNDER INTO BUILDINGS... SINK INTO THE VERY SOIL, ARE A MENACE TO ALL..."

OUR MEDICAL MEN, OUR SCIENTISTS ARE BAFFLED! ONLY *YOU,* WHO SAVED OUR CIVILIZATION FROM DECAY AND REVIVED ITS SCIENCE, CAN FIND A CURE!

TRUSTING CHILD! HOW CAN I REVEAL TO HER THAT *I* AM THE CAUSE OF THE AFFLICTION?

I SECRETLY LEFT A GERM "TIME BOMB" ON LEXOR, WHICH LATER TRIGGERED OFF THE *GIANTISM* PLAGUE!

SHOULD I BE AGAIN IMPRISONED ON EARTH, I KNEW MY LEXORIANS WOULD TRY TO FREE ME...

...AND RETURN ME TO MY ADOPTED PLANET, WHERE I'D QUICKLY HEAL THE VICTIMS WITH THE ANTIDOTE I SECRETED IN MY HIDDEN LABORATORY!

BUT I NEVER EXPECTED MY RESCUER WOULD BE MY OWN *DAUGHTER!* HOW SHE RESEMBLES MY BELOVED WIFE! IT WILL BE SO GOOD TO SEE HER AND ALL THE OTHERS AGAIN!

BUT THERE ARE TRAGIC SURPRISES AWAITING THE CUNNING SUPER-CRIMINAL AND THE STOWAWAY *SUPER SONS* ON LEXOR! FOR MILLIONS OF MILES LATER...

OUR *GREAT LUTHOR* HAS RETURNED... DELIVERED BY HIS *DUTIFUL DAUGHTER!*

NOW THE MALADY WILL BE CURED!

HAIL, LUTHOR!

SUDDENLY...

FATHER-- *LOOK OUT!*

KRAAACCCKK

FORGIVE ME, GREAT LUTHOR! THE SICKNESS ...I CANNOT CONTROL MYSELF!

NEVER MIND, MY GOOD FELLOW! I'LL HAVE YOU AND ALL THE OTHERS CURED IN NO TIME!

BUT WHERE IS MY WIFE? *WHERE'S ARDORA?*

MOTHER! SHE'S ALSO A VICTIM! BUT SHE WASN'T SICK WHEN I LEFT!

LEX.... *MY HUSBAND! HELP...* ME!

THIS IS TERRIBLE! BUT DON'T DESPAIR, WIFE! I AM HERE NOW!

NEVER FEAR, MY TWO ARDORAS! I AM OFF TO MY LAB TO QUICKLY PREPARE AN ANTIDOTE--FOR AM I NOT THE GREATEST SCIENTIST IN THE UNIVERSE?

OH, YES--YES, FATHER, AND THEN WE'LL BE ONE HAPPY, REUNITED FAMILY!

UNNOTICED IN THE FUROR OVER LUTHOR'S RETURN, TWO STOWAWAYS HAVE SLIPPED OUT OF THE SPACE CRAFT...

OKAY, SO OUR DUTY'S TO TAKE LUTHOR BACK TO EARTH JUSTICE--BUT HADN'T WE BETTER FIRST LET HIM CURE THIS AWFUL PLAGUE?

AGREED! MEANTIME, WE'D BETTER KEEP WELL-HIDDEN!

WHREEE

WHREEEEEEOOOWWWWWW

THOSE FREAKY FLOWERS--WAILING LIKE SIRENS!?

LET'S CLEAR OUT OF HERE!

THE EVIL SUPERMAN HAS RETURNED TO LEXOR! THE SIREN FLOWERS REACT TO HIS COSTUME'S COLORS!

SEIZE HIM AND HIS COMRADE!

REEEEEOOOOOOOWWW

THEY THINK I'M DAD! BUT EVEN WITH MY HALF SUPER STRENGTH, I CAN TOPPLE THEM BACK LIKE DOMINOES!

DIDN'T STOP HIM?

UFFFFFF I'M STAGGERED--?

WHOKK

AND AS BURLY ATTACKERS SWARM OVER THEM...

SUPES? WHY DON'T YOU CLOBBER THESE GORILLAS?

I.... I FORGOT! THIS PLANET'S RED SUN... IT ROBS ME OF MY POWERS JUST LIKE IT DID DAD!!

NOT LONG AFTER...

YOU WILL REMAIN PRISONERS IN THE FORCE FIELD UNTIL MY FATHER RETURNS AND DECIDES YOUR FATE!

ARDORA! I REALIZE NOW YOU BROUGHT YOUR FATHER HERE FOR A GOOD CAUSE--BUT LOOK AT THE MEANS YOU USED!

YOU BROKE EARTH'S LAWS, ENDANGERED LIVES, AND BETRAYED US, WHO BEFRIENDED YOU!

TO SAY NOTHING OF TRAMPLING ON THE LOVE I FEEL FOR YOU! I FORGIVE YOU BECAUSE YOU'RE CONFUSED AND UPSET OVER YOUR MOTHER!

I DON'T NEED YOUR FORGIVENESS...OR YOUR LOVE!

I'VE HEARD ENOUGH!

CLEVER PSYCHOLOGY, PAL--THAT PHONY I-STILL-LOVE-YOU-DOLL ROUTINE GOT HER GOING... BUT NOT ENOUGH!

IT WASN'T PHONY! I STILL FEEL THAT WAY ABOUT ARDORA! SHE'S A GREAT GIRL!

SHAMEFUL SON OF A SHAMEFUL FATHER! IT WASN'T ENOUGH *SUPERMAN* PURSUES AND PERSECUTES GREAT LUTHOR...

...NOW *YOU* FOLLOW IN HIS HATED FOOTSTEPS!

WHAT A CRAZY MIXED-UP PLACE! HERE, *SUPERMAN* IS *BAD,* AND *LUTHOR* IS *GOOD!* AND *WE'RE* SUFFERING FOR IT!

THAT'S NOT ALL! FOR HELPING LUTHOR ESCAPE, OUR DADS WILL PROBABLY NOT LET US BE SUPERHEROES AGAIN... *IF WE EVER GET BACK TO EARTH!*

"... AND THE SINS OF THE FATHERS WILL BE VISITED ON THE SONS!" MEANWHILE, BEYOND THE CITY, ONE FATHER HAS FOUND--CALAMITY!

A *METEOR*... IT WRECKED MY LAB! ITS RADIATION HAS RENDERED MY ANTIDOTE *USELESS* AGAINST THE PLAGUE!

IT WOULD TAKE *WEEKS* TO MAKE MORE OF THE COUNTERAGENT! BY THEN, THE GIANTISM EFFECTS WILL HAVE BECOME PERMANENT! MY BELOVED WIFE... THE OTHER LEXORIANS... THEY'LL BE DOOMED TO SPEND THE REST OF THEIR LIVES IN THAT AWFUL BLOATED STATE!

WHAT HAVE I DONE? I SHOULD NEVER HAVE TRIGGERED THE PLAGUE SO I'D BE RESCUED FROM EARTH JUSTICE, WHICH I WELL DESERVED!

IT WAS SELFISH--

SELFISH AND *WRONG!*

ARDORA!

I HURRIED HERE BECAUSE YOU MIGHT'VE NEEDED HELP MAKING THE ANTIDOTE! I TRAINED TO BECOME A GOOD SCIENTIST SO YOU'D BE *PROUD* OF ME!

NOW, I FIND IT WAS ALL *WASTED!*

THE *SUPER SONS* HELPLESS CAPTIVES, AND THE REAL LUTHOR EXPOSED! WHO NOW CAN SAVE THE INNOCENT PEOPLE OF LEXOR? THE ANSWER IN *PART 3...NEXT!*

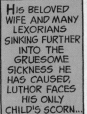

His beloved wife and many Lexorians sinking further into the gruesome sickness he has caused, Luthor faces his only child's scorn...

SHOW ME THAT THE MAN WE ALL WORSHIP STILL EXISTS! MAKE THE ANTIDOTE *AGAIN!* WITH MY HELP, IT MIGHT BE COMPLETED IN TIME!

I....I MEAN, WE...SHALL TRY, DAUGHTER!

Immediately, intensely, the two set to work! Desperate hours pass--and then!

THE REMEDY CAN BE MADE IN A *TENTH* THE TIME IF WE HAD THIS ELEMENT, ACCORDING TO MY FINDINGS!

YOU'RE A PERCEPTIVE, SHREWD SCIENTIST, ARDORA, BUT THAT EXISTS *ONLY* IN THE VENOM OF THE LEXORIAN *TERROR LIZARD*...

...WHICH LIVES IN THE *LOST ZONE,* FROM WHICH *NO ONE RETURNS!* IF THIS MACHINE WHICH ONCE GAVE ME *TEMPORARY* SUPER POWERS STILL WORKED, I'D *DARE* TO GO THERE, BUT...

FATHER! YOUNG *SUPERMAN* HAS SUCH POWERS!

YES, YES! I COULD FILTER OUT THE *RED SUN* EFFECTS SO HE'D REGAIN THEM...BUT MY GREATEST ENEMY'S SON WOULD *NEVER* HELP US!

THAT REMAINS TO BE SEEN! COME, FATHER!

I'VE BEEN WRONG ABOUT SOME THINGS, AND I'VE HURT YOU-- BUT *WILL YOU HELP?*

TO SAVE YOUR MOTHER AND OTHER INNOCENT VICTIMS? OF COURSE!

So shortly...

THE YELLOW SOLEX LIGHT BATH WILL ENABLE YOUR SKIN TO FILTER OUT THE RED SUN'S RAYS! BUT THE *LOST ZONE* IS A *DEADLY* PLACE!

THAT WON'T STOP US, LUTHOR!

US? YOU'RE NOT GOING, CHUM! YOU'LL BE IN THE WAY!

WHAT DO YOU MEAN? WE'RE A TEAM, AREN'T WE? TRY AND STOP ME!

PLEASE! TIME IS PRECIOUS! LIVES ARE AT STAKE!

NOT LONG AFTER, AN *IDENTIFIED FLYING OBJECT* HURTLES TOWARD THE *LOST ZONE!*

WE'LL JUST ZIP IN, LOCATE THE LIZARD, AND ZIP OUT...

KWAAAMMM

...AGAIN-- OOOUUFF

A *MAGNETIC SKY BARRIER!* THOSE WRECKED SHIPS TELL THE TALE! IT'S ALL *OVERLAND* FROM HERE ON!

I'M WITH YOU, PAL!

ACROSS DESOLATE, PARCHED BADLANDS' THE DUO GOES, THEN INTO CLUTCHING, BOILING BOGS...

I KNEW YOU'D NEED ME ON THIS TRIP! MORE TO THE *RIGHT,* SUPES!

SUDDENLY, AS THEY EMERGE...

YEEOW

SUPES CAN'T FLY IN THIS MAGNETIC SKY, BUT THIS THING CAN! GOT TO BE A REASON!

THIS GIZMO... MUST BE SOMETHING THE BUG EVOLVED TO CANCEL THE MAGNETISM! I'LL JUST...CANCEL....IT!

INSTANTLY, THE FLYING NIGHTMARE RELEASES THE JUNIOR *BATMAN* AND...

YEEOW! WHAT'D I DO? NEXT STOP... OBLIVION!

I *TOLD* YOU YOU'D GET IN MY WAY!

AND AM *I* GLAD YOU GOT IN *MINE!*

BETWEEN TOWERING CRAGS THE DUO CONTINUES...

KRAAK

AVALANCHE!

ROWNWAAARR

WHAT ARE YOU DOING--?

ROWNWAAAARRRR

FLATTEN!

WITH A ROARING THUNDER LIKE THE END OF A WORLD, THE AVALANCHE FILLS THE NARROW VALLEY...

ROWWAAARRR

AND THEN...

WHEW! THAT WAS CLOSE!

I FEEL FUNNY... HOPE I'M NOT LOSING MY SUPER POWERS AGAIN...

SUPES! YOUR FACE AND BODY! THAT GIANTISM DISEASE... YOU'RE GETTING IT!!

OH, NO!

SUPERMAN'S HEIR SINKS HEAVILY ONTO A LARGE ENCRUSTED ROCK...

IT'S MOVING ...THE TERROR LIZARD!!

THE HUGE BEAST LUNGES TO ATTACK...

CLOBBER IT!

CAN'T! I'M GROWING BIGGER... AND MY COSTUME'S... CHOKING ME!

THOUGH NOT MADE OF EXPANDABLE KRYPTONIAN FABRIC LIKE HIS FATHER'S, JUNIOR'S COSTUME IS STILL INCREDIBLY STRONG...

SUPES! IT'S AFTER ME!

CAN... HARDLY... MOVE!

WITH A LAST EFFORT, A PONDEROUS ARM IS THRUST INTO THE LIZARD'S SLAVERING MAW...

Y-YOU'RE SHRINKING DOWN TO *NORMAL*?

THE ANTI-GIANTISM EFFECTS OF THE VENOM!

LUCKY I REMEMBERED IT! NOW TO PUT OLD FANG TO SLEEP AND HEAD OUT OF HERE!!

KWOKK

SOME TIME LATER...

SMART THINKING, YOUNG MAN! ALL I NEED REMOVE IS ONE PINT OF YOUR BLOOD THAT CONTAINS ENOUGH VENOM TO MAKE THE ANTIDOTE FOR ALL THE PLAGUE SUFFERERS!

AND AFTER ALL THE VICTIMS HAVE BEEN INJECTED WITH THE SERUM...

THAT WRAPS IT UP, CHUM! EVERYONE'S CURED AND LUTHOR'S FAMILY REUNITED!

FOR LUTHOR NOW, IT'S BACK TO EARTH! WE MAY HAVE A PROBLEM ...BECAUSE HE'S SURE TO *RESIST* AND HIS PEOPLE WILL ASSIST HIM!

LUTHOR IS LEAVING *WILLINGLY*?

WHAT ELSE CAN HE DO? MY *X-RAY VISION* SHOWS ARDORA IS *MAKING* HIM DO IT WITH A WEAPON AT HIS BACK!

THANK YOU, ARDORA! I KNOW HOW MUCH THIS COST YOU!

I OWE IT TO YOU FOR WHAT YOU DID! THIS WAY, AFTER MY FATHER PAYS HIS DEBT ON EARTH, HE CAN RETURN HERE TO US!

UNTIL THEN, REMEMBER ME... REMEMBER ARDORA!

WHO COULD FORGET LUTHOR'S DAUGHTER? CERTAINLY NOT THE *SUPER SONS* WHO'LL RETURN IN FUTURE ISSUES OF... *WORLD'S FINEST!!*

END

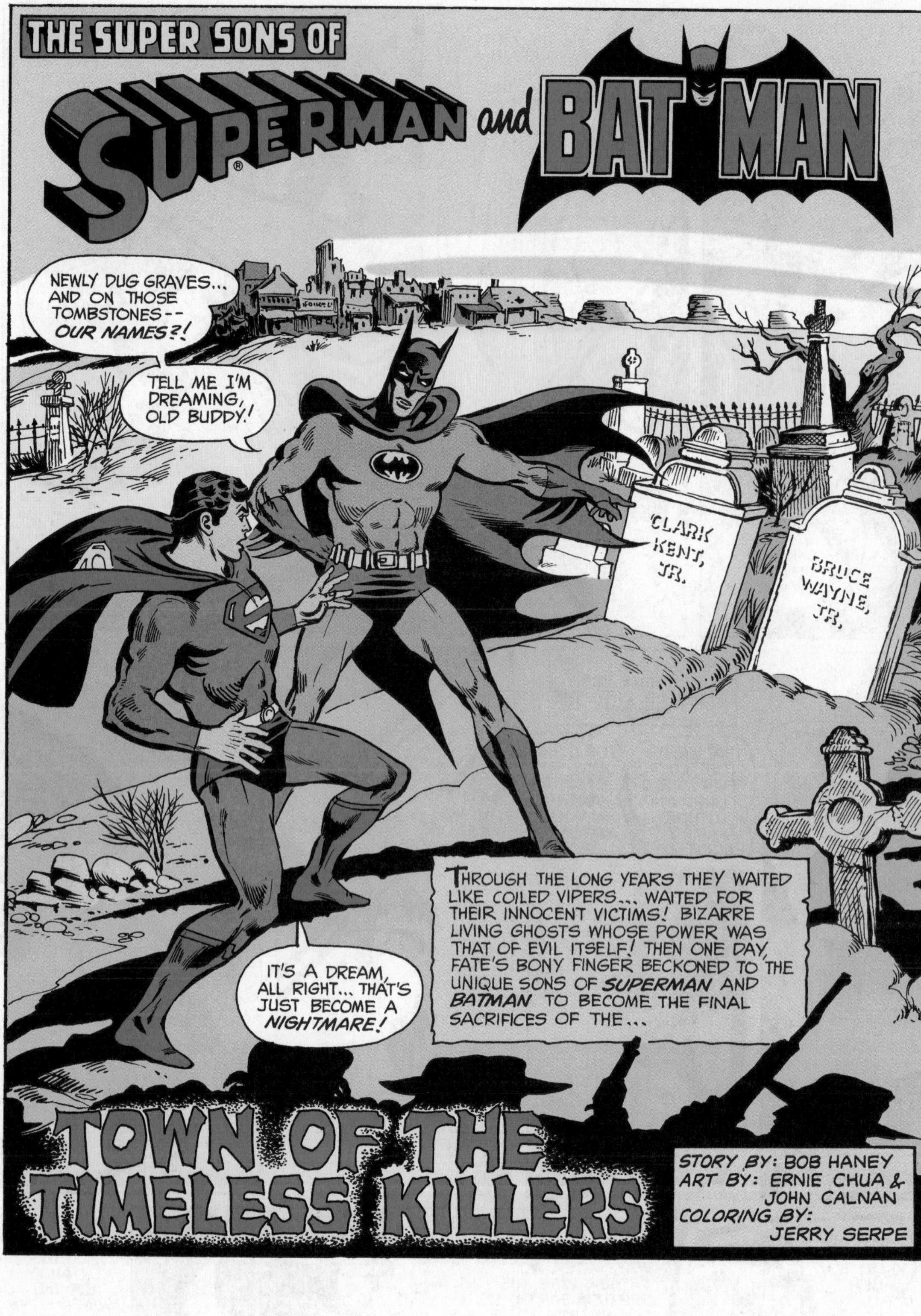
THE SUPER SONS OF
SUPERMAN and BATMAN
NEWLY DUG GRAVES... AND ON THOSE TOMBSTONES-- OUR NAMES?!
TELL ME I'M DREAMING, OLD BUDDY!
CLARK KENT, JR.
BRUCE WAYNE, JR.
IT'S A DREAM, ALL RIGHT... THAT'S JUST BECOME A NIGHTMARE!
THROUGH THE LONG YEARS THEY WAITED LIKE COILED VIPERS... WAITED FOR THEIR INNOCENT VICTIMS! BIZARRE LIVING GHOSTS WHOSE POWER WAS THAT OF EVIL ITSELF! THEN ONE DAY, FATE'S BONY FINGER BECKONED TO THE UNIQUE SONS OF SUPERMAN AND BATMAN TO BECOME THE FINAL SACRIFICES OF THE...
TOWN OF THE TIMELESS KILLERS
STORY BY: BOB HANEY
ART BY: ERNIE CHUA & JOHN CALNAN
COLORING BY: JERRY SERPE

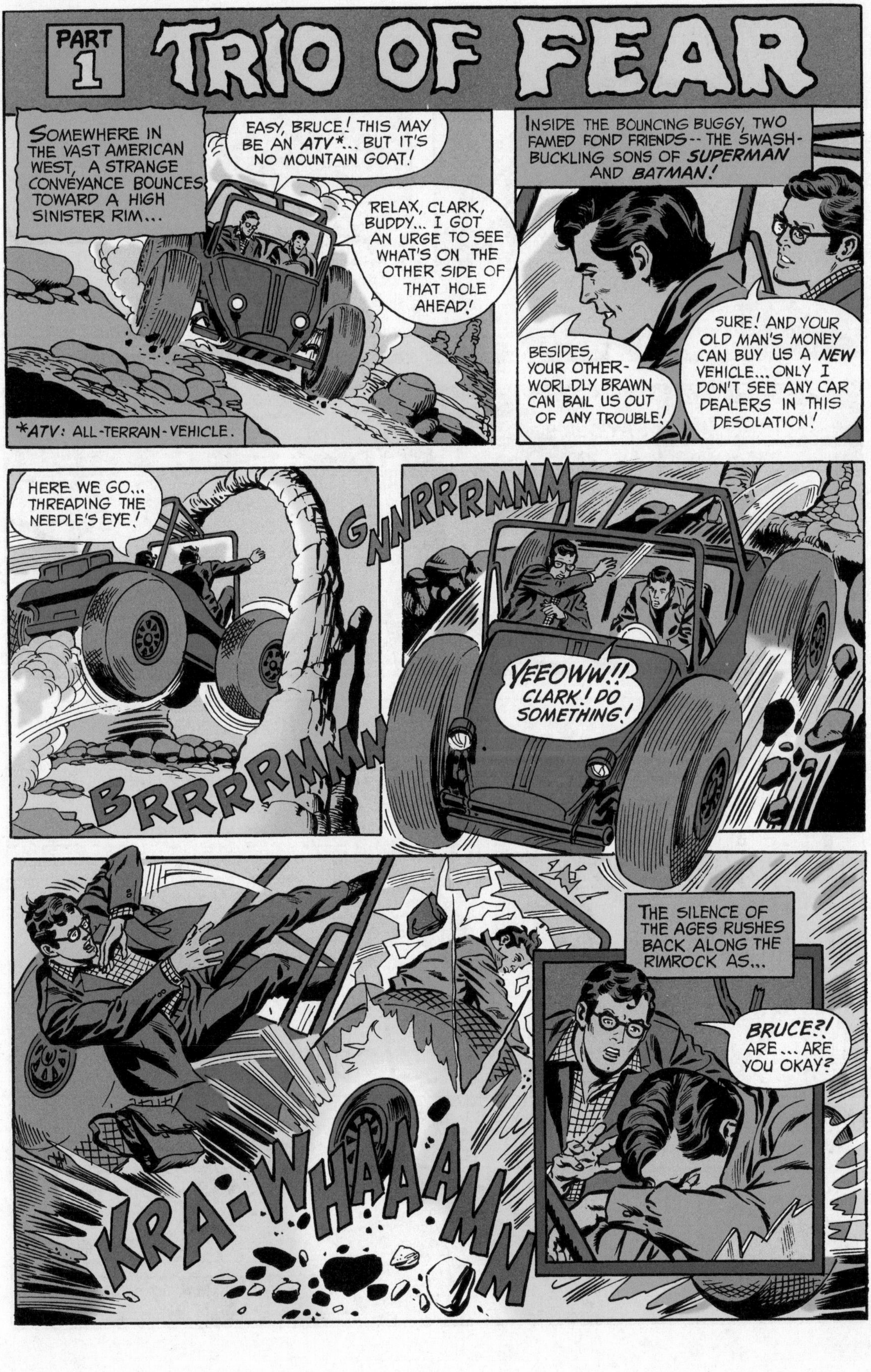
PART 1
TRIO OF FEAR
SOMEWHERE IN THE VAST AMERICAN WEST, A STRANGE CONVEYANCE BOUNCES TOWARD A HIGH SINISTER RIM...
EASY, BRUCE! THIS MAY BE AN ATV*... BUT IT'S NO MOUNTAIN GOAT!
RELAX, CLARK, BUDDY... I GOT AN URGE TO SEE WHAT'S ON THE OTHER SIDE OF THAT HOLE AHEAD!
*ATV: ALL-TERRAIN-VEHICLE.
INSIDE THE BOUNCING BUGGY, TWO FAMED FOND FRIENDS -- THE SWASH-BUCKLING SONS OF SUPERMAN AND BATMAN!
BESIDES, YOUR OTHER-WORLDLY BRAWN CAN BAIL US OUT OF ANY TROUBLE!
SURE! AND YOUR OLD MAN'S MONEY CAN BUY US A NEW VEHICLE... ONLY I DON'T SEE ANY CAR DEALERS IN THIS DESOLATION!
HERE WE GO... THREADING THE NEEDLE'S EYE!
BRRRRMMM
GNNRRRMMMM
YEEOWW!! CLARK! DO SOMETHING!
KRA-WHAAAMM
THE SILENCE OF THE AGES RUSHES BACK ALONG THE RIMROCK AS...
BRUCE?! ARE... ARE YOU OKAY?

I... I'M OKAY, I THINK... EXCEPT MY SPINE FEELS LIKE A COOKED NOODLE!

SUDDENLY, I *DIDN'T* HAVE MY *POWERS!* ALL I COULD DO WAS LEAP CLEAR AT THE LAST SEC!

SOME *SUPER PAL!* WHY DIDN'T YOU PULL US OUT OF THAT *KAMIKAZE DIVE?*

ORDINARILY I COULD CRUSH THIS ROCK TO POWDER...

STRANGER THAN REAL, MAN!

WHAT'S THAT DOWN BELOW? A TOWN... TUCKED AWAY IN THIS HIDDEN VALLEY? MAYBE WE CAN GET *NEW* WHEELS THERE!

BUT AS THE TWO TRUDGE DOWN INTO THE VALLEY FLOOR...

ENTERING DRY GULCH

BOOT HILL

A... *GHOST TOWN*... WITH THE USUAL *BOOT HILL* CEMETERY!

I DIG OLD WESTERN STUFF! LET'S RESEARCH THOSE MARKERS!

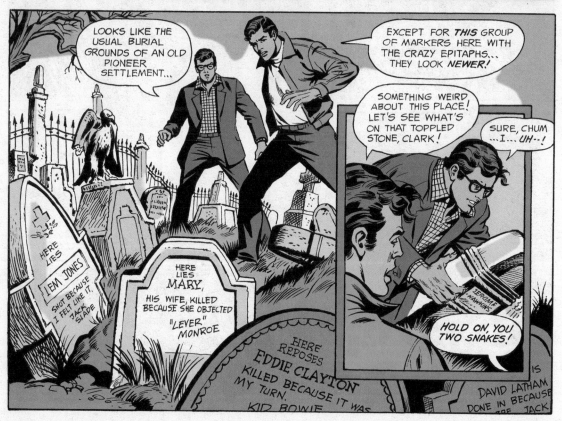

LOOKS LIKE THE USUAL BURIAL GROUNDS OF AN OLD PIONEER SETTLEMENT...

EXCEPT FOR *THIS* GROUP OF MARKERS HERE WITH THE CRAZY EPITAPHS... THEY LOOK *NEWER!*

SOMETHING WEIRD ABOUT THIS PLACE! LET'S SEE WHAT'S ON THAT TOPPLED STONE, CLARK!

SURE, CHUM ...I....UH--!

HOLD ON, YOU TWO SNAKES!

HERE LIES LEM JONES SHOT BECAUSE I FELT LIKE IT, JACK SLADE

HERE LIES MARY, HIS WIFE, KILLED BECAUSE SHE OBJECTED "LEVER" MONROE

HERE REPOSES EDDIE CLAYTON KILLED BECAUSE IT WAS MY TURN. KID BOWIE

DAVID LATHAM DONE IN BECAUSE JACK

HEY, THIS PLACE *ISN'T* DESERTED! THAT CHARACTER MUST BE AN ACTOR IN A MOVIE MADE HERE!

HI, FELLA! I'M CLARK KENT, JR. AND THIS IS BRUCE WAYNE, JR.!

I'LL HAVE BOTH YOUR NAMES CUT ON YOUR TOMBSTONES...REAL PRETTY! CATCH THAT KNIFE, BOY! *YOU'LL* DIE FIRST!

YOU KIDDING...?

KID BOWIE NEVER KIDS! NOW, CROW BAIT--FIGHT!

AAAAHH.!!

I...I'M CUT...BLEEDING! UUUHHHH.!!

CLARK! HE'S FAINTING!

THE NEXT MOMENT....!

I....I CAN'T BELIEVE THIS IS *HAPPENING!* MUST GET HIM AWAY FROM THAT MADMAN!

RUN, COWARDS! I'LL GET YOU YET!

BUT AS THE SHOCKED SON OF THE GREAT *BATMAN* FLEES WITH HIS BURDEN...

STOP RIGHT THERE, RANNY --AN' FACE ME!

GOOD GOD! *ANOTHER* CRAZY MAN!

BRUCE WAYNE JR, CAN FEEL THE WAVES OF COLD HATE COMING DOWN THE DUSTY STREET FROM THE FRIGHTENING FIGURE...

MY FRIEND'S HURT ...AND I'M UNARMED!

I'LL TOSS YOU A WEAPON! JACK SLADE ALWAYS GIVES HIS VICTIMS A FAIR CHANCE!

HERE! GRAB THIS AND DROP YOUR PAL!

MY ONLY CHANCE...TO MAKE THAT ALLEYWAY...!

YEOW

BWEE TZPP

THOSE ARE JUST CHASER SLUGS! "LEVER" MONROE LIKES HIS RABBITS REALLY DODGIN' BEFORE HE ZEROS IN!

POW POW

POW

BEOW ZIIIP VEEIP

MUST FIND COVER! THIS TOWN'S CRAWLIN' WITH INSANE KILLERS!

BULLETS... STITCHIN' A LINE RIGHT BEHIND ME!?

SAFE HERE ...BUT FOR HOW LONG?

WE KNOW YOU'RE HIDIN' SOMEWHERE! BUT IT'S NO USE! YOU CAN'T LEAVE DRY GULCH ...AN' YOU CAN'T ESCAPE US! YOU GOTTA DIE!!

IS THIS THE BEGINNING OF THE END FOR THE SUPER-SONS-- NOW REDUCED TO SKULKING FUGITIVES? PART 2 NEXT!

LATER, WHEN MERCIFUL DARKNESS HAS FALLEN OVER *DRY GULCH*-- INSIDE A DANK OLD TANK...

WHERE AM I?

HUNG UP... IN A WATER TOWER!

MY SHOULDER BANDAGED...? BRUCE MUST'VE DONE IT!

BUT WHERE IS HE...?

YOUR PARTNER, CLARK? HE'S SLIPPING LIKE A SHADOW PAST THREE UNBLINKING KILLERS WHO PATROL THE PRECINCTS OF THIS INCREDIBLE PLACE...

HE DOESN'T SEE ME...GOTTA CUT THROUGH THE GRAVEYARD NEXT--!

GOT PAST 'EM ALL! NOW TO SCRAMBLE UP OVER THE RIMROCK AND GET HELP SOMEWHERE!

WHUFFF

OHHH--!

AMAZING! A...A KIND OF *INVISIBLE* WALL ALL ALONG THE RIMROCK *STOPPING* ME FROM GETTING OVER IT!

PLUNGING THROUGH THE ROCKY *NEEDLE EYE* GOT US *IN*...BUT LIKE THOSE KILLERS SAID, THERE'S NO WAY *OUT!*

MUST GET BACK TO CLARK!

NOT LONG AFTER...

BUT WE *MUST* GET OUT! I'M WOUNDED... AND I NEVER SAW MY OWN BLOOD BEFORE! AND, BRUCE, I...I'M--

SCARED? YEAH, SO I NOTICE! LOSING YOUR SUPER POWERS HAS BLOWN YOUR MIND! NEVER HAVING HAD ANY, I'M NOT AS AFFECTED!

LISTEN, SOONER OR LATER, WE'VE GOT TO FACE THOSE THREE KILLERS... EVEN IF THEY *ARE* A HUNDRED OR MORE YEARS OLD!

HUH?

"I DID SOME CHECKING IN THE TOWN'S OLD NEWSPAPER OFFICE! A CENTURY AGO, A CAVE-IN IN THE LOCAL LEAD MINE RELEASED THAT WEIRD FORCE FIELD, TRAPPING EVERYONE IN THE VALLEY!".

"THE INHABITANTS MIGHT'VE LIVED OUT THEIR LIVES, AS PEACEFUL PRISONERS OF THE FORCE FIELD, EXCEPT THAT JACK SLADE, ONE OF THE OLD WEST'S WORST GUNMEN, STUMBLED INTO THE VALLEY!"

"THEN KID BOWIE AND 'LEVER' MONROE, A SHARPSHOOTING GAMBLER, HAPPENED ALONG, AND, TOGETHER, THOSE THREE ASSASSINS WIPED OUT THE TOWNSPEOPLE!"

"THE OUTSIDE WORLD FORGOT THE TOWN EXISTED! THE FORCE FIELD SIDE EFFECTS PROBABLY MADE THAT MURDERING TRIO LIVE DECADES BEYOND THEIR TIME--AS YOUNG AS THE DAY THEY CAME HERE!"

AND THEY KILLED EVERYONE WHO HAPPENED ALONG SINCE-- FOR THE SHEER EVIL JOY OF IT! THAT EXPLAINS THE *NEWER* TOMBSTONES AND STRANGE EPITAPHS!

AND THAT FORCE FIELD MUST EXPLAIN THE LOSS OF MY POWERS! IT'S ALL SO MIND-BOGGLING... BUT ARE YOU SURE IT'S TRUE?

MONROE, THE RIFLE FREAK, WAS ONCE A NEWSPAPERMAN! HE'S KEPT A RECORD OF EVERY VICTIM'S FATE FOR ALMOST A *CENTURY*, IN THE NEWSPAPER MORGUE FILES!

BRRRR! *MORGUE* IS THE WORD FOR IT! BUT WHAT DO WE DO NOW?

WE'VE ONLY *ONE* CHOICE, CLARK--*FIGHT!*

FIGHT...?

RIGHT ON! THERE COMES A TIME WHEN THE BAD GUYS OF THIS WORLD LEAVE YOU NO OTHER OUT!

BUT MY DAD, *SUPERMAN*, TAUGHT ME ONE GREAT LESSON! THERE'S ALWAYS *ANOTHER* WAY TO DEFEAT EVIL, RATHER THAN *VIOLENCE!*

"LIKE THE TIME HE OVERCAME A HOSTAGE-HOLDING CRIMINAL BY MELTING HIS GUN WITH HIS *HEAT-VISION*..."

SURE, THAT WAS *EASY* FOR *SUPERMAN!* MY DAD, THE *BATMAN* TAUGHT ME DIFFERENT...

"THERE WAS THE TIME HE WAS FORCED TO USE SUDDEN VIOLENCE ON A SNIPER..."

BATMAN! YOU KNOCKED THAT SNIPER OFF THE ROOFTOP!

DIDN'T MEAN TO... ONLY MEANT TO STOP HIM FROM KILLING THE NEXT INNOCENT VICTIM IN HIS SIGHTS--*YOU!*

I...I CAN'T AGREE! THERE MUST BE SOME OTHER WAY TO DEFEAT THESE RUTHLESS CUT-THROATS!

HOW? WITHOUT YOUR POWERS, WE'RE JUST TWO MORE CANDIDATES FOR BOOTHILL...UNLESS WE FIGHT!

HELP!

A GIRL... RUNNING!

PLEASE! SOMEONE... HELP!!

A MOMENT LATER...

THIS WAY-- QUICK!

YOU WERE BACK-PACKING IN THE AREA AND STUMBLED INTO THE VALLEY?

EXACTLY, AND THREE AWFUL MEN THREATENED ME! I RAN FOR MY LIFE! BY THE WAY, I'M SUSIE WELLS!

YOU'RE OKAY WITH US, FOR NOW, DOLL!

WELL, CLARK --YOU CONVINCED? WE GOTTA FIGHT THOSE GOONS TO SAVE SUSIE AND OUR-SELVES... AS WELL AS ANY FUTURE TRAVELERS!

YES, ANYTHING'S BETTER THAN FEELING THIS FEAR!

DAWN COMES WITH A BRILLIANT HOT-WHITE SUN RISING OVER THE RIMROCK...

AND IN THE DUSTY STREETS, WHERE AGELESS ASSASSINS HAVE PATROLLED ALL THE LONG NIGHT...

KID BOWIE! I'M CALLING YOU FOR A FIGHT TO THE FINISH!

DON'T KNOW WHERE YOU GOT THAT FANCY OUTFIT, BUT I'LL CUT IT AND YUH TO RIBBONS!

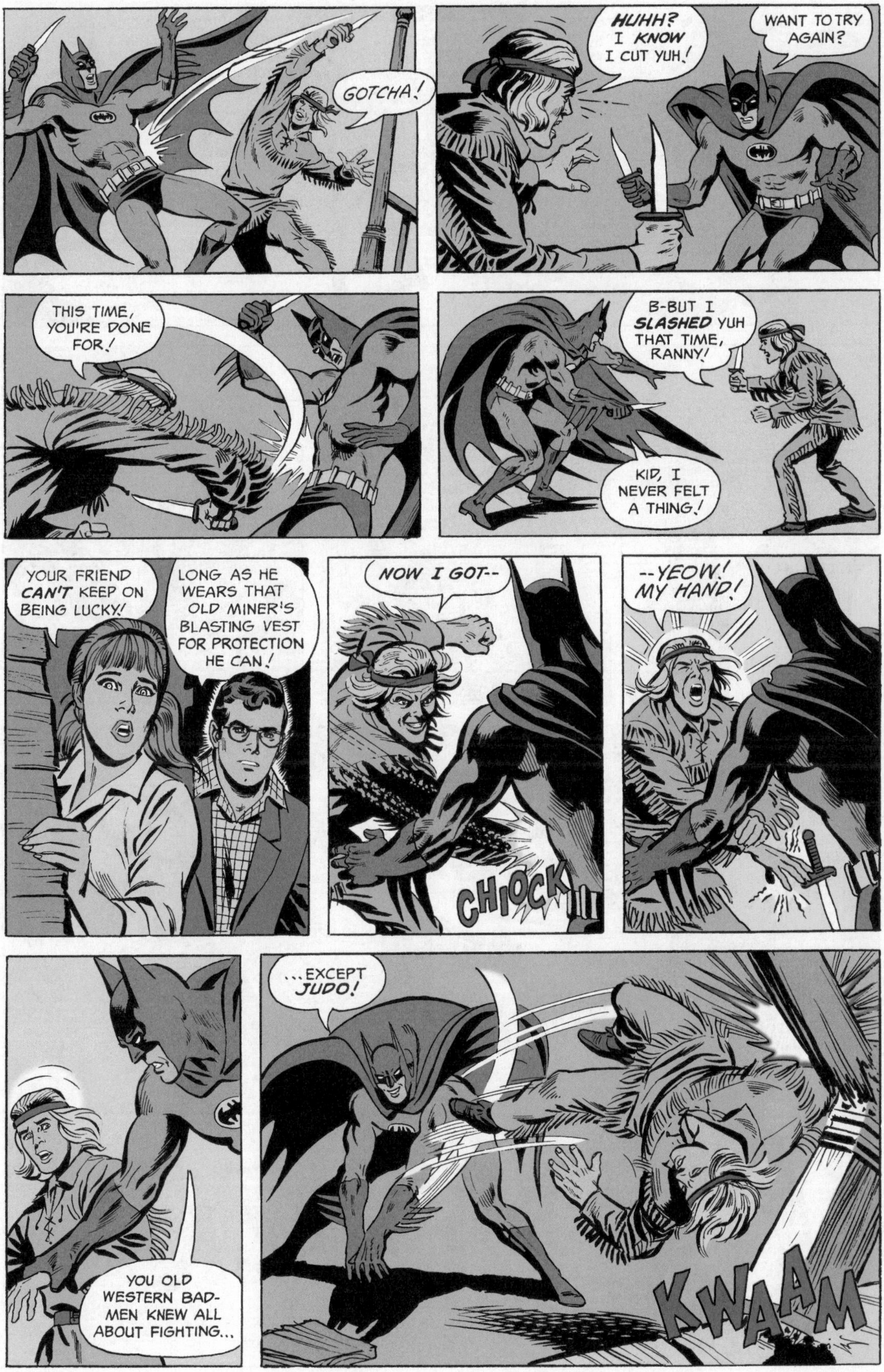
GOTCHA!
HUHH? I KNOW I CUT YUH!
WANT TO TRY AGAIN?
THIS TIME, YOU'RE DONE FOR!
B-BUT I SLASHED YUH THAT TIME, RANNY!
KID, I NEVER FELT A THING!
YOUR FRIEND CAN'T KEEP ON BEING LUCKY!
LONG AS HE WEARS THAT OLD MINER'S BLASTING VEST FOR PROTECTION HE CAN!
NOW I GOT--
CHIOCK
--YEOW! MY HAND!
YOU OLD WESTERN BAD-MEN KNEW ALL ABOUT FIGHTING...
...EXCEPT JUDO!
KWAAM

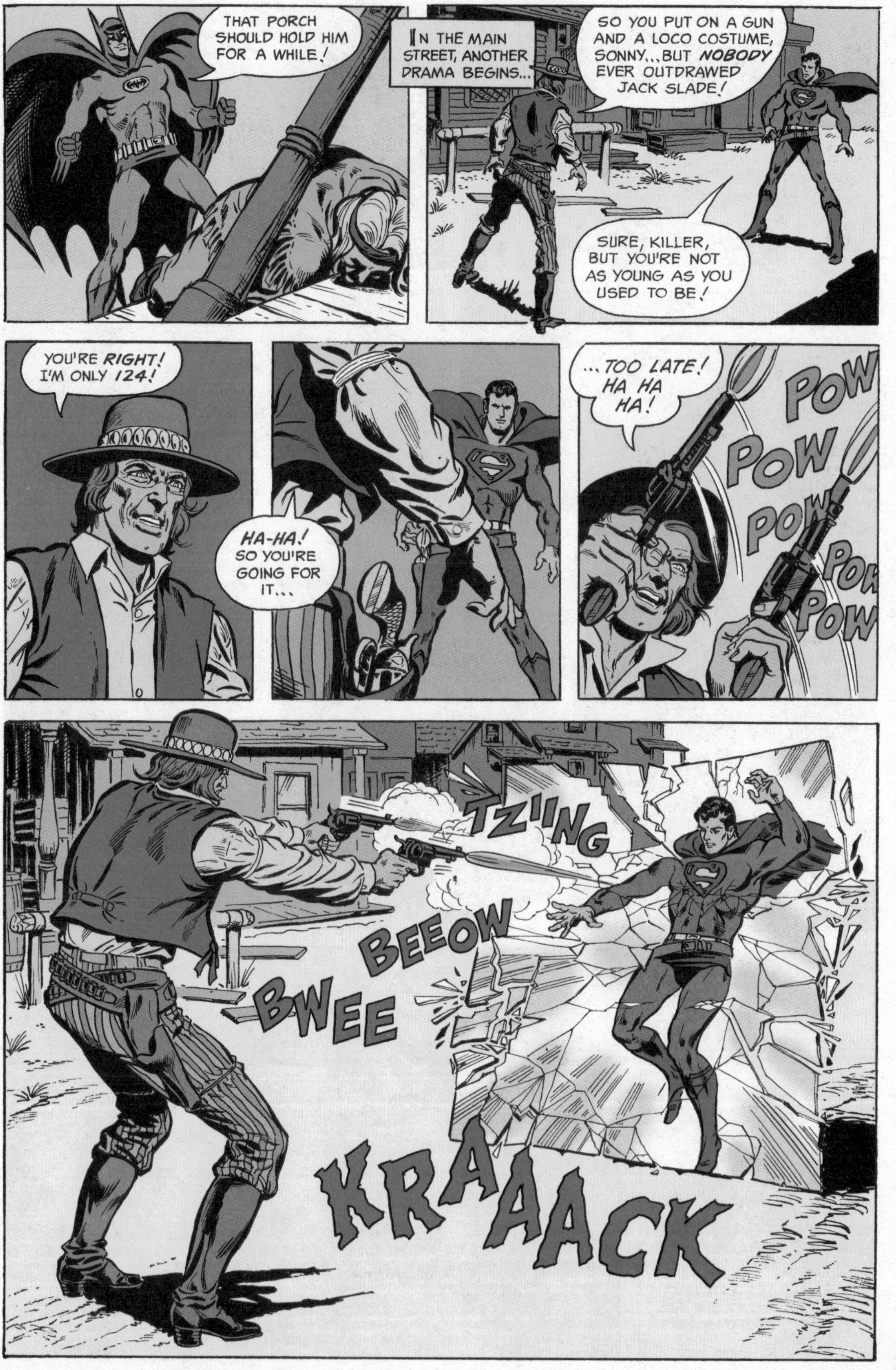
THAT PORCH SHOULD HOLD HIM FOR A WHILE!
IN THE MAIN STREET, ANOTHER DRAMA BEGINS...
SO YOU PUT ON A GUN AND A LOCO COSTUME, SONNY...BUT NOBODY EVER OUTDRAWED JACK SLADE!
SURE, KILLER, BUT YOU'RE NOT AS YOUNG AS YOU USED TO BE!
YOU'RE RIGHT! I'M ONLY 124!
HA-HA! SO YOU'RE GOING FOR IT...
...TOO LATE! HA HA HA!
POW POW POW POW POW
TZING
BEEEOW
BWEE
KRAAACK

A...A MIRROR!!

AND FAST AS YOU ARE, SLADE, YOU CAN'T TURN AND GET ME...

...BEFORE I DRILL YOU!!

POW POW

OUT LIKE A *LIGHT* FROM THOSE BULLETS I MADE FROM *CANDLE WAX* LAST NIGHT! HE'LL BE OKAY WHEN HE COMES TO!

GOOD THING I DIDN'T HAVE TO FACE HIM DIRECTLY IN THAT WALKDOWN! GOT *SOME* OF MY CONFIDENCE BACK NOW!

SUDDENLY!

THAT RIFLE FREAK! ALMOST FORGOT ABOUT HIM!

HE REMEMBERED US IN SPADES!

BEEOW   VIP   ZING

HIDE, RABBITS! BUT THE INSTANT YOU SHOW A HAIR... I'LL BLAST YUH!

*T*WO DOWN-- ONE *MORE* FORMIDABLE FOE TO GO! CAN THE *SUPER SONS* VANQUISH HIM... AND AN EVEN GREATER MENACE IN *PART 3... NEXT?*

THE LAST AND DEADLIEST OF THE TOWN'S TERRORS SWEEPS OVER THE STREET WITH RIFLE FIRE...

VIP BWEE ZIIP

SUPES AND SUSIE TOOK COVER ACROSS THE WAY! BUT WE CAN'T SKULK HERE FOREVER!

WE HAD NO PLAN FOR GETTING MONROE... I'VE GOT TO COME UP WITH SOMETHING!

I'VE GOT IT! WHAT SUPES SAID ABOUT MONROE REMEMBERING US... IN SPADES!

MONROE! YOU'RE A GAMBLER! I HAVE A SPORTING BET FOR YOU!

SALOON

COME ON OUT! I'LL HOLD MY FIRE!

NO TRICKS! I'M RELOADED AN' I GOT THE SHARPEST EYES IN THE WEST!

YOU'LL NEED 'EM! I'M HOLDING ALL THE SPADES OF A DECK!

IF YOU CAN SHOOT A SPADE OUT OF EACH CARD ...ONE BY ONE... WE'LL SURRENDER! IF YOU CAN'T, YOU LET US GO FREE!

HE'S GAMBLING OUR LIVES WITH THAT MADMAN!?

I THINK HE'S WONDERFUL AND BRAVE!

I TAKE YOUR BET, SONNY! HERE'S MY FIRST SHOT!

KA-POW

THAT'S IT... I GOT 'EM ALL! 13 SHOTS... 13 SPADES! YUH GOTTA SURRENDER, SONNY!

HUH? WHERE'D YOU GO?

RIGHT HERE, MONROE!

I'LL NAIL YUH--

KLIK

KLIK

IT'S EMPTY!

BUT MY BOOTS AREN'T, KILLER!

WOK

219

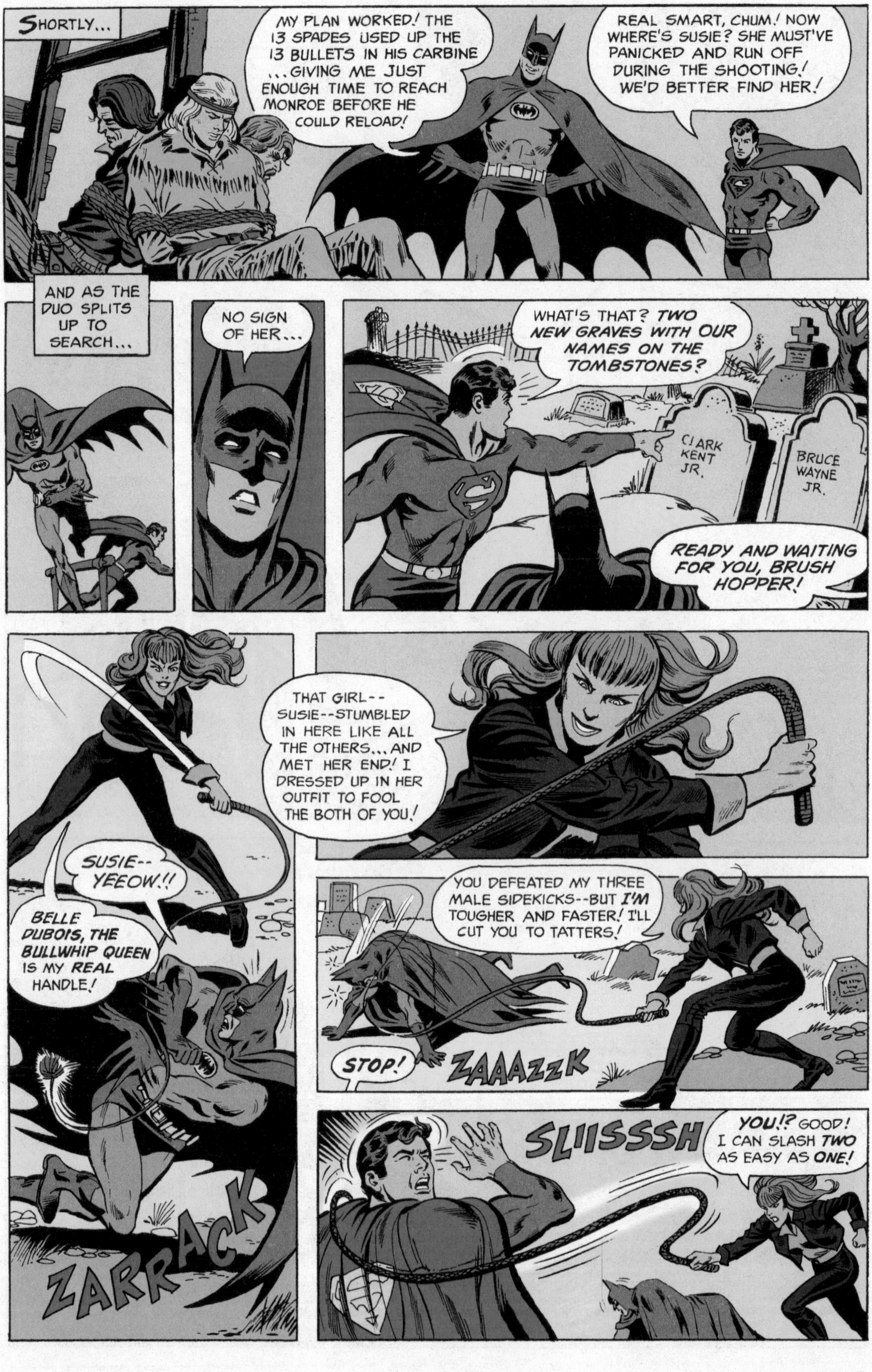
SHORTLY...
MY PLAN WORKED! THE 13 SPADES USED UP THE 13 BULLETS IN HIS CARBINE ...GIVING ME JUST ENOUGH TIME TO REACH MONROE BEFORE HE COULD RELOAD!
REAL SMART, CHUM! NOW WHERE'S SUSIE? SHE MUST'VE PANICKED AND RUN OFF DURING THE SHOOTING! WE'D BETTER FIND HER!
AND AS THE DUO SPLITS UP TO SEARCH...
NO SIGN OF HER...
WHAT'S THAT? TWO NEW GRAVES WITH OUR NAMES ON THE TOMBSTONES?
CLARK KENT JR.
BRUCE WAYNE JR.
READY AND WAITING FOR YOU, BRUSH HOPPER!
SUSIE-- YEEOW!!
BELLE DUBOIS, THE BULLWHIP QUEEN IS MY REAL HANDLE!
ZARRACK
THAT GIRL-- SUSIE--STUMBLED IN HERE LIKE ALL THE OTHERS... AND MET HER END! I DRESSED UP IN HER OUTFIT TO FOOL THE BOTH OF YOU!
YOU DEFEATED MY THREE MALE SIDEKICKS--BUT I'M TOUGHER AND FASTER! I'LL CUT YOU TO TATTERS!
STOP!
ZAAAZZK
SLIISSSH
YOU!? GOOD! I CAN SLASH TWO AS EASY AS ONE!

SUPES! MY LOYAL BUDDY... RUNNING IN FEAR!

KRAACK

BUT THE HALF-KRYPTONIAN SON OF THE MIGHTY *SUPERMAN* SUDDENLY STOPS, WHIRLS, AND...

SLASSSH

GRUNNCH

YOUR *POWERS*... YOU GOT 'EM *BACK*? BUT HOW...?

I'VE ONLY GOT THEM AS LONG AS I STAND ON THIS *PARTICULAR* GRAVE!

REMEMBER, I LIFTED ITS TOPPLED MARKER EASILY...WHEN KID BOWIE FIRST SHOWED UP!

BUT EVERYTHING THAT HAPPENED MADE ME FORGET IT...TILL JUST NOW!

WHY DOES STANDING ON THAT SPOT BRING BACK YOUR POWERS?

HOLD IT! I KNOW! HAWKINS-- I READ ABOUT HIM IN THE NEWSPAPER FILES! HE WAS *DRY GULCH'S* RICHEST CITIZEN!

HE HAD *SOIL* FROM HIS BIRTHPLACE BACK EAST SHIPPED HERE SO HE COULD BE BURIED IN IT WHEN HE DIED!

HAS TO BE IT! THAT EARTH HASN'T THE SAME POWERS-ROBBING PROPERTIES OF THE VALLEY SOIL!

SHORTLY

BY USING THAT SAME GRAVE AS A *SPRINGBOARD*, I CAN HAUL YOU AND OUR FOUR PRISONERS OUT OF THIS WEIRD VALLEY TO JUSTICE!

HAD TO MAKE ONE STOP! *THERE!* WITH MY POWERS REGAINED, I'M FILLING THE VALLEY SO OTHER INNOCENT TRAVELERS CAN'T EVER WANDER INTO IT!

ROWWRRRR

AND SOME TIME LATER...

A BEWITCHED VALLEY... GUNMEN OVER A HUNDRED YEARS OLD? COME ON, FELLERS--

TAKE A LOOK AT OUR PRISONERS, SHERIFF!

GOOD LORD!

AND STILL LATER...

WELL, HE SURE HAD TO *BELIEVE* OUR STORY WHEN HE LOOKED IN THE WAGON!

BRRR! TAKING THOSE KILLERS AWAY FROM THE VALLEY'S SPECIAL AURA ENDED THEIR LIVING ON BORROWED TIME!

THAT VALLEY WAS LIKE SOME *REVERSE* SHANGRI-LA, WHERE INSTEAD OF *GOOD*, ALL THAT FLOURISHED WAS... EVIL!

AND NO MATTER *WHERE* YOU FIND EVIL, YOU'VE GOT TO *FIGHT* IT!

THE END

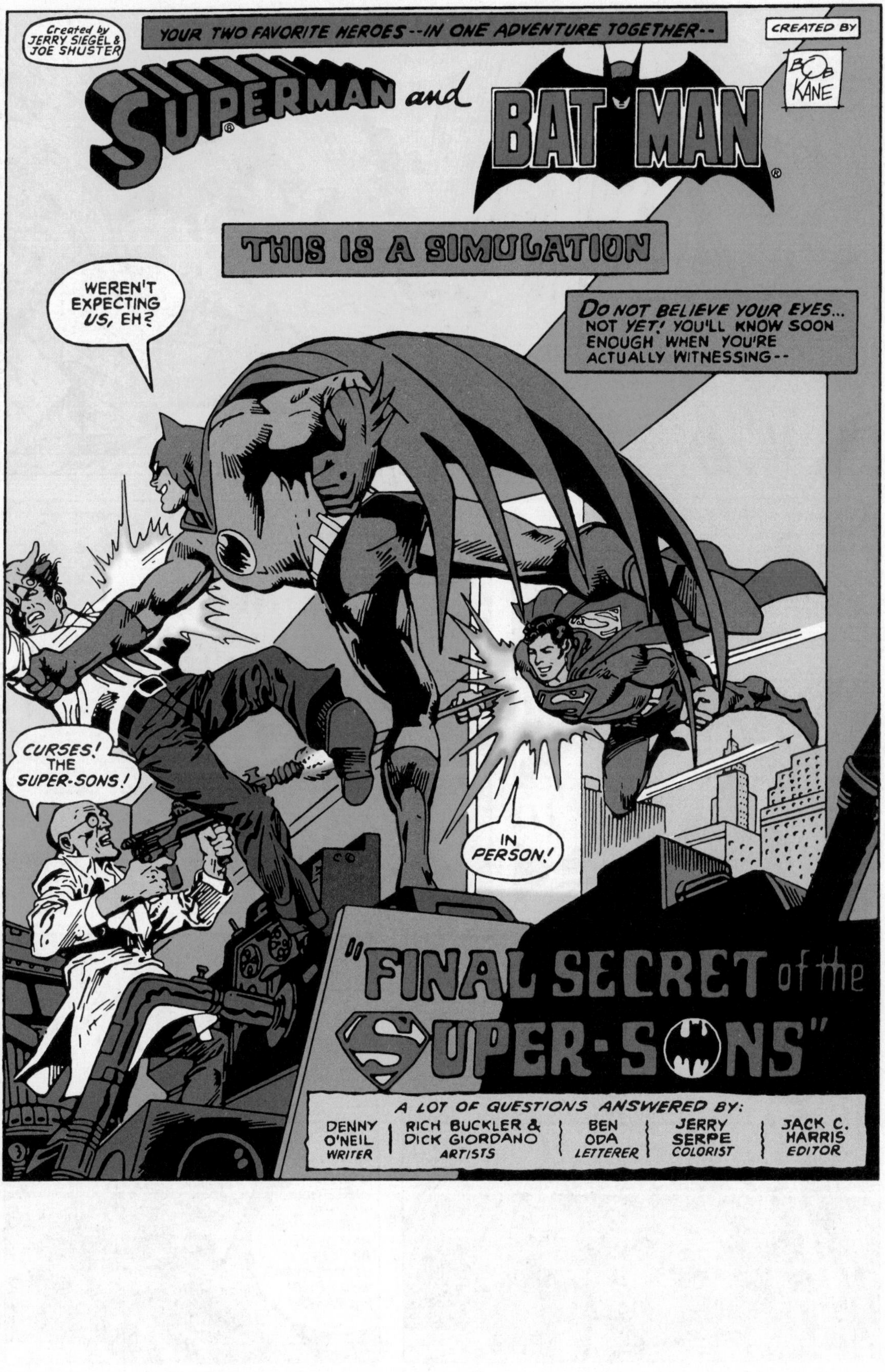
Created by JERRY SIEGEL & JOE SHUSTER
YOUR TWO FAVORITE HEROES--IN ONE ADVENTURE TOGETHER--
CREATED BY
BOB KANE
SUPERMAN and BATMAN
THIS IS A SIMULATION
WEREN'T EXPECTING US, EH?
DO NOT BELIEVE YOUR EYES... NOT YET! YOU'LL KNOW SOON ENOUGH WHEN YOU'RE ACTUALLY WITNESSING--
CURSES! THE SUPER-SONS!
IN PERSON!
"FINAL SECRET of the SUPER-SONS"
A LOT OF QUESTIONS ANSWERED BY:
DENNY O'NEIL WRITER
RICH BUCKLER & DICK GIORDANO ARTISTS
BEN ODA LETTERER
JERRY SERPE COLORIST
JACK C. HARRIS EDITOR

INTERFERE WITH MY PLANS TO RULE THE *WORLD*, WILL YOU?

IF I POSSIBLY *CAN!*

EAT *DEATH...* IN THE FORM OF MY *NEGATIVE MESON DISINTEGRATOR BEAM!*

NEGATIVE MESON-DISINTEGRATOR BEAM? PROBABLY TOOK LONGER TO SAY *IT* THAN TO *INVENT* IT!

SMASH

IN *ANY* EVENT, IT'S *FINISHED*-- AS ARE *YOU!*

AND AS IS THIS *CASE!* LET'S CART DOCTOR SIVANA TO THE *HOOSEGOW* AND TREAT OUR-SELVES TO SOME *MALTS!*

WELL, THAT ANSWERS YOUR *QUESTION*, BATMAN!

NO SURPRISE! I *FIGURED* OUR *SUPER-SONS* COULD DEFEAT CAPTAIN MARVEL'S OLD FOE *DOCTOR SIVANA*--

--ASSUMING THE SUPER-SONS *EXISTED!*

IT'S *FUN* RUNNING THE *SIMULATIONS* ON YOUR *SUPER-COMPUTER!*

SOMETIMES I WISH WE HAD *REAL* SONS, INSTEAD OF THE COMPUTER'S *MOCK-UPS!*

PERHAPS--

BUT WE *DON'T!* INSTEAD, WE HAVE OUR *TASKS*-- AND WE'D BETTER STOP *PLAYING* AND BEGIN *WORKING!*

2

However... since Superman has not *reprogrammed* his computer, it *continues* to play the drama even though the heroic pair no longer *observes* ...

Supey, I have *news* for you! Incredible news!

Lay it on me, pal!

I was wondering why we'd never *heard* of this *Dr. Sivana* before this morning, so I did some *computations!*

I've *checked* and *rechecked* my results-- and the only *answer* is that before this *morning*-- he didn't *exist*--

-- and super-buddy-- *neither did we!* Unbelievable as it is, we're only *two dimensional* creatures living in a *three dimensional* universe!

Play that back for me again--in *English!*

Sivana was *invented* by some device very much like *this* one -- and we're *trapped* inside the *same* device!

Near as I can figure it, we're being *tested!*

I think you've *supped* the proverbial *cog*, but I'll take your *word* for it!

Hang *on!* If we're in some kind of *trap*, we're gonna get *out!*

There has to be...

...an exit...

...someplace!

At *tremendous* speed they travel... *overloading* the computer circuits--

3

ALONE, SUPERMAN JR.'S ACTION WOULD DO NO *HARM!* BUT LUCK--OR *FATE*--INTERVENES...

...FOR *SUPERMAN* IS DUMPING A LOAD OF *RADIO-ACTIVE ORE* INTO THE *DISINTEGRATION PIT* AT THE BOTTOM OF HIS *FORTRESS OF SOLITUDE*...

...CAUSING A *FINAL* OVERLOAD IN THE COMPUTER WHICH CONTROLS EVERYTHING IN THE FORTRESS...

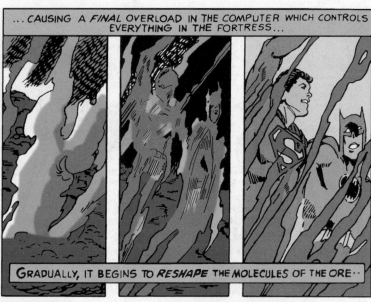

GRADUALLY, IT BEGINS TO *RESHAPE* THE MOLECULES OF THE ORE--

...FORMING THEM INTO FAMILIAR SHAPES..!

WE'RE *FREE!* HOW'D YOU *MANAGE* IT, SUPEY?

TO TELL THE TRUTH-- WHICH IS ALL I *EVER* TELL--

--I'M NOT *SURE!*

AND I DON'T *CARE!* C'MON, PAL --

--LET'S *SPLIT!*

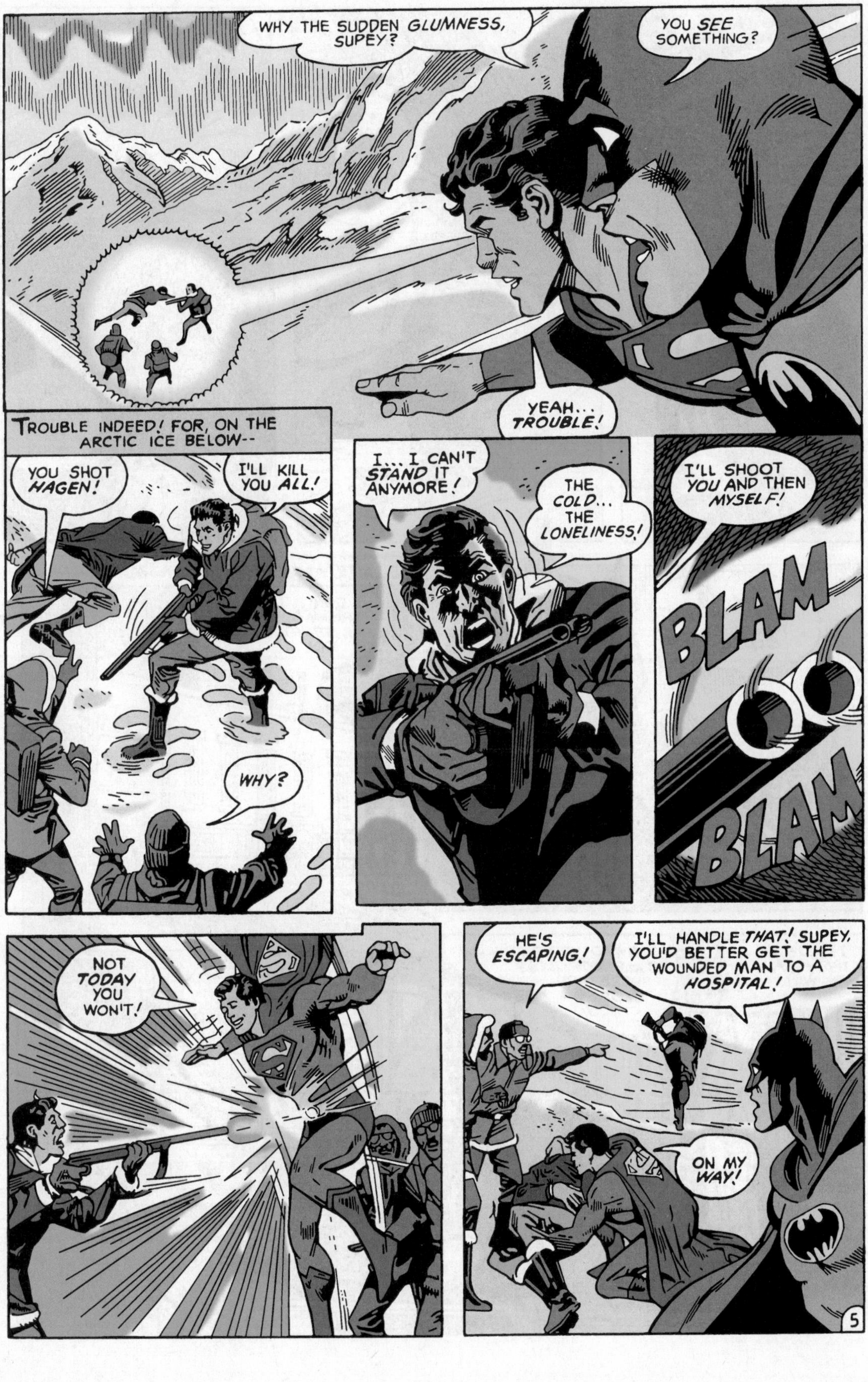
WHY THE SUDDEN GLUMNESS, SUPEY?
YOU SEE SOMETHING?
YEAH... TROUBLE!
TROUBLE INDEED! FOR, ON THE ARCTIC ICE BELOW--
YOU SHOT HAGEN!
I'LL KILL YOU ALL!
WHY?
I... I CAN'T STAND IT ANYMORE!
THE COLD... THE LONELINESS!
I'LL SHOOT YOU AND THEN MYSELF!
BLAM
BLAM
NOT TODAY YOU WON'T!
HE'S ESCAPING!
I'LL HANDLE THAT! SUPEY, YOU'D BETTER GET THE WOUNDED MAN TO A HOSPITAL!
ON MY WAY!
5

SECONDS LATER...

DO YOURSELF A FAVOR--

--DON'T MAKE THINGS WORSE BY TRYING TO RUN!

AND DON'T SIGN ON FOR ANOTHER ARCTIC EXPEDITION! YOU DON'T HAVE THE TEMPERAMENT FOR THIS KIND OF GIG!

NICE WORK, BATMAN!

YOU ARE THE BATMAN, AREN'T YOU?

FUNNY... I ALWAYS THOUGHT YOU WERE OLDER!

SOMETIME LATER, AT METROPOLIS CENTRAL HOSPITAL...

I DON'T THINK THIS WOUND IS SERIOUS, DOC!

HOSPITAL

I'LL DECIDE THAT! BY THE WAY...

...WHY'D YOU BRING HIM TO METROPOLIS? THERE ARE CLOSER CITIES!

I DON'T REALLY KNOW!

SUPERMAN! I HEARD YOU'D ARRIVED HERE AND I WANTED TO ASK...

6

OH! YOU *AREN'T* SUPERMAN!

NO... I'M HIS *SON!*

HIS... *SON?*

WHO'S THE PRETTY *LADY,* DOC?

LOIS LANE! SHE'S A REPORTER WITH THE *DAILY PLANET*-- AND A FRIEND OF YOUR *POP'S!*

DON'T YOU KNOW *THAT?*

LOIS!

GET BACK TO THE OFFICE *PRONTO!* ALL *HELL* IS BREAKING LOOSE IN *GOTHAM CITY* AND THE *ARCTIC!*

MR. EDGE WANTS YOU TO HELP HANDLE THE *PHONES!*

IN *GOTHAM*--

THINK WE *DITCHED* 'EM?

I *HOPE* SO! 'CAUSE THE COPS ARE GONNA BE REAL *PEEVED* ABOUT THE MESS WE LEFT ALL OVER THAT BANK FLOOR!

NOT AS *PEEVED* AS *I* AM!

7

WUMP!

THE BATMAN!

HOW?

YOU'LL NEVER *KNOW*, PUNK!

YOU'LL *ROT* IN PRISON NOT KNOWING!

SOK!

HOLD IT!

COOL YOUR ACT OR THE LADY HERE BUYS THE *WHOLE PACKAGE!*

YOU WIN--FOR *NOW!*

AS FAR AS *YOU'RE* CONCERNED, I WIN FOR *ALWAYS!*

BETTER FINISH ME WITH THE *FIRST* SHOT! YOU WON'T *GET* A SECOND!

GO ON... TALK *TOUGH!*

BLAM

8

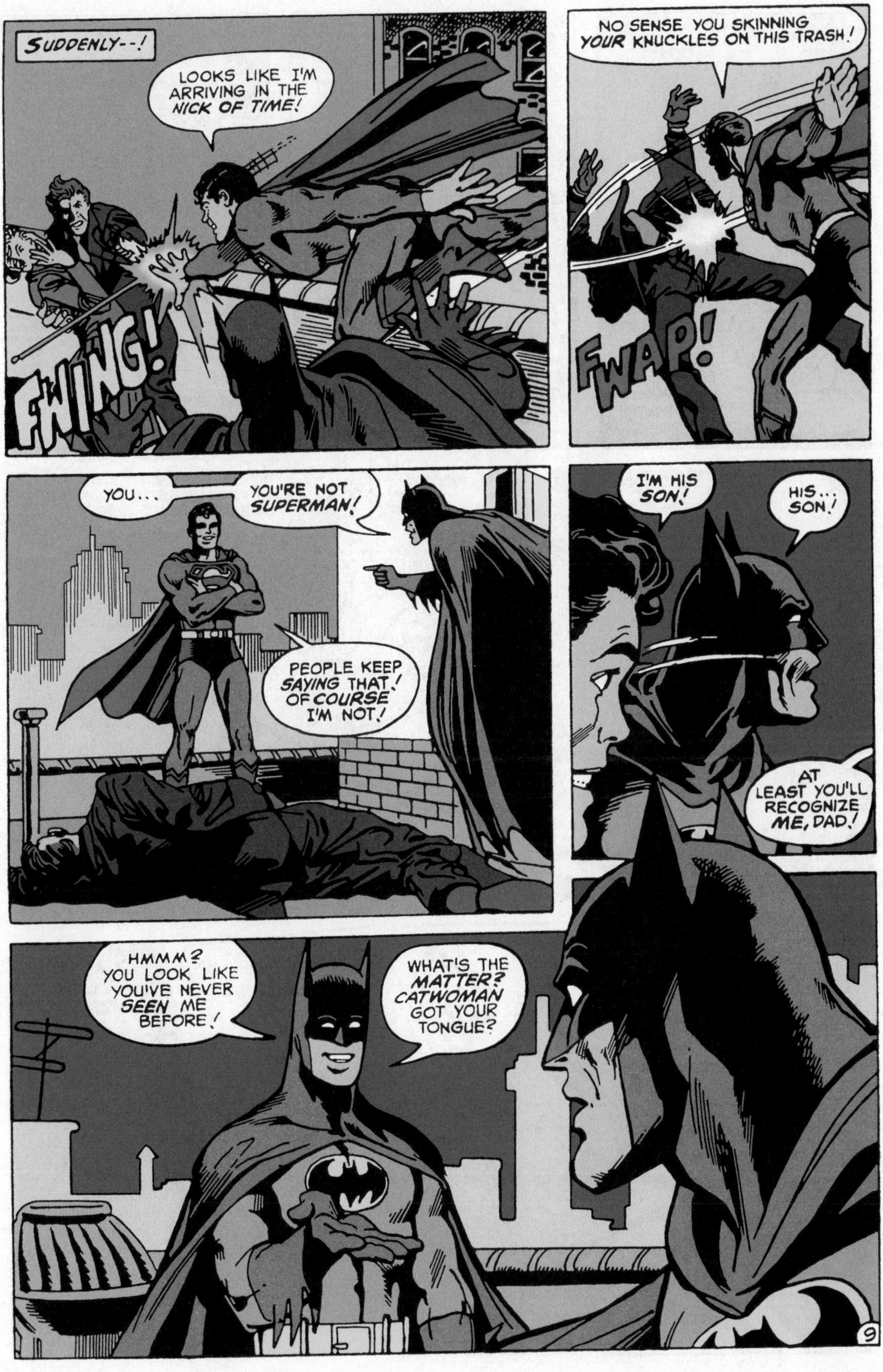
SUDDENLY--!
LOOKS LIKE I'M ARRIVING IN THE NICK OF TIME!
FWING!
NO SENSE YOU SKINNING YOUR KNUCKLES ON THIS TRASH!
FWAP!
YOU...
YOU'RE NOT SUPERMAN!
PEOPLE KEEP SAYING THAT! OF COURSE I'M NOT!
I'M HIS SON!
HIS... SON!
AT LEAST YOU'LL RECOGNIZE ME, DAD!
HMMM? YOU LOOK LIKE YOU'VE NEVER SEEN ME BEFORE!
WHAT'S THE MATTER? CATWOMAN GOT YOUR TONGUE?
9

GIVE ME A MOMENT...

AND IN THE ARCTIC--

THE *TUNDRA* AROUND MY FORTRESS IS *CRUMBLING!* DOESN'T MAKE *SENSE!*

I *CHOSE* THIS REGION FOR ITS *STABILITY!*

NO TREMENDOUS PROBLEM!

ALL I HAVE TO DO--

--IS SHOVE THE HUNKS OF GEOGRAPHY *TOGETHER*--

--AND *SEAL* THEM WITH MY *HEAT VISION!*

10

MAYBE THE INSTRUMENTS INSIDE THE *FORTRESS* WILL TELL ME HOW THAT *HAPPENED!*

THIRTY SECONDS LATER--

HARD TO *BELIEVE* IF THIS READOUT IS *CORRECT*--

BEEP BEEP BEEP

THE *SEISMO-ALARM!* THERE'S MORE *EARTHQUAKE* ACTIVITY IN THE VICINITY!

NOT *EARTHQUAKE*, SUPERMAN --

AVALANCHE!

THIS WHOLE *GLACIER'S* BREAKING UP *AROUND* US!

WE'LL BE *CRUSHED!*

KRAK-RAK

KRAK

NOT IF I--

--SMASH THE ICE CHUNKS--

--TO A FINE *MIST!*

KRAK-RAK-RAK

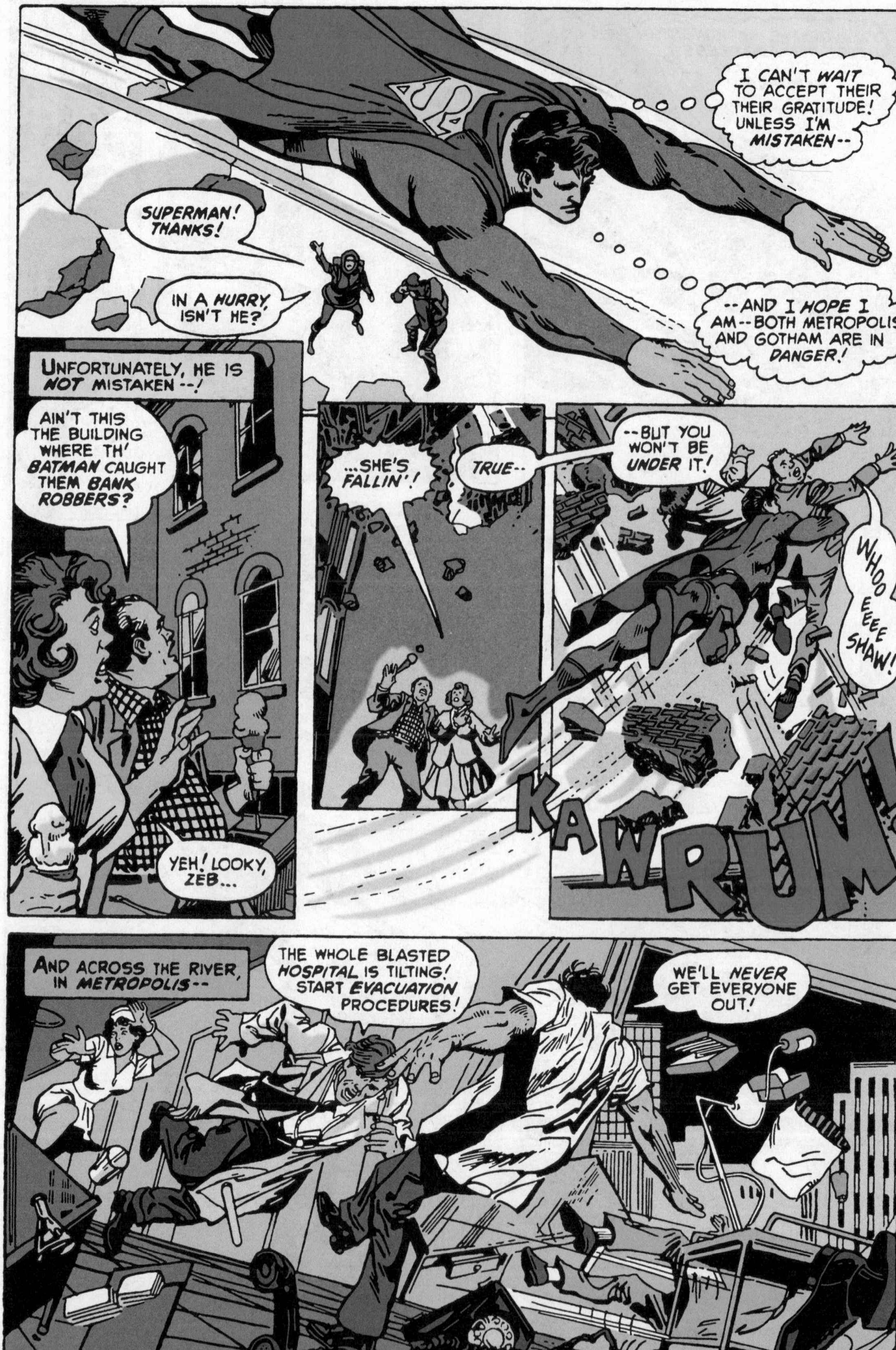

I CAN'T WAIT TO ACCEPT THEIR THEIR GRATITUDE! UNLESS I'M MISTAKEN--
SUPERMAN! THANKS!
IN A HURRY, ISN'T HE?
--AND I HOPE I AM--BOTH METROPOLIS AND GOTHAM ARE IN DANGER!
UNFORTUNATELY, HE IS NOT MISTAKEN--!
AIN'T THIS THE BUILDING WHERE TH' BATMAN CAUGHT THEM BANK ROBBERS?
YEH! LOOKY, ZEB...
...SHE'S FALLIN'!
TRUE--
--BUT YOU WON'T BE UNDER IT!
WHOOEEEESHAW!
KAWRUM!
AND ACROSS THE RIVER, IN METROPOLIS--
THE WHOLE BLASTED HOSPITAL IS TILTING! START EVACUATION PROCEDURES!
WE'LL NEVER GET EVERYONE OUT!
12

WITH MY *HELP* YOU WILL!

A FAST AND *FURIOUS* FOUR MINUTES PASS, AND··!

THIS IS THE *LAST* OF THEM!

CAN YOU SAVE THE *BUILDING?*

I'M AFRAID *NOT*, DOCTOR!

SURE WE CAN, POPS! YOU AND I WILL DO OUR *SUPER-STUFF* WHILE THE *BAT-GUY* HERE--

GET *AWAY!!*

WHOMP!

WHAT THE *HECK* IS GOING ON?

YOU OUTTA YOUR EVER-LOVIN' *KRYPTONIAN MIND*, POPS?

HEAD FOR MY *FORTRESS!* THAT'S THE ONLY PLACE WHERE THE EARTH IS *SAFE* FROM THE *BOTH* OF YOU!

THE *BATMAN* AND I WILL *JOIN* YOU THERE!

13

SOON... THIS COMPUTER *PRINT OUT* TELLS THE STORY, BATMAN!

I'VE ALREADY *FIGURED* A LOT OF IT, SUPERMAN!

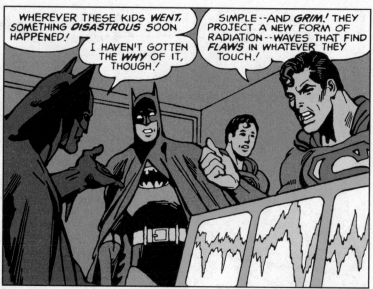

WHEREVER THESE KIDS *WENT,* SOMETHING *DISASTROUS* SOON HAPPENED!

I HAVEN'T GOTTEN THE *WHY* OF IT, THOUGH!

SIMPLE--AND *GRIM!* THEY PROJECT A NEW FORM OF RADIATION--WAVES THAT FIND *FLAWS* IN WHATEVER THEY TOUCH!

THEN THE FLAWS ARE *INCREASED!* SO MINUTE PROBLEMS IN THE TUNDRA OUTSIDE AND THE BUILDINGS BECAME *MAJOR* PROBLEMS!

NEXT... *DISASTER!*

THE FULL *SCIENTIFIC* EXPLANATION IS *BEYOND* ME--

--BUT THE FINAL RESULT IS *OBVIOUS!*

ASSUMING WHAT YOU SAY IS *TRUE*--

--WHAT THE HECK ARE WE SUPPOSED TO *DO?*

RETURN TO WHERE YOU *CAME* FROM!

THE *DISINTEGRATION PIT?*

FORGET IT, CHARLIE!

14

HOW CAN YOU TELL US TO... TO *DIE*? WE'RE YOUR *SONS*!

WITH ALL MY HEART--

--I WISH THAT WERE *TRUE*!

BUT IT *ISN'T*! YOU'RE CREATIONS OF MY *COMPUTER* AND STRAY MOLECULES FROM THE *PIT*!

OKAY, WISE-MOUTHS, *PROVE* IT!

ONE QUESTION SHOULD DO THAT!

WHO ARE YOUR... *MOTHERS*?

WHY, MY MOM IS... IS...

I CAN'T *REMEMBER*!

BECAUSE YOU *HAVEN'T* ANY MOTHERS! WHEN WE PROGRAMMED YOU INTO THE COMPUTER, WE DIDN'T *GIVE* YOU ANY! THE FACT WASN'T *IMPORTANT* TO THE SIMULATION WE RAN!

I GUESS THE SENIOR CITIZENS HAVE A *POINT*, SUPEY! I GUESS WE ARE *MENACES*!

AW-- I DIDN'T *REALLY* WANT TO EXIST ANYWAY!

JOIN ME IN A LITTLE DISINTE-GRATION?

GOODBYE!

WE *HAD* TO DO IT! WE HAD NO WAY OF *PROTECTING* THEM-- OR OTHERS *FROM* THEM!

I THINK THEY WERE ALTERING THE NATURE OF *REALITY* ITSELF...

SUPERMAN... SAVE THE EXPLANATIONS, OKAY?

END

15

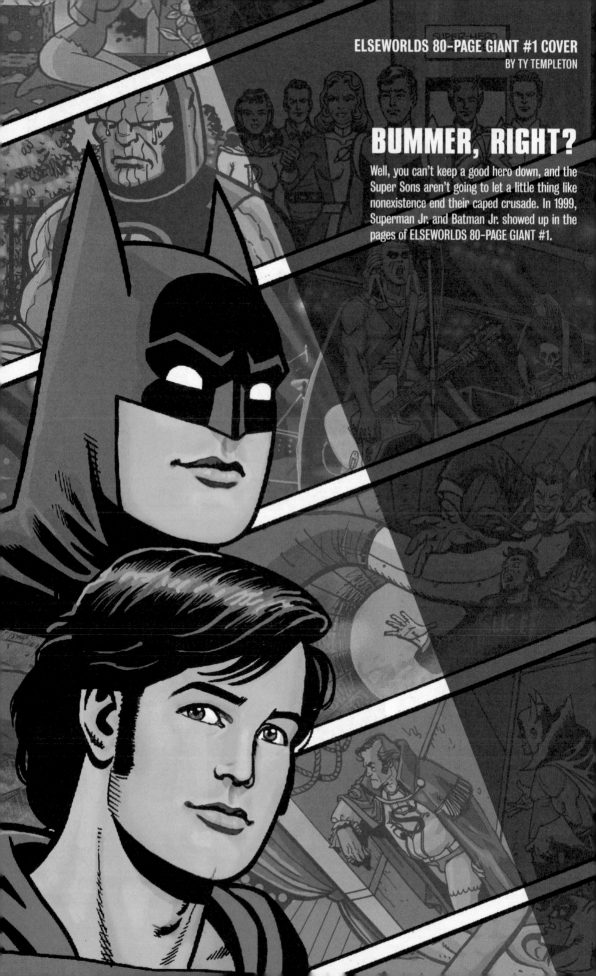

ELSEWORLDS 80-PAGE GIANT #1 COVER
BY TY TEMPLETON

BUMMER, RIGHT?

Well, you can't keep a good hero down, and the Super Sons aren't going to let a little thing like nonexistence end their caped crusade. In 1999, Superman Jr. and Batman Jr. showed up in the pages of ELSEWORLDS 80-PAGE GIANT #1.

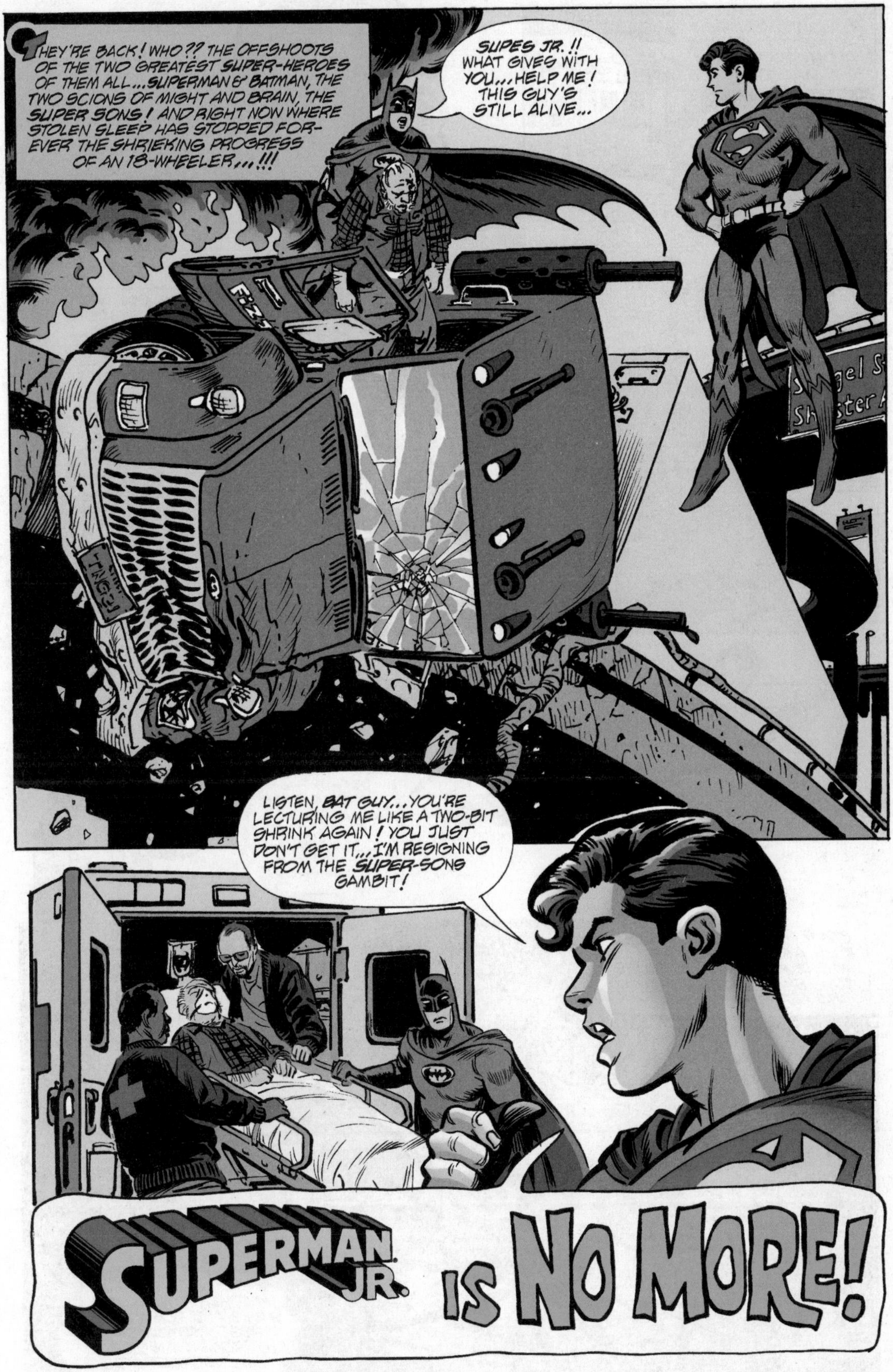
THEY'RE BACK! WHO?? THE OFFSHOOTS OF THE TWO GREATEST SUPER-HEROES OF THEM ALL...SUPERMAN & BATMAN, THE TWO SCIONS OF MIGHT AND BRAIN, THE SUPER SONS! AND RIGHT NOW WHERE STOLEN SLEEP HAS STOPPED FOREVER THE SHRIEKING PROGRESS OF AN 18-WHEELER...!!!
SUPES JR.!! WHAT GIVES WITH YOU...HELP ME! THIS GUY'S STILL ALIVE...
LISTEN, BAT GUY...YOU'RE LECTURING ME LIKE A TWO-BIT SHRINK AGAIN! YOU JUST DON'T GET IT...I'M RESIGNING FROM THE SUPER-SONS GAMBIT!
SUPERMAN JR. IS NO MORE!

YEAH, WE'VE ALL HEARD THIS BEFORE... BUT THIS IS DIFFERENT... VASTLY DIFFERENT!!

WHAT?? HOW CAN YOU RESIGN FROM SOMETHING YOU WERE BORN TO DO...?

BORN TO DO... RIGHT! BORN TO DO HALF OF WHAT MY OLD MAN DOES... EVEN NOT THAT! HELL, I'M LUCKY IF I CAN HAUL MY 'SUPER BUTT' UP TO A THIRD OF THAT...

TAKE YOU, BAT DUDE. SOMEDAY YOU'LL BE EVERYTHING YOUR OLD MAN WAS... AND IS... MAYBE BETTER! BUT I'LL NEVER BE MORE THAN A SUPERMAN IMITATION... A PALE SHADE OF BIG DAD!

WHAT'S THE PERCENTAGE... THAT DRIVER WAS WELL WITHIN YOUR POWERS TO SAVE...!

SURE, BUT WHAT ABOUT THOSE OTHER TIMES... WHEN WE'LL NEED THE OLD SUPER STUFF...

MY OLD MAN WILL BE AROUND... FOREVER! HE'LL DO THE JOB! SEE YA, BAT GUY!

IS THIS THE END OF OUR TEAMWORK... THE END OF EVERYTHING...??

GOOD QUESTION, BAT GUY! THEN, A FEW DAYS LATER, WHERE AN AWESOME FIGURE TOWS UNMITIGATED DEATH INTO FAR, FAR SPACE!!!

ANOTHER FEW MILLION MILES AND MOST OF THESE ATOMIC AND HYDROGEN MISSILES WILL BE DETONATED HARMLESSLY...

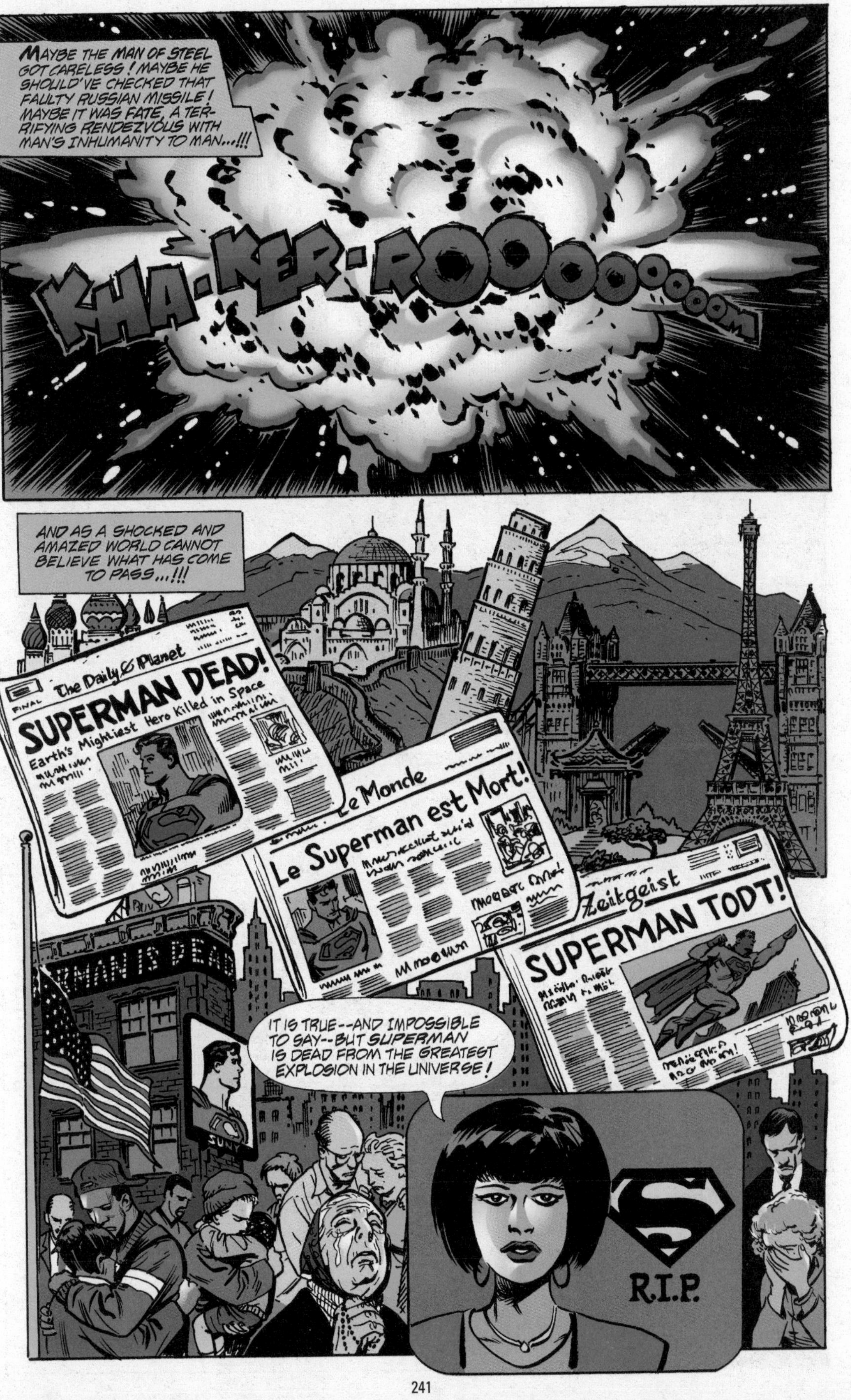
MAYBE THE MAN OF STEEL GOT CARELESS! MAYBE HE SHOULD'VE CHECKED THAT FAULTY RUSSIAN MISSILE! MAYBE IT WAS FATE, A TERRIFYING RENDEZVOUS WITH MAN'S INHUMANITY TO MAN...!!!
KHA-KER-ROOOOOOOOOOM
AND AS A SHOCKED AND AMAZED WORLD CANNOT BELIEVE WHAT HAS COME TO PASS...!!!
The Daily Planet
FINAL
SUPERMAN DEAD!
Earth's Mightiest Hero Killed in Space
Le Monde
Le Superman est Mort!
Zeitgeist
SUPERMAN TODT!
IT IS TRUE--AND IMPOSSIBLE TO SAY--BUT SUPERMAN IS DEAD FROM THE GREATEST EXPLOSION IN THE UNIVERSE!
R.I.P.

THERE ARE BILLIONS OF MOURNERS BUT NONE MORE SORROWFUL AND CONTRITE THAN A CERTAIN YOUNG MAN AND HIS MOTHER...

DAD...DAD...I'D GIVE ANYTHING TO SEE YOU... HEAR YOU...FEEL YOUR STRENGTH AGAIN...!!

THEY SAID YOU COULDN'T DIE... WOULD BE PART OF EARTH'S DEFENSES FOREVER...THEY WERE WRONG! I GUESS ALL THOSE MISSILES GOING UP AT ONCE WAS TOO MUCH EVEN FOR YOU--!

NEVER TO BE FORGOTTEN

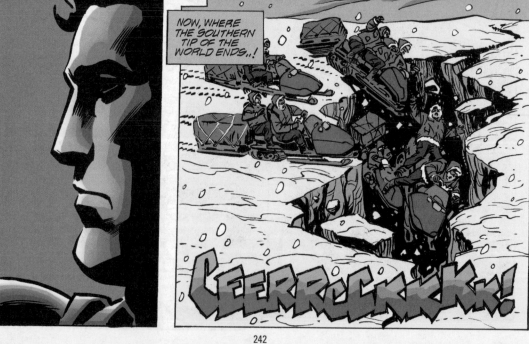

YES, THOUSANDS AND THOUSANDS OF TONS OF ATOMIC AND HYDRO-GEN POWERS EXPLODING AT ONE INCREDIBLE INSTANT WAS TOO MUCH EVEN FOR THE MAN OF STEEL.

NOW, WHERE THE SOUTHERN TIP OF THE WORLD ENDS..!

CEERRUCKKK!

AND ALMOST AS QUICKLY AS IT HAD OPENED TO SWALLOW THE SOUTH POLE EXPEDITION, THE MAW OF THE MOST FORLORN PLACE ON EARTH CLOSES AGAIN...!!

KHA-LUUMMMFFF--!!

SNOW, PYRAMIDAL FLAKES THAT FALL NEARLY EVERY LONG, LONG DAY, COVERING ALL, IT'S AS IF THE MACHINES AND MEN WHO RODE THEM NEVER PASSED THIS WAY!

YET ANOTHER DISASTER IN A WORLD WHICH SHOULD HAVE HAD ENOUGH! LATER, AS SEARCH PLANES DEPLOY...!!

THERE IT IS, BAT JR.,...A THOUSAND SQUARE MILES OF FROZEN REAL ESTATE!

A SHORTCUT TO THE POLE... BUT OUR SCANS SHOW DOZENS OF CREVASSES! THEY COULD BE IN ANY ONE...IF THEY'RE STILL ALIVE!

JENKINS

I'VE GOT TO TRY A MAN-ON-FOOT SEARCH...!!

ALLEZ-OOP!

THEIR RADIO MUST BE DEAD! NOTHING FROM ANY OF THIS...!

...NOTHING!

SUDDENLY!

WHAT IN HADES!!??

VURRRUPP!

SUPES??!!

OH, SORRY ABOUT THAT... BAT GUY!

I...I DON'T BELIEVE IT! YOU... HERE!!!

WE GET AROUND, WE JUNIOR-STYLE SUPERMEN!

HOLD UP A MIN-! DAMN! HE'S GOING AT THIS REAL ESTATE LIKE A GIANT SNOW MOLE--!

SOON...!!

BLAST! NO ONE... NOTHING!??

BUT THEN, MILES AWAY...!

HEAT! UNLESS THERE'S A PENGUIN ROASTING MARSHMALLOWS DOWN HERE...

...I'VE FOUND THEM!

SUPES JR.!! GOOD GOD... WE'RE SAVED!

SHORTLY...

THERE'S ONE OF US STILL MISSING... HE WAS LAST IN LINE...

ALIVE... OR DEAD... I'LL DIG HIM UP--!

THREE DAYS DOWN IN THIS FROZEN TRAP COULD BE THE END FOR ANYONE...EVEN IF HE'S YOUNG AND IN SHAPE--!

SOMETIMES, YOU ARRIVE, BUT TOO LATE...!!

THERE HE IS... LOOKS BAD!!

GATHERING THE LIMP FORM TO HIS BRAWNY BODY...!

IT WOULD'VE TAKEN WEEKS TO FIND THAT POOR GUY... IF EVER !!

SHORTLY...

OKAY, SLUPES, WHAT'S THE TRUE POOP ON THIS--??

SIMPLE, BAT GUY! WHEN DAD DIED... I REALIZED I WAS THE ONLY SUPERMAN! THERE COULD BE NO COMPETITION! FOR BETTER OR WORSE I WAS HEIR TO A GRAND TRADITION--!

THERE IS NO MISTAKING THE VOICE--THE SHEER PRESENCE--OF THE MAN WHO HAS HEARD EVERY WORD OF THAT CONFESSION--!!

A TRADITION THAT CRIED OUT FOR CONTINUANCE INTO THE TWENTY-FIRST CENTURY,...AND BEYOND! AND TO FLESH OUT THAT TRADITION I HAD TO TAKE AN ACTIVE, LIVING PART--!

SWELL WORDS, YOUNGSTER! I COULDN'T HAVE SPOKEN THEM BETTER MYSELF... EVEN IF I WERE STILL ALIVE--! HA! HA! HA!

D-DAD??

YOU...YOU'RE ALIVE!! NOT A PHANTOM....OR TRICK...??

NO TRICK, SON! MY AH...DEATH... WAS FAKED, OF COURSE! A BIT DRASTIC BUT IT WORKED, YES?

AND YOU'VE GOT YOUR 'PARTNER' IN THE OLD SUPER-HERO GAME TO THANK--OR BLAME-- IT WAS HIS IDEA...!

YOU ??!! AND I THOUGHT YOU WERE MY FRIEND--!

I AM...WHO BUT A TRUE FRIEND WOULD RISK ALL TO TURN YOUR MIND AROUND--!!

MY MIND'S TURNED, ALL RIGHT! YOU KNOW, DAD, I ENJOYED BEING THE "ONLY" SUPERMAN AROUND, BUT I DON'T DIG IT AS A STEADY DIET!

RIGHT, SON, YOU LEAVE THE BIG STUFF FOR ME... I'M GOOD FOR A FEW MILLION YEARS YET! HA! HAH! HA!

IT IS LATER, AND AS WASHINGTON, D.C. SPOTS A FAMILIAR FOURSOME FLYING ABOVE ITS MARBLED MONUMENTS...!!

MY GOD! IT'S...THEM !!

GLORY BE!

AND GLORY BE TO ALL YOU RABID FANS WHO WISHED FOR THE FABULOUS SUPER SONS TO RETURN! PEACE AND BROTHERHOOD BE WITH YOU!

THE END

WORLD'S FINEST #215　　　COVER BY NICK CARDY

WORLD'S FINEST #216　　　COVER BY NICK CARDY

WORLD'S FINEST #221　　　COVER BY NICK CARDY

WORLD'S FINEST #222　　　COVER BY NICK CARDY

WORLD'S FINEST #224   COVER BY NICK CARDY

WORLD'S FINEST #228   COVER BY NICK CARDY

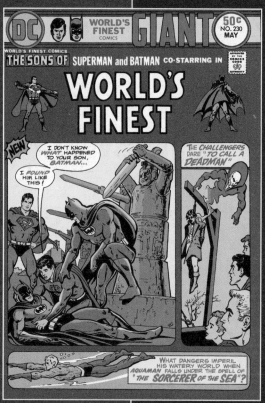

WORLD'S FINEST #230 COVER BY ERNIE CHAN

WORLD'S FINEST #231 COVER BY ERNIE CHAN

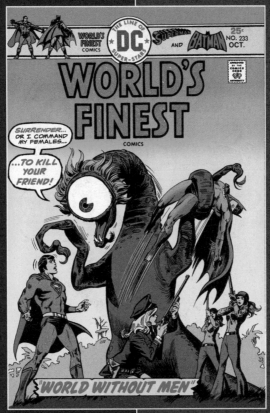

WORLD'S FINEST #233　　　COVER BY DICK GIORDANO

WORLD'S FINEST #238　　　COVER BY ERNIE CHAN
AND JOHN CALNAN

WORLD'S FINEST #242

COVER BY ERNIE CHAN
AND JOHN CALNAN

WORLD'S FINEST #263

COVER BY ROSS ANDRU
AND DICK GIORDANO

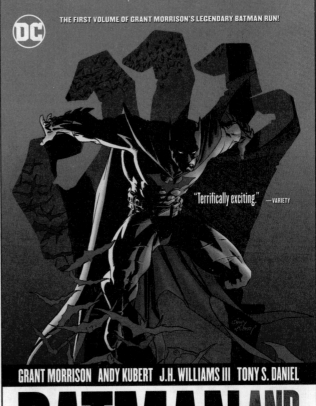
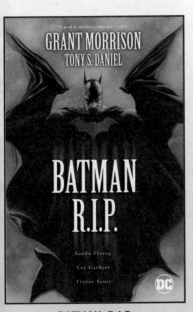